Basketball
WARFARE

Life in the Big East Conference

Published by McNamara Publishing
Rumford, Rhode Island

Visit us online for more information at www.bigeastbook.com

ISBN: 978-0-9791552-0-8

Cover photo: Tom Maguire
Typeset and Printed Narragansett Graphics, Coventry, Rhode Island, USA

Thanks

This project turned into both a labor of love and a curse. Thanks to the untrusting world of book publishing, I quickly realized that a quest for the best result possible would come through my own making. That meant getting a bit too much of an education in the business of books but thanks to the help of some key people, I'm happy with the final product and hope the reader is as well.

First of all, I have to thank the basketball coaches, sports information directors and league administrators from the Big East Conference. I've known and worked with many of these people for the last 20 years but never more intimately. Special thanks go out to some of the main subjects in the book who went above and beyond in giving their time and patience, including Jim Boeheim, Jim Calhoun, Rick Pitino, Tim Welsh, Jay Wright, John Thompson III, Mike Brey and Mike Tranghese. A special thanks goes out to the Godfather of the Big East, Dave Gavitt, for his incredible foresight and guidance over the last 30 years.

A few behind-the-scenes supporters were vital, most importantly Bill Reynolds of The Providence Journal. His constant kick-in-the-pants, lunch-time talks moved this project to the finish line. I also appreciate the help and guidance of Art Martone, Dick Weiss, Mike Waters, Randy Smith, Jeff Jacobs, Bob Ryan, John Akers and Dan Wetzel.

Finally, a publisher is only as good as his printer and Jaime Wilson of Narragansett Graphics in Rhode Island is a true pro. I also want to thank everyone who found this book through the Internet. This avenue is the future of book publishing and can put more aspiring authors into print than ever before. Consider yourself a trailblazer and enjoy the book.

To Mom & Dad, my biggest fans.

Preface

The ball, as well as the hearts and hopes of thousands of basketball fans back in the state of Connecticut, hung on the rim at the Verizon Center for what seemed like forever.

Denham Brown, one of seven seasoned stars staring his final collegiate game in the face, had just flown down the left sideline with the destiny of his University of Connecticut basketball team in his hands. The Huskies, the number-one team in the country in eyes of many experts, were somehow trailing the George Mason Patriots, perhaps the biggest Cinderella in the modern history of the NCAA Tournament, 74-72. Only five seconds remained.

The Patriots Tony Skinn, an 81 percent foul shooter, had just handed the Huskies a chance at a last gasp by missing the front end of a one-and-one at the free throw line. Rudy Gay rebounded the miss and quickly passed to Marcus Williams. UConn's most feared player in the clutch pushed the ball to the middle of the floor and hit Brown as he approached the 3-point line. A Canadian blessed with Michael Jordan-type athleticism, Brown caught the ball, took three dribbles and found himself up in the air and gliding towards the hoop. He was met by an army of bodies and tangled arms yet found a way to free his right hand and reverse the ball underneath the basket.

Brown spun the ball off the backboard and as it settled down on the orange rim, the shot seemed ready to drop to the floor. The players and coaches on the Connecticut bench stood behind Brown with both hope and fear filling their eyes. The coaching staff, led by Hall of Famer Jim Calhoun, appeared frozen in their sharp suits, waiting as time stood still. Brown's teammates were scattered along the bench. Some jumped in the air with towels over their heads, peaking out just a bit to see if the final shot would fall. Others were sprawled on the floor, looking up with wide eyes as their dreams lay in peril.

Behind the bench stood waves of UConn fans, including big-money boosters surrounding Calhoun's wife and son in the first few rows and crazed students sitting 50 rows back. They'd driven six hours just so they could tell all their friends back in Storrs that they were in The House when the Huskies fulfilled their Final Four destiny.

After all, this was UConn, the team that virtually every expert tabbed to win it all back in October when practice first began. UConn, the team with veteran stars everywhere including Gay, the smooth All-American forward, and Williams, a point guard who Calhoun had called "the best passer we've ever had at Connecticut." Up front, UConn had two more future NBA first-round picks in junior Josh Boone and the long-limbed, 6-11 center Hilton Armstrong. Complementing the group were two battle-tested seniors in Brown and dangerous shooter Rashad Anderson.

In a college basketball world where the premier players jump to the pros seemingly before they know where the best dining hall is on campus, the Huskies are an anomaly. Four key players come from a talented senior class. Two juniors and Gay, a sophomore, played the season with an eye on a move to the NBA in June. Sure enough, come draft night in June, four UConn players heard their names called in the first round and five were gone in the first 40 picks. No college team has ever enjoyed so many red carpet celebrations.

The seven veterans knew that this was their season, their time, their chance to run through the competition and win the national championship. All season long, opposing coaches pinned the ultimate label on the Huskies, calling them "the most talented team in the country." Everyone from Big East rival Jim Boeheim at Syracuse to television's talking heads picked UConn in the fall, again in the cold of the winter and once more on the eve of the national championship tournament.

Leading one of the nation's best coaching staffs was Calhoun, a fiery 64-year old with a thick Boston accent who'd take turns berating and praising his veteran team, often times within 10 seconds of each other. A common critique of the Huskies was that Calhoun had too many players and his shuttling of one substitute into the game after another limited the group's ultimate effectiveness. Yet UConn was in the Elite Eight, playing for a Final Four berth and owning a gaudy 30-3 record. Clearly, Calhoun's methods were working.

No team in America came into the NCAA's more battled-tested. Connecticut won the prestigious Maui Classic in November and nonleague victories over Louisiana State and Indiana only cemented UConn's standing as the team to beat. More importantly, the Huskies beat back the competition in the Big East. Like its glamour team, the Big East entered the season with a target on its back. The league had just emerged from its most trying period, a two-year passion play sparked by the Atlantic Coast Conference's raid of three of the Big East's marquee schools in 2003. The ugly mess, which centered on an unseemly chase for football bowl and TV money, captivated the attention of big-time athletics around the nation and threatened the Big East's ultimate survival.

The schools that remained in the conference regrouped and added some starry new friends, most notably basketball powers such as Louisville, Marquette and Cincinnati. The result was a new basketball super conference, a 16-team conglomerate that became a joy for fans and TV executives but a nightmare for coaches.

"This will be the greatest basketball conference ever," said Louisville's Rick Pitino. "Great for the fans and the players and the worst for the coaches. There are no easy games in this league."

Connecticut, as expected, emerged as the league's top team but only after one of the greatest regular seasons in Big East history. Villanova joined UConn in the national top five most of the regular season. In fact, the Wildcats and Huskies ended the regular season ranked No. 1 and 2 in the polls and both earned coveted number one seeds in the NCAA Tournament. As many as seven Big East teams were ranked for several weeks in a row and a record eight Big East teams were invited to the NCAA's. The league was blessed with great talent as 11 of the first 40 players taken in the NBA Draft owned Big East roots.

Basketball Warfare is a look not only at this historic season but also how, and why, the Big East finds itself in a bloated position today. The league features an odd mishmash of large, state universities with dreams of football glory and small, Catholic colleges defined by their basketball success. Keeping all 16 disparate schools happy is next to impossible and the story of the conference's growth is the focus of the first part of the book.

How the Big East grew from a fresh, seven-team group in 1979 to a 16-school monster over 25 turbulent years illustrates the story of modern collegiate athletics. A league founded on the promise of basketball brilliance was frequently pushed to the edge by the overwhelming pressure of college football's financial monster. Basketball Warfare will explore each of these showdowns and provide a window into the backroom deals that ultimately shaped today's multibillion dollar world of college athletics.

Basketball Warfare tries to capture the subculture that defines college basketball, from the Hall of Fame coaches to the All-American players and the recruiting wars that make the sport a year-round obsession in places such as Syracuse, Louisville and Hartford. It is impossible to feature every school in a conference as large as the Big East but Basketball Warfare offers a glimpse at a cross section of teams, plus larger looks at the Big East's heavyweights.

While the action on the court was memorable, the book doesn't offer a game-by-game account of the season. Instead, a few key games highlight the exploits of the special players and coaches in a season that ranked among the best in Big East history. A special focus is paid to both the Big East and NCAA tournaments and few schools care about college basketball in March more than the University of Connecticut. So when UConn faced a life-and-death challenge from George Mason, the eyes of the nation were on Denham Brown's reverse layup in the giant arena in downtown Washington, D.C. In the blink of an eye, Brown's shot hung on the rim, the final horn began to blare and the basketball somehow reversed its course and dropped through the net.

"It seemed like it was up there forever," Brown said. "I flipped it up there, fell to the floor and looked up and then it went in. Then things got crazy."

Even though the clutch layup only forced overtime, UConn's players and fans broke out in celebration. The Huskies had dodged a major bullet, taking the best shot from the underdog Patriots in an atmosphere where the rest of the college basketball world stood firmly in the corner of the biggest Cinderella team in the last 25 NCAA Tournaments.

The Connecticut coaches quickly moved to rein in the players. As his assistants pulled the players to the sideline, Calhoun grabbed his white, plastic clipboard and began filling it with markings. He knew his Huskies needed more than this last-second bit of heroics to punch their ticket to the Final Four. Now his team was going to take care of its business, once and for all. George Mason's Cinderella story was about to end.

Or maybe not.

Who would, and wouldn't, hold membership cards in the Big East has been an issue around the Eastern collegiate sports scene for nearly 30 years.

Back in the late 1970s, Eastern basketball operated in a twilight zone of sorts. While national powers such as UCLA (Pac-10), North Carolina (ACC) and Kansas (Big 8) thrived out of the cover of time-tested conferences, Eastern schools enjoyed success on a wing and a prayer. Sure there were great, national teams, such as Villanova's 1971 national runners-up (later vacated by Howard Porter's ineligibility); the 1973 Providence College team led by hometown stars Ernie DiGregorio and Marvin Barnes, Dave Gavitt's best club; and Syracuse's surprising 1975 Final Four team. Put those schools in a conference and it would rank with the nation's best. But instead the region's powers lacked a home that would provide the financial backing and national clout to sustain far-reaching success.

Most of the basketball schools in the East played out of a loose government called the Eastern Collegiate Athletic Conference, or the ECAC. The East was roped off into tiny quadrants for post-season play with most of the winners advancing to the NCAA's. But the death-knell for the ECAC came when it issued an edict in the late-1970s that ordered schools to begin playing more games against teams in their own area. For a school like Providence, that meant inserting New Hampshire and Maine onto a schedule that was featuring national programs such as DePaul, Louisville and North Carolina.

"That was not where we were headed and not where anyone with national hopes wanted to go," said Gavitt, the coach and athletic director at Providence.

Gavitt thought the time could be right to form a more exclusive Eastern basketball conference and his first calls were to St. John's and Georgetown. St. John's wasn't thrilled with the idea. Athletic director Jack Kaiser was intrigued but coach Lou Carnesecca was very leery. Little Louie liked ruling New York, picking many of the premier city recruits and rolling up plenty of wins at Alumni Hall on the school's Queens campus.

During that time period, Carnesecca found himself on a flight home with Gavitt to Kennedy Airport from Turin, Italy after an international coaching clinic. During a long delay, Gavitt spent the time selling his coaching rival on the idea of an Eastern league. "You always have some doubts, sure," Carnesecca said. "I had it pretty comfortable, so to speak. Dave has his ways, though. Dave likes to say he convinced me on the Big East after a couple glasses of vino flying back from Italy. There's some truth to that."

Georgetown was an easier sell, in part because coach John Thompson played for Gavitt when he starred at Providence in the early 1960s. "Georgetown was for it as long as we were committed to making it the best league in the country," Gavitt said.

Gavitt, Kaiser and Georgetown AD Frank Rienzo kept the idea quiet and decided to include Syracuse's Jake Crouthamel after an ECAC meeting in Hershey, Pa. Crouthamel was a college pal of Gavitt's from their days at Dartmouth College and excited about the idea. The four athletic directors began holding meetings on the sly at a hotel at LaGuardia Airport in New York on an almost weekly basis in the spring of 1979.

"Jake likes to say we never had any food at those meetings," Gavitt says, "but they were productive. The problem was word got out and that really brought a lot of pressure on us because other people wanted to be included."

Gavitt's objectives in filling out the rest of the league were clear. "My game plan was we needed to cover all the big markets. We already had New York and Washington but I felt we needed Boston, Philadelphia and another school in New York, plus anyone else who would bring great value," he said.

Syracuse's Crouthamel didn't want his school to be the only non-Catholic partner and he helped push Gavitt's next two targets, Rutgers and Temple. But both backed away. "They made it clear that they wanted to be where Penn State was, so we moved on," Gavitt said.

Once Seton Hall (instead of Fordham) committed to moving their games to the Meadowlands, the Pirates happily joined St. John's as the 'other' New York school. Villanova was the clear-cut second choice in Philadelphia and it accepted the offer with the provision of remaining in the Eastern Eight for one more season.

That pushed the league to six schools and set up a showdown in New England. Four schools - Boston College, Holy Cross, Connecticut and Rhode Island - were all in the mix. "We had two problems there," said Gavitt. "First, there was a lot of resistance to being a New England-dominated league, much like the ACC was in North Carolina. Syracuse, St. John's and Georgetown weren't in favor of that at all so it became clear we could only take two more schools in New England.

"But the four schools were friendly and made a gentlemen's agreement to act in unison so no one would be left out. They knew we only wanted two of them and the other two would be left behind. So basically, they told us, 'Take all of us or take none of us.'"

Whittling the four down to two proved to be fairly simple. With Providence already in, that made rival Rhode Island a non-starter. The Boston market made BC a quick pick but Holy Cross was a Gavitt favorite and owned a strong program at the time. Gavitt also was the first to spot the great promise that Connecticut brought to the table.

"We had to call their bluff," said Gavitt, "so I called Ronny Perry at Holy Cross and it became clear that Father (John) Brooks (the school's president) wouldn't do it. So I called Bill Flynn (at BC) and he called Ron Perry and they came aboard with Holy Cross' blessing. I sold Connecticut to everyone else and had a lot of support from Jake (Crouthamel) because Syracuse didn't want to be in an all-Catholic league. I called and got John Toner (UConn's AD) off the golf course and gave him just a few hours to decide. He called Mo Zarchen at Rhode Island and Connecticut accepted."

With seven schools out of the box in 1979-80 and eight in year two with Villanova coming on board, the initial seasons of the Big East were marked by a freshness, and sense of promise, that everyone felt could grow into something special. A huge early move was the creation of a Monday Night Game of the Week TV package with the William B. Tanner Company. At media day in 1981, the Big East announced that 52 of its 56 league games would be televised. Many landed on ESPN, a fledgling cable network based in Bristol, Conn., that was thirsting for programming. College basketball quickly became its marquee product and the Big East filled its airwaves as much as any conference.

The dominant teams right out of the gate were longtime rivals Georgetown and Syracuse. The Hoyas entered the league with a loaded deck and won the initial title thanks to the well-rounded exploits of John Duren, Craig Shelton and Eric 'Sleepy' Floyd. The Orange went 26-4 in the first season led by front-court stars Roosevelt Bouie and Louis Orr. One of the losses came on Feb. 12, 1980 when Georgetown stormed back from 14 points down and stunned the 'Cuse at Manley Field House. The loss snapped a 57-game winning streak in the building, which was due to close at the end of the season and make way for the Carrier Dome. At his post-game press conference, Thompson uttered the immortal words, "Manley Field House is officially closed!"

Thompson's most important win came off the court in the recruiting wars. In the spring of 1981, Georgetown secured the services of Patrick Ewing, the era's Lew Alcindor. Then St. John's outmuscled Duke for sweet-shooting Chris Mullin. Those two signings catapulted the Big East to the top of the national scene almost instantly and gave Gavitt the product he desperately needed to make the TV networks swoon.

For two years, that blissful ignorance may have filled the minds of coaches, media and most fans in the East but it didn't take long for Gavitt and his assistant commissioner, Mike Tranghese, to spot storm clouds on the horizon. And deep in the middle of those clouds was a large, brown football that threatened to blow the fledgling league to bits.

•

When the Big East formed in 1979, only two of the seven schools – Boston College and Syracuse – played big-time football and neither played it very well. Syracuse was in the process of a transition from historic, but archaic, Archbold Stadium to the East's first domed stadium, the Carrier Dome. BC battled a long, losing history on the gridiron and plenty of apathy in a region that could care less about college football or the always-struggling New England Patriots.

After Syracuse's unbeaten, national championship season in 1959 and trip to the Sugar Bowl in 1965, the Orange played in two bowls over the next 20 years. The Eagles didn't play in a bowl from 1943 to the arrival of Doug Flutie in 1982, a whopping 39 years.

Basketball at both schools enjoyed much more success and the dawn of the Big East fit the needs of both wonderfully. But it didn't take long for football to crash the party. The first, and ultimately perhaps the most important crisis of all, according to Tranghese, came in 1982. Joe Paterno, the legendary Penn State coach, lorded over the dominant Eastern football program at the time. He was also PSU's athletic director and, along with Notre Dame, led the nation's preeminent Independent football programs. But Paterno saw a future taking shape around conferences, especially through multimillion dollar TV rights fees. He surmised that if Penn State came together with Syracuse, BC and Pittsburgh, the group would form the core of an all-sports league that could also feature Rutgers, Temple, West Virginia and possibly Maryland. So his grand design was to steal the two football schools away from Gavitt's infant venture.

What happened next is one of those classic which came first, the chicken-or-the-egg scenarios. What is clear is that Penn State wanted an all-sports conference with BC and Syracuse involved. Paterno has spoken of that dream many times, most recently at the 2003 Big Ten media day. What Paterno rejects is that his school lobbied to become a full-fledged Big East member.

"Joe was trying to form his own conference, an all-sports conference," said Syracuse's Crouthamel. "We liked the Big East for what it was doing with our basketball but we were in the minority on the football side so we wanted another football school and we clearly wanted Penn State. We were all playing each other at that time anyways."

Paterno did meet with Gavitt in Hartford in early 1981 and told Gavitt of his plans. According to Big East people, Gavitt talked to Paterno about his school's fit in the Big East and left that meeting feeling he could add Penn State to the league. He took that idea back to the membership. Paterno disagrees and insists he never sought a move to the Big East.

"I talked to them about what I thought would be in the best interest of the East and that would be an all-sports conference," Paterno said in 2003. "John Toner, who was the athletic director at Connecticut and an old friend of mine, was involved in that. We talked and they wanted to know if we had any interest in the Big East? I said, 'No, we were only interested in an all-sports conference.' I went home and I got several telephone calls, including one from Bill Flynn, who at that time was the athletic director at Boston College, trying to talk us into going into the Big East or apply to the Big East because they wanted to deter my efforts to get an all-sports conference. They were scared to death."

Gavitt says Paterno flew in from State College and the two men met for the better part of an afternoon together at Bradley Airport. "Joe called and asked if we could talk about Penn State getting into the Big East for all his sports except football," Gavitt recalls. "His idea of an all-sports conference wasn't moving forward because Syracuse and BC weren't comfortable with his revenue sharing proposal. He didn't want to share bowl money."

Even though Gavitt was no football fan and needed to be sold that adding a football power – and a relatively worthless basketball option – like Penn State would increase the Big East's value, he clearly hoped to kill Paterno's plans for a rival conference. Tranghese also listened to Paterno's pitch and shared the old coach's vision of a football-basketball hybrid but wanted those teams to play under the Big East's banner. Gavitt was eventually swayed, so the young conference's two leaders went about selling the idea of adding a football school to the mix.

But Penn State had little support. No formal vote was taken but Providence (via Gavitt's vote), Connecticut and Seton Hall joined BC and Syracuse in backing a move to approach Penn State. However, Georgetown, St. John's and Villanova resisted and the 5-to-3 count fell one affirmative vote short.

"I get much of this secondhand because it was Dave who was dealing with Joe but I do know that in the summer of 1981 we had a special meeting at the Logan Hilton in Boston to specifically discuss adding Penn State. That was probably the first crisis in the history of our league," said Tranghese. "The minutes will never reflect the vote but we went around the room to the eight members and we had to have six votes. Dave was smart enough to not advance it unless he had the votes and it went round and round and round. Dave voted for it with Providence's vote but there just wasn't enough support. Some people say Dave should've pushed harder but, hey, it didn't happen."

Paterno insists he never knew of a vote because his school never applied for membership. But what the vote clearly centered on was finding a consensus on whether Penn State had enough support for admission.

"This isn't pointing fingers. What happened, happened," Paterno said. "When they called me, I said, 'Look, we are not interested.' They may have had a vote and said, 'We are going to try to get Penn State.' They may have taken a vote on their own, but we have never applied and showed any interest in the Big East as far as basketball. The only interest we had was in an all-sports conference."

Nearly 30 years later, it's probably just semantics. But what is clear is Penn State would have fit quite nicely in the Big East and BC and Syracuse would've fit equally well in an all-sports conference with Penn State acting as the gridiron anchor.

"I thought the reason for rejecting Penn State at the time was very narrow. It was like 'hey, we're a basketball conference. What do we need them for?'

Georgetown and Villanova and St. John's looked at it as an act of intrusion but in reality I viewed it as an act of preservation," said Tranghese.

Twenty-six years later, Tranghese still recalls one exchange in the board room that day. The words will stick in his head forever.

"I was working for Dave at the time and I never said a lot at those meetings unless called upon, really," he says. "At the end of the Penn State meeting, Dave turned to me and said 'you haven't said a word. What do you think?' And I said 'we will rue the day over this decision.'

"I said it and I believed it and I understood what it meant," he said.

Now Gavitt had a major problem brewing. Paterno turned up the heat on Syracuse's Crouthamel and BC's Flynn, two men who loved college football and knew finances cold. The Big East had created a unique revenue sharing vehicle whereby everyone enjoyed in the collective success of the league. Paterno wasn't enamored by this idea, especially when it came to football and bowl money. Remember, the Nitts and Pittsburgh were the only true national programs in the East at the time so the idea of Paterno giving a slice of his bowl cash away to BC and Rutgers wasn't an easy one to swallow.

"After we couldn't agree on Penn State, Jake (Crouthamel) thought we were done," said Gavitt. "I thought Syracuse would take the Penn State deal although it was a bad one. It was clear to me that Penn State was a negative with a lot of our people."

That made Pittsburgh Gavitt's next target. Unlike Penn State, Pitt offered a combination Gavitt knew he could sell to the basketball schools. The Panthers played in a media center, owned a basketball program with a good history and was just a few years removed from a national football title with Heisman Trophy winner Tony Dorsett running the ball. That welcome bonus would clearly appease the football fears of both BC and Syracuse.

"Dave was able to convince everyone that this other idea (Pittsburgh) was better than doing nothing," said Tranghese. "Our schools had talked to Penn State about doing something else but what occurred was BC and Syracuse saw that they were already part of something that was really growing on the basketball side and could see its value long-term. Whenever they talked about football, the access to football revenue sharing was minimal. That was the mistake from Penn State's end."

Adding Pitt was no slam dunk, however. The Big East's AD's gathered in Boston to discuss expansion but an anti-Pitt (or really anti-football) element in the room remained quite palpable. Gavitt seethed, according to Tranghese.

"Coming back from that meeting, I never saw Dave so mad," Tranghese said in *Big Hoops*, an excellent Big East history written in 1989 by Bill Reynolds. "We both knew that if Pitt didn't get in, BC and Syracuse would side with Penn State and there would be two leagues. When Dave got back, he called the schools opposing him and said he wanted to see the basketball coaches and AD's in his office the next day. He told them that if Pitt didn't get in, there would be two leagues and the talent would get divvied up. Both leagues would be good but neither would be able to compete with the ACC."

That argument made sense to some old-line basketball people, especially Georgetown's Thompson and Villanova's Rollie Massimino. Another vote was taken and this time Gavitt got his way. Pittsburgh was welcomed as a new member for the 1982-83 season.

Over in Happy Valley, Paterno was livid. He couldn't understand why the Big East's football schools would choose to stay put and reject his plan. After all, he led the East's premier football program, the one with the 90,000 seats, the one with the national pedigree and the one the TV networks craved. But in the 1980s, basketball was King in the East. Football was something schools played in Texas, Nebraska and Florida.

Before a game at Boston College just after Pitt was added to the Big East's mix, Paterno was asked why the East didn't have a football league.

"Football conference?" Paterno was quoted in a Providence Journal article. "Listen, I just spent nearly two years of my life trying to put that together. We missed the greatest opportunity we'll ever have to promote our game, but the people to blame for it are those who were more concerned with their basketball programs. BC and Syracuse decided to stay with the Big East and they talked Pitt into going with them."

In the same story, Tranghese lashed out at Joe Pa. "Joe lost the battle and now he's pointing fingers at a lot of people when he should be pointing one at himself. He had all the cards. If they had gone about it correctly, maybe there would be a league today. But they made the administrative errors. It was their fault," he said then.

Tranghese was referring to the botched revenue sharing model where Paterno and Penn State wouldn't budge from a decision to lord over his school's bowl money. Today he also realizes that the voting strength of the basketball coalition and Gavitt's trademark salesmanship skills carried the day.

"When we couldn't get Penn State that's when Pitt came about and once the Pitt people found out that there had been discussions about adding Penn State, that led to an open mind on their part," Tranghese said. "Penn State hadn't won in basketball and our people questioned their ability to compete in basketball. They didn't come from a large market, per se. And people didn't even know how to get there. No one questioned Pitt's ability to compete in basketball. They had just come off winning the Eastern Eight and they were from a large market."

The Big East did go on to rue the day that it rejected Penn State, just as Tranghese predicted. Then again, the college sports world felt tremors many times over because of that historic decision.

"If you look back on it, that move would've changed the face of college athletics," Tranghese said. "Football expansion was all driven by Penn State moving to the Big Ten. We might still be sitting here in 2006 with a whole slew of football independents: Miami, Florida State, Notre Dame, Syracuse, Pitt and Penn State. Who knows what might have happened? That single non-action on the part of our membership in 1981 has had an incredible ripple effect. It pushed Penn State to the Big Ten. It pushed Florida State to the ACC and Miami to the Big East.

"In retrospect, if everyone could've taken a deep breath and gone back and known what they know now, a lot of those decisions would be dramatically different."

With nine members and players such as Ewing, Mullin and Ed Pinckney in place for the 1982-83 season, the Big East was prepared for basketball glory. These stars seemed to pop up on ESPN nightly and the country couldn't get enough of the NCAA's basketball tournament every March. In a basketball world, Gavitt's Big East was positioned for stardom.

But the times, like the rest of the country, were about to change.

Up until the early 1980s, the NCAA controlled the bargaining rights for televised college football. The organization sold the idea that its 'market power' was dominant since all of the country's elite programs – from Nebraska to Alabama, Texas to Notre Dame – belonged to the same bargaining unit. These deals limited the nation's powers to three regular season appearances per season, but the schools didn't seem to care when the big checks rolled in. The networks were relatively happy to deal with just one player at the bargaining table and college football dominated the Saturday afternoon ratings, mostly through regionalized doubleheaders. In the East, that meant a Penn State-Syracuse game at noon and Notre Dame-Southern California at 3:30. ABC, with Keith Jackson and Chris Schenkel calling most of the action, purchased the NCAA's national contract in 1966 and reigned supreme as college football's TV home.

However, a storm was brewing down South and into the lower Midwest where college football dominates talk around the dinner table and the fishing holes year round. College hoops was simply a bridge between the New Year's Day bowls and spring football in locales such as Baton Rouge, La., College Station, Texas, and Gainesville, Fla. Schools in these parts thought that they should be on national TV more than three times a season, especially when they owned powerhouse teams. Under the NCAA's regionalized plan, a huge game like the 1967 epic Notre Dame-Michigan State clash wasn't seen nationally. In 1981, the Oklahoma-Southern Cal game matching Marcus

DuPree and Marcus Allen wasn't televised in Southeastern cities thirsting for the sport's best games. Instead, TV sets in the Carolinas, for example, had to suffer through Appalachian State versus The Citadel.

Under the NCAA's archaic formula, which was lorded over by long-time executive director Walter Byers, schools ranging from the Ivy League to the SEC benefited financially from football's TV deal. This drove the Big Boys nuts. From 1978 to 1981, for example, the 60 biggest football schools appeared in 54 percent of the televised games yet collected just 48 percent of the TV revenue. Under the NCAA's one school-one vote rules, the system rolled along for years with little change. With so many smaller schools holding equal voting power with the big boys, the football giants were backed into a corner. (The same was not true in basketball where individual conferences were free to cut their own TV deals for regular season action. The NCAA, of course, sold the rights to its post-season basketball tournament.)

By the early 1980s, this patently unfair system was under fire. A flash point arose in August of 1981 when 61 Division 1-A schools united under the College Football Association (CFA) banner (which notably excluded the Big Ten and PAC 10) and announced a four-year, $180 million deal with NBC that would run from 1982-85. The NCAA took this as a direct attack on contracts it had signed with ABC and CBS a month earlier that called for $263.5 million for the same four seasons. The NCAA promptly threatened to either expel or place on probation any school that chose to vote for the CFA's deal.

That threat from Byers' heavy-handed NCAA sent several football powers into a tizzy and they returned the volley with lawsuits. The most important came a few months after the proposed NBC contract when the Board of Regents of the University of Oklahoma and the University of Georgia's Athletic Association filed suit against the NCAA in federal court in Oklahoma City. The lawsuit sought to show that the NCAA's control of football's television rights violated the Sherman Antitrust Act.

With a devastating mutiny brewing, Byers convened a special NCAA Convention in St. Louis in December 1981. In order to assuage some of the football powers, he crafted a political power play that created a new subset of schools, dubbed Division 1-A. In order to live in this rarified air, football programs needed to play in a stadium with a capacity of at least 30,000 and average at least 17,000 fans. This was a direct shot at the bow of the Ivy League, ECAC and other small schools that had enjoyed their seats at the same financial table as Nebraska and North Carolina.

Penn State's Paterno, a former star player in the Ivies at Brown University, crystallized the issue when he was quoted in a history of college football on

TV titled *The 50 Year Seduction* as saying, "The Ivy League is in another world all of their own. I'm in the real world."

At the NCAA Convention in Houston in January 1982, Byers sought to hold his football TV power intact. He chose to play a trump card by offering the full membership a regulation that read, in part, "The telecasting, cablecasting, or otherwise televising of intercollegiate football games of member institutions shall be controlled by the bylaws enacted by the Association."

Even though the newly created 1-A schools all voted against the measure, it passed easily, 631-to-178, because of the one-school, one-vote system. Byers in effect showed who was boss on the issue of TV rights. But the Oklahoma-Georgia court case was not so easily overpowered. That case went to trial in June 1982 and very quickly the lawyers arguing on the schools' behalf shed a light on the NCAA and Byers' strong-armed bureaucracy. It quickly became apparent that the NCAA employed negotiating tactics that were nothing short of price fixing and when the plaintiffs claimed that freeing conferences to cut their own football TV deals would increase both rights fees and the number of exposures for schools, the courts listened intently.

The judge hearing the case, Juan Burciaga, was brought in from New Mexico when it became clear that no jurist in the state of Oklahoma could be found without either a Sooner bumper sticker on their car or season tickets in their pocket. On Sept. 14, 1982, Judge Burciaga ruled against the NCAA and its television practices and called it "a classic cartel" that operated in violation of antitrust laws. The NCAA quickly appealed the decision but the proverbial Genie was out of the bottle. The unsettled nature of college football's future sparked rumors and desperate actions. Penn State's Paterno, for example, knew once and for all that he needed a conference home for his program but the Big East's door remained shut. He cast his eye toward the Big Ten but found little interest there, either.

With little say in the fracas, the Big East sat on the sidelines and watched as their rivals placed their golden goose football programs in danger. Finally, in June 1984 the Supreme Court acted on the case. In a 7-to-2 decision, the high court agreed that the NCAA acted like a cartel and was fixing the price in its network deal.

"Because it restrains price and output, the NCAA's television plan has a significant potential for anticompetitive effects. The findings of the District Court indicate that this potential has been realized," wrote Associate Justice John Paul Stevens. "The District Court found that if member institutions were free to sell television rights, many more games would be shown on television, and that the NCAA's output restriction has the effect of raising the price the networks pay for television rights. Moreover, the court found that by fixing a price for television rights to all games, the NCAA creates a price structure that is unresponsive to viewer demand and unrelated to the prices that would prevail in a competitive market. And, of course, since as a practical matter all member institutions need NCAA approval, members have no real choice but to adhere to the NCAA's television controls."

Justice Byron 'Whizzer' White, an All-American running back at the University of Colorado, wrote in the minority and defended the NCAA and its attempts to protect amateurism.

"Although some of the NCAA's activities, viewed in isolation, bear a resemblance to those undertaken by professional sports leagues and associations, the Court errs in treating intercollegiate athletics under the NCAA's control as a purely commercial venture in which colleges and universities participate solely, or even primarily, in the pursuit of profits. Accordingly, I dissent," White wrote.

The old running back ended his argument with a string of sentences which were dismissed at the time but ring very true in 2006. He somehow saw a day where money flowed only to the schools with the best teams, where coaches jumped from job to job in search of the next million dollar contract and where crowds of 100,000 packed stadiums that dwarfed those in NFL cities. White may have been prophetic, but at the time he was clearly a voice in the wilderness drowned out by college football's riches.

"When these values are factored into the balance to offset any minimal anticompetitive effects of the television plan, the NCAA's television plan seems eminently reasonable," he wrote. "Most fundamentally, the plan fosters the goal of amateurism by spreading revenues among various schools and reducing the financial incentives toward professionalism....In short, "the restraints upon Oklahoma and Georgia and other colleges and universities with excellent football programs insure that they confine those programs within the principles of amateurism so that intercollegiate athletics supplement, rather than inhibit, educational achievement."

"The collateral consequences of the spreading of regional and national appearances among a number of schools are many: the television plan, like the ban on compensating student-athletes, may well encourage students to choose their schools, at least in part, on the basis of educational quality by reducing the perceived economic element of the choice, it helps ensure the economic viability of athletic programs at a wide variety of schools with weaker football teams; and it promotes competitive football among many and varied amateur teams nationwide. These important contributions, I believe, are sufficient."

•

The aftereffects of 'NCAA vs. Board of Regents,' would haunt college athletics for the next 25 years. The Big East saw its membership twisted and torn over the money needed to support the football beast from 1983-2003. From the outside, the conference thrived. And while largely true, life was never smooth sailing for Gavitt or Tranghese because of the divergent wishes that placed the basketball-only schools on a collision course with their football brethren.

Soon after the court victory, the CFA's predictions of heavenly economic gains never materialized. The NCAA negotiated pacts worth $66 million for the 1983 football season but in a free-for-all created by the Supreme Court decision heading into 1984, the CFA struck a deal worth only $13 million and the Big Ten-Pac 10 rights went for just $10 million. The deregulation allowed the major networks, along with cable giants ESPN and WTBS, to flood the market with more college football games than ever. But that proliferation hit the schools in the pocketbook with sharply lower rights fees. It didn't take the colleges long to realize they had severely wounded their golden (TV) goose.

"I was on the last NCAA Football committee and the last CFA TV committee. Those are two notable lasts," said Syracuse athletic director Jake Crouthamel. "Quite simply, if you are a single entity selling to multiple bidders, you have leverage. If you become multiple entities selling to few buyers, they hold the cards. That's what happened with the NCAA and the price (for football rights) went down dramatically. It caught us dumb guys in college football by surprise."

It also didn't take long for the loss of dollars to begin crippling the budgets in the nation's biggest athletic departments. Women's sports enjoyed skyrocketing growth in the 1980s despite little, or no, increase in revenue from TV or attendance. Title IX restricted schools' ability to slow the expansion of women's sports so by the late 1980s many Olympic men's sports such as gymnastics and wrestling found their way to the chopping block.

An interesting paradigm developed, too. While the bean counters experienced sticker shock, football fans were thrilled and began to stay home in front of their TV's on Saturday afternoons and evenings more than ever before. But the extra TV games created a culture where the only college football that truly mattered was the kind played on TV. Attendance at games in the Ivy League and at the service academies – once among the biggest names in the sport – plummeted as fans in the East stayed home in droves to watch budding stars such as John Elway, Jim Kelly and Doug Flutie throw the ball like arrows on a slingshot.

Some schools thrived under the new setup. Notre Dame cemented its place as America's Team. Restricted to three national games a year under the NCAA's plan, the Golden Dome, Touchdown Jesus and Gerry Faust's Fighting Irish saw eight of their games on TV in 1984.

While football's TV paydays dwindled, basketball's grew to unprecedented heights. In 1988, CBS paid the NCAA a whopping $163 million to televise the next four NCAA Tournaments. That amounted to an 85-percent increase from the previous contract. A key player in the negotiations, incidentally, was the Big East's Gavitt.

In 1989, ABC held the Big Ten-Pac 10 football contract at $17 million a season. The CFA, made up of the rest of the 1-A powers (including BC, Pitt and Syracuse), shopped its deal at the same time and reached a crossroads. Current partner CBS was offering a robust $150 million over five years, or $30 million per season.

CFA executive Chuck Neinas had heard that ABC and NBC were both interested in the package so he weighed offers from both networks. ABC saw this as a chance to own both contracts and become 'The Home of College Football,' so it offered a staggering $210 million. But while the extra millions lit up the eyes of athletic directors, ABC's deal would cut back on the number of national TV games the CFA teams enjoyed with CBS and instead opt for a weekly regional package of games.

That set up a clear choice of taking the extra revenue or keeping the added exposure. In January 1990, the CFA's television committee signed off on the bigger dollars and went with ABC. But almost as soon as the ink was dry, the most important football school in the country realized it had made a mistake in agreeing to the deal.

Notre Dame and its President, The Rev. E. William Beauchamp, saw football as the university's Golden Goose. Getting the goose on TV as often as possible was important to alumni, as well as the school's 'Subway Alumni' of fans around the country with no direct tie to the school except their Irish heritage and love of football. TV was terribly important to the school's coffers.

Under the CFA's new deal with ABC, Notre Dame would see its national exposure diminish. This, the Good Father determined, was not good. Just after the CFA deal was announced, Irish athletic director Dick Rosenthal met with Ken Schanzer, an NBC Sports' executive, regarding the Irish's basketball deal. But eventually the talk moved toward football.

The talks moved quickly, eventually involving NBC head Dick Ebersol. Less than a month after the CFA deal was signed, Notre Dame and NBC agreed to a $38-million contract that covered Irish home football games from 1991-95. The Rev. Beauchamp was roundly criticized, especially since he sat on the CFA's board of directors. But without a conference holding it back, Notre Dame leveraged its free-agent status into the richest TV contract in college sports. The $7.6-million-a-year average fee NBC paid from 1991 to 1995 has risen modestly to about $9 million through 2010, or $1.5 million a game.

Notre Dame's move began the slow death of the CFA. As soon as the Southeastern Conference was free to negotiate its own TV deal in 1994, it left the group and made a killing with CBS. Between 1989-1994, an unprecedented environment emerged in big-time college sports where the best football schools were literally up for bid. And everyone was chasing football TV and bowl dollars.

The fallout was somewhat catastrophic. The Texas-based Southwest Conference, perhaps the nation's most football-centric league, eventually died when Arkansas left for the Southeastern Conference in 1992 and Texas, Texas A&M, Texas Tech and Baylor jumped to help form the Big 12.

The Big East's internal talks concerning Penn State heated up again in the late 1980s but a league with six basketball schools and three football schools didn't look like a budding football power.

"We talked about it and our directors said then that they'd be supportive of it but I remember leaving the meeting and telling Dave 'I don't believe them," said Tranghese. "I thought we were getting led down a path that would bring more disappointment. Syracuse and Boston College and Pitt were very supportive but I didn't believe the others would step up. We had nine schools then so we needed seven votes and when push came to shove, I didn't think we'd get the votes."

Penn State talked with the ACC to some degree but a strong push from the school's academic leaders ultimately landed Joe Paterno in the Big Ten. The move seemed like a perfect fit but, in retrospect, you have to wonder if the Big East wouldn't have been a better home. Paterno's winning ways slipped with the move into a competitive league and, perhaps just as importantly, the Nitts' basketball program has largely remained a nonentity.

With the conference shuffle breaking out, the Big East was dealing with another crisis. Gavitt, the league's founding father, was leaving to run the

Boston Celtics. From the moment he first approached Tranghese with the idea, the lieutenant knew his boss of the previous 20 years was ready to move on to another challenge.

"Dave came to me in April (of 1990) and told me that the Celtics had approached him. I knew after the first conversation that he was going to leave," said Tranghese. "He didn't make any decision until May at our annual meeting but it was during that period when Dave was approached by the Celtics that Penn State went to the Big Ten. So we went from the middle of May to late June when we didn't have anyone in charge and the whole world was blowing up. Everyone was panic-stricken.

"The ACC became very engaged with Florida State and had conversations with Miami. The SEC talked to Miami, Florida State, South Carolina and Arkansas. The whole thing was exploding and meanwhile Syracuse and Pitt and BC were engaged with conversations with the Metro people and no one could deal with it because there was no one fully in charge."

The Metro Conference was talking with the Big East's football schools and trying to broker a hybrid league of sorts where BC, Pitt and Syracuse would join with East Carolina, Miami, Rutgers, Temple, Virginia Tech and West Virginia in a football-only league. "This was an opportunity for Syracuse to get its football placed while still retaining membership in the Big East," said Syracuse's Crouthamel.

A more radical idea included talk of an all-sports Metro Conference that would include BC, Pitt and Syracuse from the Big East, and some combination of football Independents East Carolina, Florida State, Miami, Rutgers, Temple, Virginia Tech and West Virginia.

The Big East was ready to make some major decisions but first it had to find a new leader. And there really was only one candidate: Mike Tranghese.

"In June, I was asked to go to Logan Airport to be interviewed by our athletic directors," Tranghese said. "They had assigned questions to each AD and the first eight were rather perfunctory ones. Then it came to Jake (Crouthamel) and, as only Jake can do, he said 'what are we going to do about football?

"I said, 'if you hire me, you need to understand that we're going to add football. Because if we don't, we're going to dissolve. If you don't want to do this, don't hire me."

Tranghese laid out his plan and made it clear that he thought the league could foster a unique relationship with some schools joining as full members and others only playing football under the Big East's umbrella. The one school he targeted more than any other, however, was one far removed from the league's geographical footprint.

"I told the AD's that we had to add football because in my heart of hearts, I knew that BC, Syracuse and Pitt had no choice. They were going to be left behind," he says. "There was no doubt we had to get Miami and I told them I thought we could do it. They had won four national championships in the previous six years. Everybody wanted them but people thought Miami was a hard sell and the ACC and SEC couldn't make it work. Sam Jankovich (UM's athletics boss at the time) had been up to see Dave (Gavitt) in the past and they made it clear that they wanted their basketball to be successful again."

The existing Big East members accepted Tranghese's plans and hired him as commissioner in June 1990.

"Within two weeks of the day I took the job, we had an emergency meeting in New Jersey at the Meadowlands and I laid out exactly what we needed to do to go and get Miami," he said. "Miami was being courted to some degree by the SEC and the ACC but I just sensed that after seeing Sam that they wanted to join with us. They liked the idea of being in the Northeast marketplace and would have a hand in constructing a new football league. In the SEC they faced the large budgets of the sprawling state institutions and Roy Kramer (the SEC boss) saw Arkansas and South Carolina as better fits. The ACC, I think, had made up its mind to take Florida State. I know Gene Corrigan (the ACC commissioner) had hoped to take Miami as well but he couldn't get it past his membership. Even getting Florida State in was difficult because Duke, especially their AD Tom Butters, was really against it. But Gene got that done."

Syracuse's Crouthamel was a big proponent of the Big East Football Conference. When it was time to make the move, he said the logical place to start was in Miami. "We wanted instant recognition. That's why we took Miami. We weren't dumb," he says.

Tranghese asked two of his most impressive presidents, Father Donald Monan of BC and Syracuse's Melvin Eggers, to accompany him to Miami for a meeting with that school's Board of Trustees. The meeting went well enough that Miami was offered membership and quickly accepted an invite to be the Big East's 10th school in October 1990.

"Sometimes you want to be wanted and from day one, Miami was wanted by the Big East," Tranghese said. "To this day, I think it was Father Monan who convinced Miami to come. As I look at the annals of our league, we've been blessed with some great presidents and, for us, Father Monan was a giant. I always tell people that Boston College is a great institution today because of two people: Doug Flutie and Father Monan.

"We have become friends. We have become partners," Miami president Edward T. Foote II said at a news conference announcing his school's move to the Big East. "I have tremendous respect for the conference we're joining and the institutions it represents."

Tranghese clearly saw Miami's addition as an act of self-preservation. "To be very blunt with you, our future was at stake," he said. "If the Big East and Miami had not gotten together, I'm not sure we had an answer that would have satisfied the football concerns of Boston College, Pittsburgh and Syracuse."

With four 1-A football schools, including the nation's hottest program, the Big East was in a unique position to join the chase for football glory and dollars. Like basketball's unpredictable success a decade before, no one in the country was ready for just how successful the Boys from the East would be.

3

It's supposed to take time to put the pieces in place at the birth of an athletic conference but the Big East's football league suffered few growing pains.

In the very first year of competition, Miami went 12-0 and won the 1991 National Championship. That was a team led by the timely passing of Gino Torretta, a great kicker in Carlos Huerta and a defense spear-headed by linebackers Jessie Armstead and Michael Barrow. Two challenges in November lifted the 'Canes to glory. First was the annual grudge match in Tallahassee against No. 1 ranked Florida State. In what became known as "Wide Right I" the Hurricanes erased a 16-7 deficit in the fourth quarter and went ahead, 17-16, with three minutes left. The Seminoles drove for a game-winning field goal but Gerry Thomas' 34-yard attempt sailed wide right in the final seconds.

A few weeks later, Miami held off a late drive by Boston College to win at The Heights, 19-14, to set up a berth in the Orange Bowl. The Hurricanes captured their fourth national title in nine seasons (and third in the last five) by ripping apart Nebraska, 22-0.

Miami carried an undefeated string into the Sugar Bowl in 1992 but a stunning loss to Alabama kept the Big East from a second straight piece of the national championship. The league showed it wasn't a one-team wonder in 1993 when Major Harris and West Virginia beat UM and entered the Sugar Bowl with an 11-0 record. The Mountaineers were trumped by Florida, 41-7, but it was clear that the Big East was positioned for a sustained run of success.

The biggest key on that front became the rise of Virginia Tech. The Hokies were one of the schools Tranghese tabbed as football-only Big East members back in '91. The others were Rutgers, Temple and West Virginia. The Mountaineers were poised for success but so were the Hokies, although their record didn't show it.

"We looked at Virginia Tech like we saw Connecticut when we started out in 1979. Everything was in place. The league was clearly going to help them," said Tranghese.

What no one knew at the time was how brilliant a coach Frank Beamer would become. Hired in 1987, Beamer was largely unimpressive over his first six seasons in Blacksburg but things began to turn with a 9-3 record in 1993. By the 1995 season, Tech broke through and shared the conference title with Miami. The Hurricanes were on NCAA probation that year, so the Hokies went to New Orleans and whipped Texas in the Sugar Bowl, 28-10.

By this time, the Big East had overcome its third membership crisis. With Rutgers, Temple, Virginia Tech and West Virginia proving to be positive partners in the football league, each clamored to become full-time members. Rutgers, Temple and WVU were key members of the Atlantic 10 Conference, while Va. Tech played the bulk of its sports with the Metro Conference.

In the fall of 1993, another key development was playing out. The College Football Association's (CFA) TV contract with ABC and ESPN was about to expire. With Miami as one of the nation's hot teams, the Big East was set to join the SEC and other conferences in leaving the CFA behind in a scramble to cut their own TV deal.

The SEC had signed with CBS but that network was looking for more games to fill up its Saturday afternoons. It turned its focus to the Big East. At the NCAA Convention in San Antonio in January 1994, Syracuse athletic director Jake Crouthamel said he was approached by Neil Pilson, the CBS Sports President.

"The meeting was a shocker," Crouthamel wrote on Syracuse's Web site a few years ago. "CBS had been out of the college football business for some time with ABC/ESPN claiming all the exclusive rights. This was CBS' opportunity to get back in. It had reached an agreement with the SEC for football and basketball, and needed Big East inventory to round out its programming. CBS laid a lot of money on the table for exclusive national network rights of The BIG EAST Conference for football and basketball. We pointed out to CBS that we could not represent the non-football playing schools in the Big East for their basketball rights. The response from CBS was that it would then assume the basketball rights for the eight Big East football schools. A total mess!"

In effect, CBS was asking B.C., Pitt, Miami and Syracuse to sell their basketball rights apart from the rest of the league. Pilson's idea was dismissed in the conference office but the amount of money for football's TV rights certainly was not. The resolve of the football schools to add at least two new, full-time members (for a new total of 12 schools) grew strong but the resistance of the basketball schools was fierce, maybe deeper than it had ever been before.

At least one athletic director at the time insisted that the league would be better off splitting than adding Rutgers and West Virginia, the favorites for the new spots. "Why would we ever want to go play West Virginia," said the AD. "We already helped Miami and what have they done for us? And the facade of a rival league forming was a joke."

In order to scare the basketball schools, word was floated that Rutgers (and possibly West Virginia) were in discussions to join the Big Ten. The idea, almost laughable now, had some credence at the time and stoked fears that BC, Miami, Pitt and Syracuse could leave the Big East and form a league with Rutgers, West Virginia, Temple, Virginia Tech and perhaps Louisville and Cincinnati. That 10-team conglomerate would cripple the basketball schools' future.

"It became a pretty divisive thing," Tranghese said. "The basketball people tell the football people, 'Look, we gave you our name. We gave you our people to help you run everything. We gave you the Big East Television Network. And none of this has been in the best interests of basketball. When will it stop?"

It ultimately did stop because of college sports' two-headed monster: money and TV. By February, the football schools were assured of positive expansion votes from Connecticut and Villanova but only with the proviso that those two could join the football league if they ever elevated their programs from 1-AA to 1-A. But expansion was contingent on 7 of 10 votes and cracking another vote out of the Catholic school block of Georgetown-Providence-St. John's-Seton Hall proved futile.

That's when the football schools decided to call their partner's bluff. On Feb. 15, 1994, the Big East announced it had signed a five year contract with CBS worth $60 million. But the deal was the property of the four 1-A football schools. The six other schools - UConn, Georgetown, Providence, St. John's, Seton Hall and Villanova - now faced the choice of joining the contract through an expanded Big East or pursuing another alignment. At the time, the football schools were pushing a four-school expansion that would bloat the league to 14 schools and include Rutgers, Temple, Virginia Tech and West Virginia.

"Georgetown, Providence, Seton Hall, St. John's, Villanova and Connecticut are aware of the basketball portion of the deal," Tranghese said in announcing the CBS deal. "Whether they decide to be a part of it is a decision they have to make about membership."

If the league voted against expansion, the football side would form a new conference and the $60 million TV deal would be theirs. (A breakup actually would have triggered a clause to renegotiate the deal downward). Tranghese did say he was reluctant to sign a new network TV deal before settling his conference's membership questions but he felt time was short on wrapping up a TV deal of this magnitude.

"CBS began talking relative to football and as part of that, they put a basketball offer on the table," Tranghese said. "We were faced with a very attractive window of opportunity for a football deal and we had to decide to face it or let it go. We decided to seize the window of opportunity."

With the clock ticking on a decision, the league gathered in New York in March for the Big East Tournament. Connecticut was riding high at the time with Donyell Marshall, Ray Allen and Doron Sheffer. Georgetown and Providence ultimately matched up in the finals with Rick Barnes' Friars and rebounding machine Michael Smith winning the schools' first (and only) tourney title.

But a day before the tournament began, the presidents and athletic directors met at Lubin House, Syracuse's New York City campus. Things were not going well.

"Chancellor (Kenneth) Shaw of Syracuse hosted the meeting and it was a very, very contentious meeting," Tranghese said. "Then Chancellor Shaw basically threw all the AD's out of the room. He just said 'get out. You are incapable of solving this.'

Then he put his hand on my arm and said 'you stay right here."

Tranghese sat among the priests and academics and talked straight about the future of college sports. It was a future revolving around football and at this point the Big East's football schools were holding all the cards: they owned the TV deal, they had a powerhouse team in Miami, they would remain strong in basketball. On top of that, St. John's and Villanova had slumped badly on the court but the priests who led the Catholic schools didn't seem to grasp the strength football schools across the country had attained.

"The presidents asked me a lot of hard questions in that meeting and some of them weren't happy with some of my answers. But I told them what we had to do to survive," Tranghese said. "I told them 'you might as well just split because if you think we're going to stay together by rejecting Rutgers and West Virginia, you're wrong.

"There were presidents on the basketball side who had been painted a very optimistic picture of what their life would be alone and I told them they were dead wrong. A couple of them were upset with me but I just said 'with all due respect, I know more than the person telling you these things. You can survive but not at the level of doing what you're doing.'"

Outside the room, the athletic directors fretted. "The AD's were dismissed and they closed the door. We had put a lot of work in on this but we didn't find out about the vote until it was already taken," said Syracuse's Crouthamel.

The 10 presidents quickly agreed to not kill the conference but Georgetown, Providence and Seton Hall were staunchly against any expansion. Ultimately, Syracuse's Shaw and BC's Father Monan convinced the president at St. John's, The Rev. Donald J. Harrington, to vote their way. Rutgers and West Virginia were in.

"It wasn't a crisis but it was close to it," said Crouthamel. "It could've become a crisis but a couple of presidents from the Catholic schools understood that, depending on their vote, the whole conference could split. It could have been a painful decision."

With the Eastern media in town for the basketball tournament, the Big East held a late-afternoon news conference where the presidents and athletic directors of the 10 schools attempted to put on a happy face. It didn't work. What came across quite clearly in a ballroom at the midtown Grand Hyatt Hotel was that the Big East Conference had survived, but not without leaving some deep scars.

"We thought 12 teams would help what is best for the Big East and UConn," said Dr. Harry J. Hartley, then the president at Connecticut. "Our goal was to keep the Big East together more than anything."

Speaking with school president The Rev. Philip A. Smith on his side, Providence AD John Marinatto said, "Providence was philosophically opposed to expansion because the league was formed with basketball in mind and the membership kept growing for football reasons and was getting away from the original principles of the league. The idea of 14 schools was too obtrusive, but 12 is the more palatable of the choices."

Tranghese summed up the showdown this way: "The football schools went to war to make 14 work and they lost. Then they went for 13 and lost and were faced with a problem: Do we stay with the people we've been in business with or not? They realized they would be walking away from a lot."

Syracuse's Crouthamel lobbied hard for a 14-team league and expressed deep concern about how Temple and Virginia Tech would respond to being kept out. "I didn't feel happy about the situation we had placed them in," Crouthamel said. "We had to make tough decisions. I was instructed to call Dave Braine at Virginia Tech after that vote. That was not a very pleasant chore."

Amid the talks, the basketball schools kept mentioning the only football power they'd unanimously welcome with open arms: Notre Dame.

Sure enough, the league moved to add Notre Dame for all sports almost as soon as the ink was dry on the invites for Rutgers and West Virginia. The Irish, as usual, backed off when any talk of adding their football program to the mix was even broached. But the Irish were very interested in finding a home for all sports except football.

"It was sometimes difficult to extract a definitive answer from Notre Dame but we continued to talk to them from time to time and a positive relationship developed," said Tranghese. "The timing was right for everyone at that time and we took Notre Dame."

That made the Big East a disjointed, 13-team league beginning with the 1995-96 season. For three seasons, the conference office actually split the teams into two divisions and called one group the 'Big East 6' and the other 'Big East 7.' That only illustrated just how cumbersome the league had become but by the end of the 1990s, that issue was solved.

Virginia Tech, with star quarterback Michael Vick at the controls, was clearly tired of making plenty of money for the Big East on the gridiron but not being able to join in the conference's marquee basketball parties. The Hokies were successful members of the Atlantic 10 at the time but longed for more. In the summer of 1999, the Big East voted to accept the Hokies in exchange for an entrance fee of a reported $2.5 million.

But buried beneath the excitement of another new school joining the league were rumors circulating out of Miami and Greensboro, N.C. Some members of the North Carolina-based Atlantic Coast Conference were anxious to jump into the expansion game and the main target in their sights resided in Coral Cables, Fla. The courtship of the Miami Hurricanes had begun.

4

If Mike Tranghese learned anything in his years as Dave Gavitt's righthand man, it was that TV negotiations are both vitally important and quite simple.

"TV negotiations are not about brainpower. They are about leverage," Tranghese says.

In 1999, the Big East appeared to have a lot to offer the TV networks. Connecticut was coming off its first basketball national championship, Virginia Tech and its top 10 football program were now full-time conference members and women's sports like basketball and soccer were thriving. But the Big East quickly learned that the only ingredient that truly mattered to the TV networks was the health of a conference's football programs.

The Big East was in somewhat of a damaged state at that time. Miami and its freewheeling Hurricanes were still experiencing some aftereffects on the recruiting front of a stay on probation. The 'Canes didn't win the league or finish ranked in the top 10 for five straight years (1995-99), a development that took away a bit of that old Miami swagger. This hurt the Big East at the negotiation table, as did a shifting of priorities at CBS which quickly re-signed for the Southeastern Conference's football rights but wasn't overly excited about retaining the Big East.

That reluctance led the Big East to shop its product and ABC/ESPN became involved. The league ultimately took its football-basketball TV rights to ABC/ESPN. CBS only retained some marquee men's basketball games.

"Miami's probation status really hurt us in the value of the television agreement," Tranghese said. "We lost our leverage in '99 for two reasons: Miami was going on probation and CBS had lost the post-season (bowls) and decided to cut back on college football. CBS made a very small offer for an amount that we weren't accustomed to. So we had to go deal with ABC/ESPN in a damaged state, to some degree. We made a deal but it was far less than what we feel we could've gotten if we were healthy."

On top of the football woes, basketball wasn't thriving either. True or not, the Big East of the mid to late 1990s was perceived as a push-and-grab league filled with too many players who couldn't shoot straight.

"ABC/ESPN had all the leverage there as well because there was no other place to go at the time," Tranghese said. "We hadn't had a long run of success in basketball leading up to that negotiation period. So we made two deals that, in my view, were not great deals but we had little choice."

While schools like Providence and St. John's barely noticed what they saw as a slight financial dip, other schools weren't happy. The biggest complainer was Miami, Tranghese said.

"I will say Miami was a constant complainer at that time. They didn't want to look in the mirror. They just said it was my fault. It's ironic because that was one of the great complaints that Miami had: 'Our television contract isn't as good as everyone else's.' But they didn't want to admit that had a lot to do with their being on probation. Both the ACC and Big East were being driven by one, star power, school. The ACC had Florida State and we had Miami. And Miami going on probation dramatically affected our value."

Sam Jankovich left Miami's athletic director post to run the New England Patriots in 1993. His replacement was Paul Dee, a much more conservative, corporate administrator who did a great job of maximizing the Hurricanes' football fortunes, reviving the basketball program and lining up money for a beautiful, new on-campus basketball arena. Where Jankovich was a back-slapping, personable leader, the short, overweight Dee wore the look of a frazzled lawyer. (In fact, Dee came to athletics after serving as UM's general counsel).

As any competent jurist would, Dee always looked out for his client's best interests. And as far back as 1999, Dee openly admits that he began talking to representatives of the ACC about plans for potential expansion. Most of the talk was idle chatter, a few athletic directors getting together over drinks and chewing the fat. There's no crime in this business, for sure, but the fact that Dee was even entertaining such discussions excited the ACC and its football loyalists.

At a Big East meeting in May 1999, Dee told his Big East partners that "Miami has never been contacted by the ACC itself; Miami has never contacted the ACC; There is no timeline because Miami has never been approached by the ACC."

Those words clearly defined Dee's delineation in this matter. Talking to athletic director pals like FSU's Dave Hart and Georgia Tech's David Braine was just that, idle talk and speculation. It's not as if Dee was peppering ACC commissioner John Swofford with questions or involving his president in any way.

After a Big East meeting on Nov. 2, 1999, Miami president Edward Foote felt the urge to clear the air even more. In a statement released by UM's press office, Foote said, "The rumors that the University of Miami might leave the Big East and join the Atlantic Coast Conference apparently began some time ago as a result of some casual conversation among athletic directors. We have great respect for our friends in the ACC but we have been, and remain, happy with our Big East affiliation. We have no plans to change conferences. No one has offered us membership in another conference. We are proud to be partners with the fine institutions that comprise the Big East Conference."

What wasn't made public, however, was what Miami was telling Tranghese behind closed doors. On Nov. 30, Miami's Dee sent Tranghese a letter enumerating 16 concerns that Miami had with the Big East. The school expressed anxiety about scheduling, marketing, TV rights fees and the mechanism for schools that wished to leave the conference.

It was a soup-to-nuts laundry list that caught the Big East by surprise. The conference office felt it had stood by UM in its time of need, helping it get through probation and back into the top 10. Yet instead of any gratitude, Miami complained. Over the next year and a half, the Big East and Miami discussed these concerns, many of which sought to improve Miami's financial package. In a lawsuit Miami filed against the Big East in October 2003, it claimed "almost no progress was made to address at least 14 of Miami's 16 concerns."

By the summer of 2000, the ACC was clearly developing into a league divided. On one side were football athletic directors like Hart and Braine who openly wondered about their fate in a world now dominated by the Bowl Championship Series and its more than $100 million in payouts. The nine-school ACC was guaranteed a place at the BCS trough but no one besides Bobby Bowden's Seminoles had developed into a consistent, national program. More troublesome was the fact that some ACC schools (namely Duke) considered football a nuisance of sorts that simply tore attention (and millions of dollars in facilities and coaching staff salaries) away from their heavyweight basketball programs.

Clemson, FSU and Georgia Tech led this football faction. On the other side were traditional basketball schools Duke and North Carolina. Maryland, North Carolina State, Wake Forest and Virginia alternated allegiances between the two groups but all four schools realized the importance of football's money to their athletic futures.

The dollar signs available for the premier football powers were skyrocketing thanks to the dawn of the BCS. Full shares for the Orange-Sugar-Fiesta-Rose bowls approached $12 million per team and rose to $17.8 million in 2005. That was real money, the type that separated the haves and have-nots in college sports in lightning-quick fashion. The ACC was assured of one of those payouts but its chances at multiple BCS bids seemed slim as long as the bulk of its football programs continued to founder.

The ACC also took notice when the SEC and the Big 12 decided to hold conference championship games. These games held the promise of delivering a $10-12 million, single day payoff for the conference. Under NCAA rules, a league could only hold a championship game if it had 12 members. That left the nine-member ACC out in the cold.

Dee kept talking, and listening, to his ACC friends as he surveyed the changing football landscape. At the dawn of the new millennium, his Hurricanes and Virginia Tech were clearly driving the Big East's football bus. Although Syracuse, West Virginia, Pittsburgh and Boston College made some national noise from 1997-2002, those schools never produced a team that finished in the top 10 in the polls. The bottom half of the Big East was pillow-soft with Temple serving as a joke of a 1-A program and things promised to get even softer if Connecticut joined the league, something Miami wanted no part of.

A fateful change in Miami's athletic future occurred on June 1, 2001. That's when Foote retired and Donna Shalala stepped into the corner office. An Ohio native who did graduate work at Syracuse's Maxwell School of Citizenship and Public Affairs, Shalala was regarded as a dynamo in the fields of public education and government. She became the chancellor at both Hunter College in New York and the University of Wisconsin-Madison and became a national figure in 1993 when President Bill Clinton appointed her the Secretary of Health and Human Services. She served throughout Clinton's two terms.

Just as Shalala arrived, Miami's football fortunes began to rise. The Hurricanes were 11-1 and finished second in the nation in 2000 and then swept to the National Championship in '01 under first-year head coach

Larry Coker. That team finished with a 12-0 record and a Rose Bowl win over Nebraska.

Two months after that game, Shalala met with the other Big East CEO's in March 2002. During the meeting, Shalala was asked to speak about Miami's commitment to the league. She said, in words reflected in the meeting's minutes, that "in the strongest terms possible, emphatically stating that the University of Miami is in the Big East Conference and has no interest in leaving it for any other conference."

This reassurance was welcomed by the other presidents and chancellors, including West Virginia's David Hardesty. Hardesty sent Shalala a letter on the day after the meeting (March 7, 2002) where he wrote: "I want you to know how important your statement at the Big East meeting yesterday was to the entire league. It is a significant act of leadership on your part, and your election as our representative to the Equity Conference Group reflects the support you already have within the Big East....I look forward to working with you in the years to come and enjoy what you bring to our group very much."

What wasn't known then was that Miami's issues with the Big East, raised in its 'Letter of Concern' written back in 1999, were still largely unresolved. In the Oct., 2003 lawsuit, Miami stated that "Miami was committed at that time (2002) to continue negotiating with other conference members to improve The Big East and address the concerns set forth in the Letter of Concern."

On the gridiron, Miami kept rolling. The Hurricanes made a valiant run at a second straight national title in 2002. Behind running back Willis McGahee and quarterback Ken Dorsey, the 'Canes entered the Fiesta Bowl as favorites to beat Ohio State. But in one of the greatest college football games in the last 25 years, the Buckeyes outlasted Miami in double overtime, 31-24.

What the college football world didn't know at the time was that a move was already afoot that promised to send shock waves from coast to coast. With Miami's value as a football powerhouse soaring once again, Dee's discussions with the ACC had picked up. No one in the Big East knew it, but the 'Canes were about to rock everyone's world.

•

In December 2002, just before Miami's loss in the Fiesta Bowl, the Big East held a meeting of its football athletic directors. One issue on the agenda was a discussion of the league's revenue sharing policy. From the creation of the football league, the Big East had crafted a revenue plan different from the one used in basketball where all schools evenly shared (more or less) the pot.

This was done to protect the huge bowl shares teams received and also agreed upon to appease Miami's Jankovich when the Hurricanes entered the league. For a dozen years, the unbalanced division played into the pockets of the Hurricanes who routinely advanced to the premier bowls and appeared on network TV more than any other Big East team. But in 2002, there was a move afoot to alter the revenue sharing plan and make things more equitable. The school pushing such a move, according to Tranghese, was Boston College and its AD, Gene DeFilippo.

"We had crafted a very innovative policy for revenue sharing in football and over the years some people had wanted to change it but we fought that," he said. "What was very interesting is that BC was the one that constantly wanted to change it. That would've taken Miami's share down."

Tranghese pulled Dee aside and assured him that BC's idea had little support. "I told Paul Dee that they would not get this past me. They'd have to run me over with a truck on this issue. I understood what our deal with Miami was and they had to be maintained," he said.

The revenue-sharing change never did move forward. What did occur in the winter of 2003 was a slice of heaven for the Big East. Led by precocious freshman Carmelo Anthony, Syracuse came out of nowhere and stormed through the NCAA Tournament to win its first national basketball championship in dramatic fashion at the Louisiana Superdome. A day later in Atlanta, Connecticut and its star, Diana Taurasi, beat Tennessee for its fourth national title in five years. Amid the celebration with his friends from UConn, Tranghese spoke with coach Geno Auriemma and longtime associate athletic director Dee Rowe.

"I remember telling Dee and Geno that 'this is like euphoria. This is the first time since I've been commissioner that I finally feel good about where we are.' I just felt we finally had harmony and peace and people working together."

"We were on a pretty good roll," he added. "Syracuse and Connecticut winning both titles in the same year was a great accomplishment. We were feeling good about football, too, particularly with Miami and Virginia Tech. But we felt the other teams were getting better and we were anxiously looking forward to negotiating a new football (TV) contract because we knew we were undervalued."

The highest profile coaching change in the Big East that spring was playing out at Pittsburgh after basketball coach Ben Howland left to return to his West Coast roots and coach UCLA. Pitt instantly thought about two homegrown coaches, John Calipari and Skip Prosser. Calipari had just settled in at Memphis and his penchant for flouting NCAA rules spooked Pitt a bit. Prosser, however, looked like an ideal candidate.

Pitt spoke with Prosser and sometime during the discussions, Wake Forest broke some shocking news to its coach: The Big East is a doomed league. The ACC is about to expand and take some of its marquee schools. You should stay right here at Wake.

Armed with this inside info, Prosser pulled out of the running for the Pitt job. The Panthers ended up replacing Howland with his top assistant, Jaime Dixon. Eight days after watching UConn win in Atlanta, Tranghese received a phone call from Dick 'Hoops' Weiss of the New York Daily News. He had heard rumors that ACC expansion plans may have spooked Prosser away from the Pitt job.

"I guess during the course of conversations, to entice Skip to stay, people told him 'why are you going to go there? The league is going to break up. We're going to take their members.' I didn't believe what Dick was telling me," Tranghese said.

Tranghese said he quickly picked up the phone and called DeFillipo at Boston College, someone he considered a close friend in the business.

"I called Gene DeFilippo and I could tell by the awkwardness of the call that they were involved. He didn't deny it and it was just awkward. And this was someone I was very close to," Tranghese said.

What Tranghese and the rest of the Big East didn't realize at the time was that the conference was literally asleep at the switch. Miami's leaders say the ACC contacted the school about expansion around March 2003. This timeline seems almost laughable, however, and really spins on semantics. The ACC and Miami were clearly dance partners for some time. Tranghese says the ACC even allowed Miami to view its financial records in February, a claim Miami rebuts.

But what is clear is that Swofford was doing an expert job keeping things quiet. In its 2003 lawsuit against the Big East, Miami claims it "promptly notified Commissioner Tranghese that it was having discussions with members of the ACC regarding a possible expansion of the ACC to include Miami," around March 2003. This is plainly false, however. "It certainly wasn't March, that's for sure. That news would've stayed with me. I'd recall that phone call," Tranghese said.

On April 16, 2003, the college sports world was thrown into a state of shock when Weiss' story ran in the Daily News. In it, Tranghese lashed out at the ACC. "I have no use for the ACC right now...... they're a bunch of hypocrites. They operate in the dark."

"I was shocked at the way it was being handled. Shocked that they just didn't come and tell us," Tranghese said. "People have every right to leave but when I found out from (Weiss) about the depth of the conversations, I made some pretty inflammatory comments and the ACC was pretty upset with me. It's funny, I found that curious. They're angry with me? They were operating behind our backs with our members."

The ACC's position on the matter was quite clear. They were some time away from holding any sort of vote on expansion and were simply talking to schools it thought would fit into their plans. That Miami was listening was Miami's business. That Miami chose to keep those talks quiet was apparently Paul Dee's choice.

Jake Crouthamel, the athletic director at Syracuse, was a close friend of Dee's. He said the two never shared a word on a possible Miami exit up to that point but he understood the ramifications of Miami's exit.

"The economics drove the ACC's decision, pure and simple," Crouthamel said. "This was a historically conservative conference that had trouble going from eight to nine members in 1991 (when Florida State was added) and had been discussing going to 10, mainly with Miami, ever since. But there wasn't support for it. Then, all of a sudden, they're talking about going to 12 members. That was because of television money, expanding the brand and creating a conference championship game, no question.

"From our perspective, the conference had done right by Miami and they were happy with us," Crouthamel added. "When Donna Shalala showed up, I think that changed things a bit down there. There were some personal things going on behind our backs, coming from the ACC office to Miami. Paul Dee is a good friend of mine and I've asked him about that. All he said was 'yes, there were some conversations,' and we all listen to discussions about these things."

The news began a flood of stories in newspapers up and down the East Coast about the threat of expansion, the power of money in college sports and the potential demise of the Big East. The situation was so unstable that virtually every school in the East instantly began weighing their options on conference affiliation. BC's DeFilippo personified everyone's concerns when he went on a Boston radio station soon after the news about Miami broke and said, "if Miami leaves, we'll have to evaluate our options."

So much for allegiances. Miami, after all, was Big East football's Golden Goose. The conference's financial structure in football largely relied on TV and bowl money but a league without Miami clearly didn't carry as much cache with the networks and would be in grave danger of getting squeezed out of the Bowl Championship Series.

"Obviously the threat of not playing in the BCS shook people up. It was a crazy time. No one quite knew what everyone else was really thinking," said Rutgers athletic director Bob Mulcahy.

While it seemed clear that Boston College would choose to follow Miami if asked, other schools weren't so sure. Syracuse was an obvious contender and Crouthamel knew what losing Miami and BC could do to the Big East. But if the ACC was truly interested in SU, Crouthamel's phone didn't ring.

"I was aware that we were on the table and that John Swofford wanted to talk to me but I didn't have any discussions with the ACC until about two days before we received an invitation to join," said Crouthamel. "I know Boston College was heavily involved on a regular basis. That I know of. John Swofford knew my number. I'm not hard to find."

While BC and Syracuse were hardly natural fits in a southern conference, other Big East schools looked like naturals. Virginia Tech looked an awful lot like an ACC school. Seven ACC members were within 300 miles of Blacksburg and the state's media covered the league like a blanket, always at the expense of the Hokies and the Big East. More importantly, recruits in Virginia, Maryland and the Carolinas grew up dreaming of playing in the ACC.

But Va. Tech wasn't on the ACC's initial wish list. For reasons known only to themselves, academic and athletic officials at several ACC schools began leaking expansion news to the media in almost reckless fashion. It became clear that the ACC wanted to add three schools in order to grow to 12 and play a conference championship game. But the ACC presidents were widely divided on who they should ask to join with Miami. Support for BC, Syracuse and Virginia Tech was split and ACC bylaws called for 7 of 9 votes for any new member.

Dave Gavitt, the Big East's architect and a man with deep relationships with several ACC schools, didn't see the logic in the ACC's plans.

"I'm not sure what (the ACC) is trying to accomplish," Gavitt told the Boston Globe. "All this for one football game? They are going to find out the money for a championship game is not what they think it is. But there is a bigger issue involved. Each of the leagues has its own persona, something that is unique to that league. The Big East was the Northeast configuration of schools with their own identity....The ACC has always been this nice, academically oriented league with a great basketball tradition. But what I see is three schools – Florida State, Georgia Tech and Clemson – who are all from the heart of SEC territory, seemingly forcing the football issue. But what they are doing could damage two great leagues. I just don't understand why."

Yet throughout ACC country, the horse trading had begun. John Thrasher, the chairman of Florida State's Board of Trustees, told the Jacksonville Times-Union that FSU was in favor of adding Miami, Syracuse and Boston College. Virginia, at the urging of Gov. Mark Warner, wanted to bring in Virginia Tech and not Syracuse. Georgia Tech also backed adding the Hokies. Miami wanted the ACC to include Syracuse and Boston College as part of any package. Duke and North Carolina were holding out for no expansion of any kind.

On May 16, the ACC Presidents voted 8-to-1 to enter expansion discussions with Miami, BC and Syracuse. Reportedly, Virginia was the only school against the decision. If carried out, the ACC would grow to 12 schools by the 2004-05 school year.

At that point, this was not news. ACC expansion was the talk of the industry for at least a month with one news report after another guessing about the future makeup of the major conferences. Reaction to the move was both swift and dramatic. On the plus side, you had Andy Haggard, a member of Florida State's Board of Trustees, telling the Miami Herald that "we're thrilled to have Miami joining the ACC because of the great traditional rivalry between FSU and Miami, because of what it will do for recruiting for both schools within the state and, probably, most importantly, that it now makes the state of Florida an ACC state."

Notice that Haggard, an official at an institution of higher education, had little to say about academics.

Miami acknowledged the ACC's vote and said that Dee would attend the Big East's annual meetings that began May 17. "It is our intention to give the Big East Conference a full and fair hearing regarding our continued membership," the school said.

Syracuse's road to the ACC was far from a done deal. Crouthamel saw the need to join Miami, just like Boston College did. But he couldn't make sense of the ACC's odd rules of courtship.

"I saw John (Swofford) at an NCAA meeting just we were named in the expansion plan and I pulled him aside and asked him about what everyone was talking about," Crouthamel said. "He said 'yes, this is what we're looking at in the ACC. What followed was an invitation."

Syracuse Chancellor Kenneth Shaw, a major player in the Big East, made it clear he was happy his school enjoyed some options but wasn't close to making any commitments.

"Our position really hasn't changed," Shaw told the Syracuse Post-Standard. "We think Miami's decision-making is pivotal. It may be true that if we didn't go, Miami may not go. In the short term. But eventually, if Miami wants to go, they'll do so. Miami's the school the (ACC) wants. I don't have any illusions about that."

Virginia Tech AD Jim Weaver was understandably crushed. With the Big East's spring meetings at the posh Ponte Vedra Inn and Club outside Jacksonville set to start, Weaver crystallized the Big East's feeling on the matter.

"My resolve is to work as hard as we can to keep the Big East Conference intact," he told the Associated Press. "Obviously we don't want to spend four or five days doing that and then have people say they're gone. I'd rather if they've made up their minds that they tell us up front so we can get on with life."

The ACC's vote didn't equate with a formal invitation to join. Its bylaws called for a group of league leaders to visit the campus of any prospective new school. Then a vote on each new member could be taken. The ACC scrambled to line up visitation dates for the three schools over the next few weeks.

When the Big East's athletic directors and men's and women's basketball coaches gathered in Ponte Vedra, the scene was unlike any other meeting in conference history. Not only were members of the media from Boston to Miami camped outside conference room doors, but the normal fun of arranging golf dates at the Tournament Player's Club at Sawgrass a few miles down the road was put on the back burner.

"I'm letting those other guys handle that (ACC talk). I'm playing golf," UConn coach Jim Calhoun said with a smile on the first day of the meetings.

The ringleader of the golf pairings is normally Tranghese, an avid player whose handicap has hovered around five for the better part of the last 30 years. But the commissioner was in no mood to tee it up. He says he was informed of the ACC's vote via a phone call from Swofford. He also spoke with

Miami's Dee two days before the start of the Ponte Vedra meetings. He maintains both calls came several months too late.

"Miami, I made six calls over three weeks between April and May and they never returned any of them. That's all you need to know," Tranghese says. "In fact, Paul Dee and I never had a conversation between the time Dick Weiss' story ran in the Daily News to two days before our annual meeting. He just didn't return my calls. Now they'll probably deny that but if they want to go that route, I'll dig out the phone logs.

"So we go to the annual meeting and I felt the bus was already gone. (Miami) said they were open-minded. Well, when people don't return phone calls and I can hear it in their voice, they were gone. John Swofford called me at the start of our annual meeting and said that the ACC had the votes (for expansion). Their meeting was a week before ours. So they had the votes. Was Miami gone? No, they hadn't signed. But they were gone emotionally. No doubt in my mind. Boston College was gone as well. Boston College wanted it to happen and contributed to it happening.

"Now they both had every right to do it but I think that after all that we had built and enjoyed, it's only right to be up front about your business. Boston College had been with us from Day One. Miami had been out in limbo and we helped them. They were on probation and we were incredible partners. They had a right to leave but they went and operated behind our back. As I look back on it, if Pitt hadn't been trying to hire Skip Prosser, who knows when I might have found out about it. The ACC would've gone to its annual meeting and they would've voted on it and I would've gotten a call saying 'we've got the votes' and I wouldn't have known about it. But somehow everybody paints this picture like we're the bad guys. That's Miami and the BC view, for some reason. I resent that. I have great resentment about that. We didn't do anything wrong.

"John Swofford and I talked about this later in the process and he said, 'we didn't have the votes so why would I call you?' I just said, 'John, I disagree with that. You don't go this far without knowing you have the votes. Pick up the phone.'"

On the flip side, Tranghese says Syracuse and Virginia Tech handled things more openly.

"I don't know if Syracuse was reluctant or not but I know Syracuse wasn't 100 percent there. I know Chancellor Shaw wasn't," he said. "When Syracuse was contacted, Jake called me. Like he should have. That was just before our annual meeting."

For his part, Swofford simply said he was working on behalf of the ACC presidents and dismissed the notion that the main impetus for expansion was money. "Finances are a part of it, but only a part. It's about our culture and our history being at a point in time where culture, history and tradition meet opportunity. The world never stays the same, whether we want it to or not," he told reporters in North Carolina.

While their wives enjoyed the oceanfront resort, the Big East's athletic directors spent the daylight hours squired away in conference rooms. The football AD's quickly realized that convincing Miami to stay was a long shot. Their only alternative was to turn to the root of Miami's issues: money. Tranghese crafted an improved financial package that guaranteed Miami $9 million a season through more of the conference's TV and bowl receipts. In exchange, the Hurricanes had to commit to the Big East for five seasons.

As soon as some of the AD's began emerging from their meetings, a few key points became clear. First, Miami was gone. Dee may not have told anyone so but he was asking for the world not only financially but in structure, too. Dee, BC's DeFilippo and Syracuse's Crouthamel were either heading to the ACC or staying in a dramatically revamped Big East. After a few years of rumors and innuendo, the football schools were finally ready to split from the basketball schools. At least that was the world Miami craved and Miami was clearly 'driving the bus on that issue," according to another AD in the discussions.

To his credit, Dee didn't hide his feeling on that position. "The question isn't, 'What's it going to take to keep [teams]?' The question is, 'What can we do as a league to create a future that has stability in that league for everyone, that has stability in a variety of ways?" Dee said."You have to look at where the world is going. We have two conferences (Big 12, SEC) now that have 12 members, that have been extraordinarily successful with members of that level. The SEC probably has been the most successful at it. The Big 12 has certainly done a tremendous job with bringing that into being."

In this environment, the football schools were ready to sacrifice Georgetown and Villanova in order to keep Miami. Anything for the Hurricanes and all the money and cache their vaunted football program could deliver.

But it became clear that even if Pittsburgh, Rutgers, West Virginia and the other football schools agreed to this historic move, Miami would still bolt. At one point, Rutgers AD Bob Mulcahy went at Dee and told him "to cut the crap and lay your cards on the table."

Dee wasn't Mulcahy's only target. At the meetings it became obvious that BC's DeFilippo was strongly linked to Miami and that he and Dee had worked on the issue for some time. One way out of the jam was convincing everyone that letting Miami leave wasn't the end of the world. If BC and Syracuse remained committed to the Big East, the league could expand and survive. That was Virginia Tech's bargaining position but Boston College wasn't ready to bite on that one.

"There was a moment in that meeting where I asked the question of Boston College, 'If Virginia Tech stays, will you stay?' Mulcahy said. "I said that Virginia Tech's president has committed, and will sign a contract today, to stick with us. Boston College said 'we don't believe it.'

"We were all willing to let Miami go. Boston College's response was 'we're going with Miami and we don't believe Virginia Tech.' That is wrong. I was in the conversation with the Virginia Tech president and I knew that he would sign the contract to stay with us."

On Sunday night, the group, including Miami's representatives, attended a banquet sponsored by the conference office. Later, the party moved to the hotel's bar area. At one point two coach's wives, Juli Boeheim (Syracuse) and Connie Jarvis (St. John's), hugged and laughed. Then a song came on the jukebox and the two women happily shook each other as the Sister Sledge hit 'We Are Family' rang out.

The moment stayed with others in the room because as the hours passed, it became apparent that the Big East's family was headed toward an ugly divorce.

5

By the third day of the Ponte Vedra meetings, the verbal and mental strain had reached its apex. Tranghese met with the basketball coaches on Monday morning and filled everyone in on the AD's meetings. Things weren't good, he reported, but he planned on airing a few key concerns at a new conference that afternoon.

Perry Clark, then Miami's basketball coach, was in an odd position. His school was being painted as the bad guy but no one had any issues directly with him. It was football, after all, which threatened to dramatically alter everyone's athletic life.

"The hard part is to see how our decision will affect everybody else," said Clark. "That's an uncomfortable situation."

Paul Dee sat in the most uncomfortable chair. He was the force behind expansion and was set to move Miami closer to accepting the ACC's invitation but he maintained an interest in listening to the Big East's best offer. Syracuse's Jake Crouthamel and BC's Gene DeFilippo also enjoyed options that Pittsburgh, Virginia Tech, West Virginia and the other football schools did not but everyone knew who was calling the shots.

"We will not make a decision until one other decision is made," Crouthamel said, referring to Miami's move. "Clearly Miami is driving the whole situation and has been for the last five years."

A little after noon, a clearly frustrated Tranghese walked to a podium and addressed the media. His words were direct and strong and aimed at one target: The University of Miami. He seemed to know that Miami had a foot out the door and his league's last, best offer boiled down to playing the guilt card.

"This is a crisis. Make no mistake about it. I don't hide from that fact," he said. "This is no secret. At the end of the day, the University of Miami is going to make a decision and that decision is going to drive the wagon. That's why the ACC went to them. If Miami doesn't go, there isn't going to be any expansion."

"This is not just an athletic issue. This is an institutional issue. This has incredible implications," he said. "Is (money) worth just providing a body blow to a group of schools who were there when no one else wanted Miami? When we extended the invitation to Miami there was no one else there. I remember telling President (Edward) Foote, 'this would be a union. We will help you in a lot of ways, and you will help us in a lot of ways.' And we've done that.

"So we're going to end it and damage the people who've extended this opportunity? I just find that to be unacceptable."

Tranghese then painted a picture of Miami's decision causing chaos around the country with conferences trading members like cattle.

"This will be the most disastrous blow to intercollegiate athletics in my lifetime," he said. "It's wrong. I don't want to hear about previous pieces of expansion. People were not damaged (then). No one has been hurt. People wanted to leave in those cases."

"What bothers me the most is the way this whole thing has happened. We could argue whether who has the right to do what. I've heard that what happens to us is an unintended consequence. It is not an unintended consequence. It's there, they see it and I don't sense one iota of concern about it. If I were IBM, I'd understand it. I'm not IBM. I represent 14 educational institutions. Educational institutions are supposed to be controlled by presidents. That's what I've been told for the last 10 years. Presidential control. Welcome to the world of presidential control. The (ACC) presidents are making this decision. And when presidents begin to act this way with other presidents, I think it's wrong."

Tranghese's vitriol was highlighted in some corners as words from a scorned lover. Miami was exercising its right to move in a different direction and the Big East could do nothing to stop it. Yelling and screaming and putting Donna Shalala and Paul Dee on the spot certainly didn't help the situation.

But even today, Tranghese doesn't regret the words he chose at the media conference a bit.

"They were contentious meetings but they were all a waste of time, in my opinion. We made a financial offer to Miami to make sure they were whole. That was our response. But this thing was done. It was done when we went there. You could see it in people's eyes and I knew," he said.

Everyone left Ponte Vedra the next day hoping against hope that Miami would realize life was pretty good in the East. But a meeting in early June between Shalala and the presidents of the other football schools made it clear that the Hurricanes probably could not be appeased. On June 6, Connecticut, Pittsburgh, Rutgers, Virginia Tech and West Virginia filed a bombastic lawsuit against the ACC, Miami and Boston College for conspiring to violate their legal obligations and fiduciary duties to the other members of the conference. The Big East office (or Syracuse) was not a party in the suit.

The ACC shrugged off the lawsuit as 'frivolous' and continued with its campus visits. On June 2, a delegation including Swofford and Wake Forest AD Ron Wellman visited Boston College. At a news briefing at the end of the visit, Swofford said, "I don't think there's any doubt that if this indeed works out . . . that Boston College would be an excellent fit in the Atlantic Coast Conference in every regard."

DeFilippo expressed "deep concern" for the Big East's leaders and other schools but made it clear that moving to the ACC was in his school's best interest. "The ACC does a lot for us," he said. "It secures our future. It puts us in one of the leagues that could be one of the best in the country."

A few days later, the ACC Tour hit Syracuse. Crouthamel says his department was ready, opening its financial books and exchanging ideas for the ACC's future. "We saw that as kind of perfunctory. Everybody seemed very impressed," he said.

One Syracusan who wasn't impressed was Boeheim, the most important coach on campus. He couldn't fathom a move South. "It makes no sense at all for us and BC," he said. "We're going to go from a league where we're founding members and have a lot of input to a league in the South where we have no input. It's insane."

During the heat of the turmoil, Boeheim and UConn women's coach Geno Auriemma were honored by the Winged Foot Golf Club at a dinner at the New York Athletic Club. Basketball commentator Billy Packer, a former star at Wake Forest, was the master of ceremonies and at one point in the evening he introduced Dave Gavitt, who received a hearty standing ovation. Then he took the gloves off.

"I thanked Billy for his kind words," said Gavitt, "and then I said 'Billy, when you go back to Greensboro, or wherever you live, tell those damn cotton pickers to keep their hands off our teams.'"

Despite the apparent success of the campus tours, the ACC still didn't have the votes to add the three schools. Swofford had most of the athletic directors in his pocket but the presidents at Duke, North Carolina and Virginia were resisting. In fact, the move was blasted at the presidential level in the ACC's heart, the Raleigh-Durham Research Triangle.

"This is what happens when you lay bare the fact that your purpose in this (expansion) is only one mission: that is to make money," said William Friday, the former chancellor in Chapel Hill.

As the process moved forward, it was clear the BC-Miami-Syracuse mix wasn't going to make it. Virginia President John Casteen, reportedly at the urging of Gov. Mark Warner, wouldn't support any expansion that didn't include Virginia Tech. With Duke and 'Carolina in Casteen's corner, Swofford didn't have the seven votes (out of 9) needed. That's when the ACC threw Virginia Tech into the mix. In early June, Tech was working hard to pressure BC and Syracuse to remain in the Big East. On June 9, Tech President Charles Steger went so far as to say, "if an offer [to join] came from the ACC today, we would not accept it."

After several days of rumors and leaks out of the executive suites of several ACC schools, the presidents were at a stalemate. North Carolina Chancellor James Moeser came out in favor of adding only Miami but that would bring the league to only 10 members, two shy of the 12 needed for a championship game. Finally, on June 24 the ACC made a decision. Without the votes to move to 12 schools, the ACC went halfway and offered membership to only Miami and Virginia Tech. It was a move that literally stunned BC and Syracuse.

"President (Kenneth) Shaw was on a conference call earlier in the day with the ACC people and he called me and I believe his exact words were 'it isn't going to happen,'" said Crouthamel. "I was obviously surprised he said that but I didn't really believe him until I heard from John Swofford. He called me later that evening. I was so stunned that I nearly dropped the phone."

"Am I shocked at this turn of events? No," said BC's DeFilippo. "Was I surprised and disappointed when I learned of the ACC Presidents' decision? You bet."

BC issued an official statement on the rejection that read, in part, "Our discussions with the ACC were based on a conference expansion proposal that included Miami and Syracuse. Yesterday, in the eleventh hour, the ACC instead voted to invite Virginia Tech and Miami and to exclude Boston College and Syracuse. This unexpected vote has ended our discussions with the ACC."

Virginia Tech quickly committed to the ACC but Miami's Shalala said she needed a few days to reach a decision. The Big East made a final (financial) offer to Miami at the eleventh hour but Miami ultimately accepted the ACC's invitation.

The news hit the Big East like an atom bomb. The football league was now a paper-thin six teams: BC, Connecticut, Pittsburgh, Rutgers, Syracuse and West Virginia. It wasn't a bad group but the league's BCS bid, bowl affiliations and TV contracts were all on shaky ground.

"We came out of the annual meeting in May in a crisis mode but then the ACC didn't make an announcement that they were taking our members until late June," said Tranghese. "From end of May to late June, we were talking about what to do assuming the ACC is going to take Miami, BC and Syracuse. Then the Virginia Tech people called us and were very up front about the fact that they had to be aggressive and had to find a way to be involved with the ACC. I appreciated that honesty and told them 'I don't blame you.'

"Then we have what - I don't know what you call it - a circus. The ACC touring our schools and talking publicly. Things leaking out everywhere. Then one night I'm sitting at home and I get a call from Steve Weiberg from USA Today and he asked me to comment on the fact that the ACC took Miami and Virginia Tech. I said 'what are you talking about, Steve? What about Syracuse and BC?' He said 'they took Virginia Tech and Miami. That's it.'

"What they basically did was reject two schools publicly. At that point I was shell-shocked. Now we have to regroup with a totally different set of schools than we were planning on. Virginia Tech is out and BC and Syracuse are back in. It was nuts."

The initial reaction from the remaining Big East football schools was one that lingered from the meetings in Ponte Vedra: dissolve the conference. The Football Six needed at least two new partners to grow to the eight members required to remain a BCS-level conference. Cincinnati and Louisville of Conference USA quickly emerged as the leading candidates.

The footballer's resolve was emphasized at a July 9 meeting of presidents and athletic directors at the Newark Airport Marriott. In minutes of that meeting, the first entry summarizes the spirit of the day. "Jake Crouthamel goes on record and states that if this group expands to 16, he will resign his position as AD at Syracuse. Gene DeFilippo echoes those sentiments."

The group explores three different models:

- A 12-school merging of the Big East football schools and those from Conference USA. That group included favorites Central Florida, Cincinnati, Louisville, Army and Navy, with some support for East Carolina, South Florida, Memphis, Southern Mississippi, Marshall and Alabama-Birmingham.

- A 16-school model that would feature two divisions and include the five basketball members, Georgetown, Providence, St. John's, Seton Hall and Villanova, as well as Notre Dame.

- A 8 or 9 school all-sports conference that would target Cincinnati and Louisville, with Notre Dame as a long-shot possibility.

Syracuse's Shaw asks the AD's if there is any support for the 16-team model. There was none so he urges an exploration of the 8/9 model. A quick vote is taken and comes up 6-to-0 in favor of the 8/9 model

Then the group moved on to its most important issue, a binding agreement to each other. The initial suggestion is to bump the current 1-year/$1 million withdrawal penalty up to $5 million with a 27-month waiting period. A reaction from BC's Father William Leahy in the minutes states that "Bill Leahy indicates that he never felt the Big East had a commitment to excellence and it had difficulty balancing the basketball/football issues. If people within the room at some point feel uncomfortable about the direction of the league and, secondly, is presented with an attractive alternative, they would pay the $5 million penalty and give the 27-month notice."

Syracuse's Shaw proposes that the group agree to the new withdrawal terms and the motion is quickly seconded and passed, 6-to-0.

With that in place, discussion ensues over which schools to add. First, various presidents are advised on what to say to their counterparts at the basketball schools. The minutes state that "the conversations that take place should present the break-up situation as follows:

"We as a group genuinely believe that the break-up of the Big East Conference is inevitable – and probably the best overall scenario for all parties concerned. Toward that end, we suggest that a small group of football representatives meet with a small group of basketball representatives in order to discuss the possible fallout issues associated with this. We are prepared to do what we can to minimize the negative impact that this break-up will have on your group."

The AD's then talked about potential new partners. Louisville earned full support while Cincinnati and Temple were placed in the 'considered' lot.

Those three would bring the league to nine members. Central Florida, Army and Navy were placed on the table for football only. West Virginia president David Hardesty asks for support for in-state rival Marshall but receives none. Others placed under a 'dismiss' category in the minutes were Memphis, Southern Miss, East Carolina, Alabama-Birmingham and South Florida.

At the end of the meeting, Tranghese dropped a bombshell on the group. He says that his role as the leader for all 12 remaining schools is now jeopardized by a potential split. "He states that he feels he cannot effectively continue as commissioner of the Big East Conference, either with the basketball or football schools. He feels that he will be compromised by both groups if he takes any other position," the minutes read.

The meeting then adjourned to the following morning. On July 10, the group pressed forward with plans to split. Syracuse's Shaw was asked to contact Penn State about the possibility of leaving the Big Ten and joining the Big East. Tranghese would do the same with Notre Dame. A timeframe was drawn up with the basketball schools dismissed by Sept. 15 and new candidates added by Oct. 1. Groups were also set up to explore moving the conference office out of Providence to Newark, Philadelphia or Pittsburgh and to establish criteria in hiring a new commissioner.

And a written legal agreement needed to be drawn up that outlined the $5 million/27-month withdrawal requirement.

Asked about the meeting today, Tranghese makes it clear that the presidents were missing one key ingredient: Boston College's willingness to make a new conference work.

"So we have this big meeting (in July) and the football schools decide that they were separating. That's when I told them that I'm not going to manage the dissolvement of the conference so I'd vacate the last year of my contract," Tranghese said. "I told the presidents of the football schools that they were walking down the wrong path because BC is still going to leave. The ACC had 11 schools, they wanted 12 and BC wanted to go. I knew Syracuse wouldn't because Chancellor Shaw looked me in the eye and said he was so angry about being treated the way he did that he would stay in the Big East.

"I felt we were going through all these gyrations but in my heart of hearts I knew BC was going to leave. They wanted to leave, they were actively involved with the ACC in wanting to leave and even though it was deterred by this political game with Virginia Tech, they only had 11 (schools) so you knew they had to come back."

Others wanted to take BC at its word, including Rutgers' AD Mulcahy. "After Miami and Virginia Tech left, we formed a committee of four athletic directors and six presidents and Father Leahy was one of the presidents. We met in the summer to put the (football) league together and there was a commitment by everybody in that room that we would be together. We upped the (withdrawal) penalty to $5 million so that it would be a serious detriment to anybody leaving. And everybody agreed to it. That's in the minutes," he said.

Sure enough, the ACC did revisit Boston College. But not before the Big East's football schools had a dramatic change of heart.

What the football presidents didn't originally know was that a move to dissolve the Big East would carry all sorts of issues with it. First, the Big East owned 14 'units' from the NCAA basketball tournament that were worth about $40 million. How the football/basketball split would divide that money, who would keep the Big East name and its contract with Madison Square Garden for the post-season basketball tournament were all unclear.

The key point centered around an NCAA rule that stated that a conference can remain viable in a split if it retains six members who've worked together for at least eight years. That meant the Football Six were all set but the five basketball schools were in danger of forming a new league that had no immediate automatic bids to NCAA events.

"What happened is I thought there were a lot of people sitting around the table who didn't know what the hell they were talking about at that point," said Tranghese. "(Associate commissioner) John Marinatto put together a really good document and after talking with the NCAA he laid out rules about continuity, basketball units and all of the important issues at hand."

In order to dissolve the league under its constitution, a majority vote was required. With 12 remaining members, that meant a 7-to-5 vote. That shifted the focus squarely to Notre Dame. If the Irish voted with the football group, the league could dissolve. If not, everything remained in limbo.

"To their credit, Notre Dame took a step back away from all this," Tranghese said. "I'm a big Notre Dame fan because of how they conducted themselves. Notre Dame refused to allow the other 11 schools to drag them into the middle and be the decision maker. They refused to accept that role. Notre Dame was evaluating its position and could've gone with either one of these groups. They also had a conversation with the ACC and I'm confident the ACC would've voted them in instead of Boston College. But I know Notre Dame was not going to cast a vote that would control the destiny of everyone else. They didn't see that as their role and I happened to agree with them."

Once it became apparent that Notre Dame wouldn't provide that seventh vote, the presidents began to look at the 16-team model being pushed by the basketball schools, Tranghese and Dave Gavitt. TV consultants told them that the value of a 16-team basketball league that spanned from Boston to Chicago to Washington, D.C. could be a whopper. A hoops deal without New York (St. John's), Philadelphia (Villanova) or D.C. (Georgetown) wasn't as nearly valuable.

Tranghese also sold the football schools on the ills of a 12-team setup solely for the riches of a conference championship game. First off, he noted that the extra game provided a significant hurdle in the chase for the national championship. The NCAA was also set to expand regular season football schedules to 12 games, meaning a team that played in a championship game and a bowl game would tee it up 14 times.

With no clear avenue open for a split, the football presidents also looked at the position they'd leave the basketball schools in. Pittsburgh Chancellor Mark Nordenberg and West Virginia President David Hardesty then began to push for including the basketball schools. "I don't think anyone in the room wanted to be in a position to harm some of our longtime partners," was the way Nordenberg explained the decision.

"I don't think there were any of us on the football side that wanted to do damage to the basketball schools," said Syracuse president Kenneth Shaw. "We were just wounded (by the exit of Miami and Va. Tech). It wasn't a time to wound somebody else."

Crouthamel made it very clear what a split could've done to the basketball schools. "If we had just up and left, it would've been disruptive to the point of destructive. In order to give them the opportunity to exist, if you will, and to grow, we had to expand on both sides. Our presidents were not prepared to stab them in the back the way some of the rest of us had been stabbed in the back."

With the 16-team model now in place, discussions began on finalizing the lineup of schools. At a meeting in Newark on Oct. 1, BC's Father Leahy expressed concerns about the graduation rates at Cincinnati and Louisville but those two schools drew instant support from the football side. DePaul and Marquette were quickly embraced as the new basketball members.

Ed Pastilong, the longtime AD at West Virginia, said he was convinced this was the right way to go. "I can remember distinctly the Ponte Vedra meeting and others afterwards and the first thing we had to address was whether to go football or football and basketball. Those were very trying times," he said. "But we chose to go with the basketball schools and that was a very, very intelligent decision. West Virginia was a strong proponent of keeping everyone together. The reason being we love the Northeast presence and we love being in Madison Square Garden. And schools like Georgetown and St. John's and Providence, they were the ones, along with some of the football schools, that put together the Big East. They're the originators and that's important. We were very much proponents of continuing it."

The most vital decisions came with Tranghese out of the conference room. "I had written a dissolvement document and I was very concerned about what was going to happen to our employees but in the end, I think Chancellor Shaw, Chancellor Nordenberg and President Hardesty just looked at the situation and said, 'if we're being critical of the ACC for doing this, how are we going to walk away?'" Tranghese said. "Those three just said 'we need to find a way to make this work.' So they called me in and we called a special meeting and laid out the plan for them.

"At that point I was so shell-shocked that nothing surprised me. I wasn't sold that we could survive, in all honesty. It would only work if everyone involved wanted it to work. I give the people in this (Big East) office a lot of credit. They had a lot to risk and they were working for the good of all our schools but no one came to see me and asked 'what about me and my family.' Instead they worked and put together the initial stages of our plan but the key was keeping everyone committed and I knew that probably wasn't the case."

Boston College wasn't a fan of the move. At the Oct. 1 meeting, the Big East's reorganization plans were nearing completion. But Father Leahy told his partners that his board of trustees wanted him to explore a move to the ACC once again. Minutes of the meeting state that he needed to determine the ACC's wishes "before he is willing to commit BC to an exit penalty larger than the already agreed to $5 million."

Sure enough, the ACC wasn't finished. In order to drive the revenues to make its per-school payout equal to what it was before Miami and Virginia Tech were added, the ACC needed a football championship game and a 12th member. Swofford was pursuing any avenue possible to get there, first petitioning the NCAA for a change of its rule requiring 12 teams to play a championship game and also reportedly exploring a change to the league's bylaws and reducing the percentage of votes needed for acceptance of a new member from 75 percent to 66 percent. Such a change would make it easier for BC to garner the necessary votes.

The chance of BC accepting an ACC invite always hovered over the Big East's discussions but with Father Leahy and DeFilippo involved in meetings and preparing for a new Big East, many in the conference took BC at its word. Yet on Oct. 16, the ACC offered BC an invitation to join its membership and the Eagles happily accepted. Once again, the Big East was knocked back on its heels.

"The Boston College administrators indicated to us in a face-to-face meeting that they were going to stay. And they broke that commitment. So yes, I thought they were going to stay," said WVU's Pastilong. "When you're in a room and the CEO of the college and the athletic director look you in the eye and say they're staying, I think that's the strongest statement that one can make."

Syracuse's Crouthamel was even more blunt, saying, "I don't know what we learned from it all other than who you thought were your friends suddenly became your enemies. It has nothing to do with collegiality. It has to do with money. We always thought that and we continue to prove it."

BC's Leahy called Tranghese on a Sunday afternoon and said his school planned to accept the ACC's offer. Tranghese was meeting with Nordenberg, Hardesty and officials from Cincinnati and Louisville the same day at a Hyatt Hotel in Pittsburgh

"The meetings went very well and then my cell phone rang and it was Father Leahy," Tranghese said. "He told me they were leaving and I wished him well and told him I wasn't surprised. But we had a backup plan assuming BC would leave. Monday we conference called and talked about South Florida and I was given permission to meet with them that Friday. So we had our new members in about a week, 10 days."

On Nov. 4, the Big East held a news conference at the Grand Hyatt in New York announcing the culmination of the expansion showdown. Cincinnati, Louisville and South Florida were in for all sports. DePaul and Marquette joined the basketball side and made a monster, 16-school behemoth.

"I can't express how excited we are," said a relieved Tranghese. "On the football side, we're solid and have enormous growth potential. In basketball, we're clearly as good as anyone in the country."

In the end, the Big East followed the ACC's lead and grew into a Super Conference. But instead of a goal focusing only on money and football, the Big East reacted in survival mode. Tranghese said he made sure to contact Conference USA leaders so that his cards were on the table. The Big East's new lineup provided a chance at a solid football future but what developed on the basketball side was truly exciting, or scary depending on where you sat. The 16-school setup represented more than 25 percent of the nation's TV households and stretched from Providence to Milwaukee to Tampa.

All sorts of issues needed to be worked out but on that crisp, fall day in New York big-time college sports in the East actually had a future once again. After the events of the previous seven months, this was an occasion to celebrate.

6

UCONN

As you drive into the tiny village of Storrs deep in the Eastern Connecticut woods, it's easy to feel as if you're tucked away somewhere in rural New Hampshire and not around the corner from the hustle and bustle of the Boston-to-New York corridor. Storrs is a college town in a part of the world where college towns barely exist.

Traveling along the quiet, two-lane state Route 195 through tall pine and oak forests, you pass by the brick Mansfield Center Post Office and small, rustic businesses cut out of the woods with signs like 'Storrs Family Medicine and Dentistry' hanging out front.

Civilization begins again when the Edward O. Smith High School pops up along the road. When a small, green sign dubs the pavement 'UConn Husky Way,' things begin to change a bit. Springing out of this wooded wonderland is a college campus that's clearly a mix of the past and the future. Some tired, old brick buildings that speak of a sleepy New England prep school sit next to new-age, academic warehouses named after powerhouse corporations. Traveling on one of the two main roads that twist through the campus, you dodge one construction site after another, complete with trucks and work crews and scaffolding rising to the heavens. Dimeo Construction, a Rhode Island contracting firm, seems to have its logo plastered on every corner.

As you turn another corner, an odd looking, mushroom-shaped edifice rises on the horizon. It's a building that's changed this campus more than any other. In fact, it's a building that's changed an entire, hoops-crazed state.

Gampel Pavilion is that special. Opened in 1990, Gampel was New England's first modern-day campus arena. The University of Connecticut had always enjoyed a strong, regional history playing out of its Field House, a 4,500-seat bandbox whose heyday ended in about 1972. Thanks to a push from the Big East office and a forward-looking president named Harry Hartley, UConn found a few wealthy donors who forked over the key seed money for the $28 million arena.

Gampel was on the drawing board when UConn was searching for a new basketball coach in 1986. Dom Perno, a good man but average coach and recruiter, had the bad luck of coaching the Huskies when the Big East was the baddest conference in the country. The Huskies had some good players such as Earl Kelly and Tim Coles but they were overshadowed by Patrick Ewing, Chris Mullin, Pearl Washington and the other Eastern mega-stars of the 1980's.

Many UConn fans, as well as an infamous Hartford Courant article written in 1985, wondered if the state school could ever compete in a league like the Big East. In-state recruits had paid little attention to their state university for years. Beginning back in the mid-1960s when the great Calvin Murphy left Norwalk High for Niagara, opposing recruiters plucked the Nutmeg State's best with seemingly little resistance. Great high school stars such as Bruce Campbell (Providence), Sly Williams (Rhode Island), Mike Gminski (Duke), John Pinone (Villanova), Harold Pressley (Villanova) and John Bagley, Michael Adams and Jay Murphy (all of Boston College) felt no pull to stay home. Someone, somehow, had to change that.

That someone ended up being Jim Calhoun.

In the waning days of the Perno Era, UConn athletic director John Toner happened to sit next to the opposing bench when Northeastern came to Hartford and beat the Huskies a few days after Christmas in 1985. Toner saw an aggressive, tough coach who demanded, and received, the best from his players.

"At Northeastern, Calhoun could often recruit only the second or third level players but he used excellent coaching and better conditioning to get the most out of them," Toner recalled several years later in Hoop Tales: UConn Huskies, a history of the Connecticut program.

Perno resigned at the end of that year, his fourth consecutive losing campaign. Calhoun was Toner's top candidate with Holy Cross' George

Blaney and Fairfield's Mitch Buonaguro also in the running. Calhoun remembers the search process with a chuckle, knowing he almost went the wrong way in the biggest decision of his life.

"John and I met at a halfway stop between Storrs and Boston, some place in Sturbridge," Calhoun said. "He asked me how interested I was in coming here but I was a Boston guy. I was a tenured professor and I could be the athletic director if I stopped coaching. We were going to the NCAA Tournament every year, we had Reggie Lewis and I really didn't think leaving was the best thing for me. UConn was at the bottom of the Big East."

Calhoun certainly knew all about Connecticut basketball. A tough, fast-talking Irishman from Braintree, Mass., Calhoun wasn't a big-time player and certainly didn't pop out of some Five Star Camp coaching test tube. But he grew up wired into New England's basketball subculture.

Pushed by an athletic father, Calhoun loved the Red Sox and the Celtics and played both sports at Braintree High. Standing in the outfield of a local baseball field back in 1957, a neighbor rushed to the fence and gave 15-year old Jimmy Calhoun a message.

"Jim, your father's dead. You better go home," the kid said.

That lightning bolt, delivered in the most callous way possible, was how Calhoun found out his father had died of a heart attack. The news sent Calhoun's college plans up in smoke. His new plan became supporting his mother, four sisters and little brother, just like his father told him to do.

He found a job at Settimelli Stonecutters in Quincy and came home to his mother covered in dust, like some tall, skinny ghost. But his high school coach, Fred Herget, kept in touch with him, told him not to fall into the working-class trap of chasing trouble and drinking with friends for hours after work. Calhoun listened and played extensive pickup ball with local clubs in and around Boston and was eventually discovered by the coach at American International College, a Division II school in Springfield. The 6-5 guard enjoyed a strong career, earning Little All-America honors and leaving AIC as its fourth all-time leading scorer. One of his best nights came on Dec. 1, 1964 when he poured in 27 points in a loss to UConn and its great star, Toby Kimball.

After coaching for a year at AIC, he bounced from high school jobs in Old Lyme and Westport, Conn., back home to Dedham High. He went 26-1 in 1972 and heard about an opening at Northeastern University, then a Division II school that sat a jump shot away from Boston's Fenway Park. The school had plans to move up to D-1 and needed a new, aggressive direction. Calhoun wasn't sure what he was walking into when he accepted the job but he knew he loved coaching and he certainly was aggressive. He also was a mere 29 years old.

Over 14 years at Northeastern, Calhoun turned an average, mostly white, Division II team into a traditional Eastern underdog with tough, mostly black, city kids. While seemingly no one in Boston – most of all the local press – noticed, the Huskies dominated the North Atlantic Conference and played in 5 NCAA Tournaments, beating Long Island, Saint Joe's and Fresno State. In his final three years at Northeastern, Calhoun's teams rolled to a 75-19 record. Those are numbers that get you noticed and John Toner over in Storrs, Conn., certainly took notice.

Calhoun was also a true basketball junkie, someone who scooped up morsels that fell from the minds of the area's extensive coaching tree. He spent a considerable amount of time with Dee Rowe, a legendary figure in New England coaching circles during his time at Worcester Academy and as UConn's head coach in the 1970s. That relationship with Rowe proved critical when it was time to weigh his jump to Storrs.

"I knew Jimmy and liked him a lot," Rowe said. "He was tough, fiery. I thought he'd be great for us but he was a Boston kid. He liked Boston and had done a great job at Northeastern. But Dave Gavitt and I talked to him and got the job done."

One of the biggest selling points was the untapped potential everyone in the East saw at Connecticut. The state university money, unmatched fan support and daily news coverage in almost a dozen newspapers made UConn look more like Kansas and Indiana than St. John's or Georgetown. Calhoun didn't know what the road to winning big in the Big East looked like but he knew the right coach at Connecticut had a chance.

"We had to get a better facility and needed to recruit better locally but everyone just loved the team. They wanted us to win more than anything," he said. "That's a great impetus for a coach, knowing the support is there for you to do great things."

Calhoun accepted the job and started at UConn in May of 1986 but greatness would come slowly. He won his first game against Massachusetts but then lost to Yale in New Haven, 77-75. The ride back to campus was long and quiet, but a late-night practice at the Field House was anything but.

"Coach killed everyone, the players and coaches. We caught the first taste of his temper that night and we all remembered it," center Gerry Bessilink said in *Hoop Tales: UConn Huskies*.

Losses to Boston University and Hartford in the Huskies' own Christmas tournament completed Jim Calhoun's first month as Connecticut coach. Perno did leave behind two impressive sophomores, Cliff Robinson and Phil Gamble, but when they both fell into academic trouble and couldn't play down the stretch, the Huskies were dead. A 9-19 record was justified in some quarters as acceptable for a young team with a first-year coach that lost two key players late in the season but Calhoun seethed.

He eased his temper on the recruiting trail and his first big target was Chris Smith, a high-scoring point guard from Kolbe-Cathedral High in Bridgeport. Smith was the kind of kid who had always left the state and he certainly listened when North Carolina, Syracuse and other powers recruited him. Smith was deemed so important a recruit that he had the coaching suite in Storrs redecorated. Literally.

It seems Calhoun hated the tired, old chairs and couches left over from the Perno Era. He ordered top assistant Howie Dickenman to upgrade the look before Smith and his family visited campus. The new look worked, and Calhoun celebrated when Smith answered the coach's plea to stay home and play before his mother and his friends.

Before Smith enrolled in the fall of 1988, an unexpected pleasure fell upon Calhoun and Connecticut's fiercely loyal fans. The Huskies finished last (4-12) in the Big East but a 15-14 overall record earned a bid into the National Invitation Tournament. First came a win over West Virginia, then one over Louisiana Tech. The final great game in the Field House was next and the Huskies handled Virginia Commonwealth, 72-61, to move on to Madison Square Garden. A tight win over Boston College set up a championship game match up with Ohio State. UConn won again, 72-67, and the old Garden rocked, Husky Blue and White everywhere.

"That two-week roll showed me what winning here was like. It was magical. The people couldn't believe it," Calhoun said. "The toll keepers on the Connecticut Turnpike applauded our bus as we passed on the way back to Storrs."

After winning 18 games in 1988-89, Calhoun got an unsolicited phone call from Marv Kessler, an old New York coach wired into the hoops scene through the Five-Star Basketball Camps. Kessler, who is Jewish, said he knew of a great player from Tel Aviv who St. John's was poking around with. His name was Nadav Henefeld.

"Marv asked me if I'd be interested in the Larry Bird of Israel," Calhoun said. "This is New England in 1989. Larry Bird was God. So I went over to take a look."

Henefeld ended up picking UConn over St. John's because he liked the idea of a college campus with lots of grass, plenty of trees and even a few cows. St. John's only had acres of blacktop. When he showed up in Storrs in September, Henefeld joined a team that featured Smith, Tate George and another top in-state recruit, Scott Burrell, a wonderfully talented wing athlete from Hamden who was a first round draftee of the Toronto Blue Jays. Burrell played baseball in the summers and basketball at UConn during the school year and ultimately blossomed into a pro hoops player.

UConn lost its first two Big East games but quickly began to jell. Led by the passing and defense of Henefeld, the Huskies won 10 games in a row, including an upset of No. 2 ranked Georgetown. Amid all the winning, UConn played its first-ever game in the beautiful, new Gampel Pavilion. The team rose in the polls, climbing from 13th to 8th and all the way to No. 3 after Smith and Tate George combined for 42 points in the Big East Tournament final win over Syracuse and its two All-Americans, Derrick Coleman and Billy Owens.

In the span of one magical, dream season, Calhoun's Huskies christened Gampel Pavilion, achieved the highest ranking in school history, won the school's first Big East tourney title and earned the first seed in the East for the NCAA Tournament.

The dream season continued with a play every self-respecting UConn fan simply calls 'The Shot.' Down by one with only one second left in the Sweet Sixteen against Clemson, Burrell flashed his baseball arm and fired a floor-length pass to Tate George. He caught the ball, turned and swished a deep corner jumper at the buzzer that gave UConn a stunning 71-70 win. Two nights later, the same thing happened but this time it was Duke's Christian Laettner who nailed the last-second shot and UConn's magic carpet ride ended one game short of the Final Four.

Henefeld left for the pros after that season but the 31-6 record carried a lot of weight nationally. Now when Calhoun unfolded recruiting lists, he didn't just look at kids from New England and the East. He suddenly owned the cache to recruit anyone he wanted, just like Duke and North Carolina, Syracuse and Kentucky. And to nearly everyone not named Jim Calhoun, the recruits listened.

"At the start, Howie Dickenman, Dave Leaito, Glenn Miller and the other assistants had trouble selling UConn," says Tom Moore, the program's current chief recruiter. "They weren't beating Syracuse for anyone, they weren't beating St. John's in New York City, they weren't beating Villanova in Philly. But they learned you can pick up the phone and call anyone around the country and sell the Big East. Coach Calhoun is always saying 'give it a shot."

Soon enough, those shots were landing big-time players. Over the next three years, Connecticut signed Brian Fair out of Phoenix, Travis Knight of Utah, Kevin Ollie from Los Angeles and Donny Marshall from the state of Washington. Sprinkle in a few Eastern recruits like Donyell Marshall of Reading, Pa., and all of a sudden the Huskies had as much talent as anyone in the Big East.

Those players combined to take UConn to even greater heights. Finishes near the top of the polls and deep in NCAA Tournaments came virtually every year in the 1990s and with four Big East Tournament titles, the Huskies were clearly the conference's Team of the Decade. The ever-elusive national championship came in 1999 on the shoulders of a skinny kid from Coatesville, Pa. (Richard Hamilton) and a pudgy guard from Minneapolis (Khalid El-Amin). UConn turned the trick again in 2004, led by Emeka Okafor, the dominating big man from Houston.

"The first championship was a great win, a great upset for a group of kids who really had a super year and a great run," said Calhoun. "To see what that did for the state of Connecticut and all our fans was just fantastic. But the second one, that was just damn impressive. We beat a very good Duke team in a great game in the semifinals but then just throttled Georgia Tech in the finals. That one told me we were in a select group of the very best programs in the country."

That it all happened in little Storrs, Connecticut, is nothing short of a miracle.

•

Winning national titles only made the recruiting easier and when the Big East grew to 16 schools in time for the 2005-06 season, UConn and Calhoun were ready.

The '06 season actually began the day the previous one ended at the DCU Center in nearby Worcester, Mass. That Connecticut team was stacked with good big men but troubled by shaky guard play. A 77-71 first round NCAA tourney win over Central Florida raised plenty of eyebrows but UConn was still a healthy favorite in round two against North Carolina State. Tough defense kept the Huskies in command through most of the game's first 30 minutes but when the Wolfpack's star, Julius Hodge, caught fire down the stretch, the Huskies failed to answer and lost, 65-62.

"That team had Marcus Williams at point guard and no one else who could score outside," Calhoun said. "Rudy (Gay) wasn't there every night. Josh

(Boone) wasn't there every night. Charlie (Villaneuva) had a great finish to his season but he was inconsistent. We had some tough injuries to Denham (Brown) and Rashad (Anderson) that really hurt us."

Critics in the New England media lashed out at Calhoun, questioning his team's fire and wondering why Boone, the Big East's Defensive Player of the Year, was on the bench in the final seconds as Hodge banked in a driving layup over reserve center Ed Nelson. A few weeks after North Carolina won Roy Williams his first national title in St. Louis, Villanueva announced he'd leave Connecticut for the NBA after just two seasons.

Even so, most pundits instantly installed UConn as a clear Final Four favorite in 2005-06. After all, Calhoun's stable appeared to be as full as anyone else's. First off, he had four experienced seniors and two star juniors in an era when the best players rarely lasted in school that long. Pro scouts loved Boone, a shot-blocking center, and Williams, a crafty point guard. A healthy Anderson and Brown held loads of promise and a summer of hard work was all that the immensely talented Gay needed to blossom into a star. UConn's top recruit was A.J. Price, a guard who redshirted the '04-05 season after nearly dying from a brain hemorrhage.

Clearly, the talent was in place for a banner season and with the N.C. State loss in his head, Calhoun's motivational skills were ready for action. "I can use confrontational motivation. You may not like me but I don't really care," is how he sums up his approach.

Getting this special group of players into the blocks for the 2005-06 season proved to be a major challenge. The biggest obstacle came in June, during one of the few flips of the calendar when UConn basketball isn't big news. Williams and Price, the team's two point guards, took part in a theft-and-fence scheme on the UConn campus. Police said that Thaddeus Ferguson, a man who reportedly was a friend of Williams', stole four laptop computers from rooms in the Charter Oaks Suites that belonged to incoming freshmen on the women's basketball team and a member of the women's track squad. The three men then allegedly decided to sell the computers at pawn shops in Manchester and East Hartford. The plan hit a major snag at the first stop when the store didn't buy laptops. However, a security camera recorded the visit, according to court records. The store clerk, John Muller, immediately recognized Williams.

Back on campus, the track performer, Maxine Davila, noticed that her laptop was missing. She heard from a friend that Williams may have been involved and when she confronted him, the players scrambled to return the stolen goods. Davila, however, contacted university police who found two laptops under a bed in Price's dorm room, according to the police affidavit.

By late June, rumors that Williams was in trouble on campus began circulating around the state's media outlets. The heat intensified through the summer as an investigation continued and no charges were filed. But on Aug. 18, the authorities finally indicted both Williams and Price in the theft. Williams faced four counts of third-degree larceny, which carry a penalty of up to five years in prison and $5,000 in fines. Price was charged with three counts of felony larceny and with lying to police, a misdemeanor. Both players were quickly suspended from the team by Calhoun.

The news of the arrest and arraignment made the headlines in every newspaper in Connecticut. TV crews provided blanket coverage and instantly pundits in the state and around the country weighed in on what should be done to the two players. Price, at the time, still wasn't cleared to play in the upcoming season because of his medical condition. Williams, however, just may be the best point guard in the country and clearly was the one piece Calhoun needed for his high-octane engine to run its best.

Publicly, Calhoun said he'd wait and see what the legal system ruled in the case but insisted the two players were "on suspension with me anyways," which he somehow made sound more important.

In late August, the 19-year old Williams filed an application to enter the state's accelerated rehabilitation program, a special form of probation available to first-time offenders. If he completed the program and avoided trouble for the next two years, any charges on Williams' record would be expunged. In order to be eligible for accelerated rehabilitation, a defendant must have a clean criminal record or never have used the program before.

Williams and Price also faced a private hearing before UConn's Director of Judicial Affairs. UConn's Student Code listed "attempted or actual theft of property" as a violation and authorized the school to judge student conduct independent of any criminal proceedings. Penalties could range from probation to expulsion.

With his star guard facing serious heat, Calhoun couldn't help but begin a campaign for himself – and not the courts or UConn officials – to serve as the most important arbiter in the case. "I want to be able to have the opportunity to discipline them and to bring them back and get them on track so they can understand fully that they are responsible for their actions," Calhoun told the New London Day. "I feel I can do this if the university grants me that right and the court system grants me that right… The court system, based upon precedent, will probably give me that opportunity and now I'm going to ask

– to beg - the university to grant me the opportunity to discipline them and bring them back."

Calhoun's plea wasn't received well but, then again, his words are always interpreted many different ways in the state. UConn basketball is covered by more media (nine daily newspapers regularly travel with the team) than any program in the country and because the group travels in pack-like style, it was dubbed 'The Horde' years ago. The Horde is the bane of every sports' publicist in the Big East because it gobbles up space, telephone lines and press room food wherever the Huskies play.

When UConn wins, the power of The Horde is immense and drives attention to unspeakable heights. When something controversial occurs on the beat, the Huskies are the topic du Jour throughout the state and the Marcus Williams affair is every reporter's dream.

Because the Huskies are a national title contender, the Williams decision is national news and plenty of negativity is flying around. One national columnist, Gregg Doyel of CBSSportsLine.com, called Calhoun out and wrote that "watching a leader's shameless pursuit of victory is enough to break your heart. Or turn your stomach."

Randy Smith, one of the longest-running sports columnists in the state at the Manchester Journal-Inquirer, wrote that letting Williams or Price play at all in the coming season would be inexcusable and criticized Calhoun for permitting Williams to play, calling it "the charade of helping a kid."

What many members of the press missed is that Calhoun almost can't help himself in such situations. He truly believes his way is the right way and he certainly doesn't care what people think about his line of thinking. Most of all, he doesn't understand the power of 'No comment.' He loves to talk, is good at filling The Horde's notebooks and keeps everyone coming back for more.

But on this issue, Calhoun was in a no-lose situation. If he sat back and said nothing, the media could open fire at Williams and Price. If he stuck up for them, he was only trying to win. Calhoun chose to be on the attack, his preferred mode of operation.

On Sept. 13, Williams cleared the first hurdle in his way when Superior Court Judge Marcia Gleeson placed him into the state's accelerated rehabilitation program for first-time offenders. His criminal record would be cleared if he successfully completed 18 months of probation and 400 hours of community service.

"My act was foolish, and it was selfish," said Williams, who appeared in court with his attorney and his mother, Michele. "I'd like to apologize to the four women involved. I'd like to apologize to the students on campus. I'd like to apologize to my coaches, my teammates, my family and to the state of Connecticut. I'd like to say I was wrong, with no excuses. And I'm sorry."

Gleeson later told Williams that "perhaps you've heard of the concept 'noblesse oblige,' which means: to whom much is given, much is expected. Now much is expected of you. Put your heart and soul into your community service."

Getting word from the University, however, wasn't as simple. While Calhoun's basketball suspension lasted into December, Husky fans everywhere wondered if Williams would be allowed to play. So did his coach.

"I've asked the University to say definitively what they're going to do," Calhoun said a few days before the start of practice in October. "The biggest thing right now is clearly something that happened June 8 and you get to October 11, it makes us not look as good as we should. It makes a lot of us have to answer questions that, quite frankly, we don't know the answer to."

Calhoun said he was ready to abide by whatever the decision was but he wanted closure on the case.

"If tomorrow they say the kids can play, well they can't because I'm not allowing them to play until the end of the semester. That I can tell you," he said. "They could suspend them for a year, they could suspend them for two years, they could throw them out of school. They could do whatever they want. That has not been decided. Nothing has been done yet. It's close. I would hope by the start of practice (this Friday).

"I don't want the questions. Whatever the situation is, I'm not going to have control of it. The school needs to cooperate and at least make it look like we're not dragging our feet."

On Oct. 28, the school finally acted. Price was suspended from taking classes for the fall semester, barred from campus housing for three years and kicked off the team for the season. Williams, however, got off easier. He was put on suspension for the 2005-06 academic year but the punishment was held in abeyance, meaning that if he didn't comply with the conditions of the suspension he risked being expelled from the University. More importantly, he was allowed to begin basketball-related activities on Dec. 17 and start playing games on Jan. 1, 2006.

UConn's Big East opener just happened to tip off two nights later at Marquette.

"I have said since the beginning of this process that we should never be in the business of abandoning young men who have made a mistake and I am glad that we will not be doing that," Calhoun said in a prepared statement. "I have punished them and so now has the University and hopefully in the process we can teach them that there are serious consequences when you act as selfishly as they did. I want to thank the people on this campus that did their best to make sure that the process was a fair and deliberate one. It was certainly not an easy one."

The backlash from the announcement was both swift and harsh. No one believed that Calhoun, or at least his domineering presence on campus, didn't help sway the differing penalties. Price, after all, was the unproven guard. Williams was the stud, the missing piece to a championship puzzle. Calhoun fought back, as expected.

"Jim Calhoun was not involved, ok? What conspiracy did you think happened? I'd have to get the board of trustees to lie, the president to lie, the governor to lie," he said. "Over the last few years, 63 kids were accused of fourth degree felonies on campus. Four were thrown out of school, about 60 remained. Is Marcus lucky? No. He wasn't treated any differently."

Since June, rumors and uncertainty over Williams' fate were a daily part of Calhoun's life. But with the start of the season just three weeks away, he knew the score. He wouldn't have his veteran point guard for a trip to the Maui Classic or any of the first 11 games. New guards Craig Austrie and Rob Garrison needed to fill in the gap. Even so, his team was ranked third in the country and appeared poised to make another run at the national championship. Finally, all the pieces were in place.

$$\boxed{7}$$

Recruiting

If there is any coach who knows his school's place in the college basketball hierarchy, it is Jim Calhoun. Spurred on by the 1990 Dream Season and its wonderful fallout, Calhoun brazenly rolled the dice and targeted hot-shot recruits around the country. When they listened to his Boston-staccato pitch with open ears, UConn had its entrée into the elite group of national powers.

Calhoun told recruits about this magical place called Storrs, a town where there was no football, no big city and no distractions. It was a place that revolved around basketball and dreams. If you worked hard and followed the coach's word, you'd play on national TV, win a lot of games and land in the NBA. And, sure enough, he was right.

"At first you weren't sure what to think because Coach Calhoun talked so fast," said Travis Knight, a center from Utah who went on to play in the NBA. "But he was so intense, you believed what he said."

Over the years, the coach's recruiting pitch changed. As Knight, Donyell Marshall, Ray Allen and Rip Hamilton moved on and grabbed the NBA's riches, Calhoun realized he could get involved with just about any prospect he wanted to. After all, he could throw the biggest trump card of all on the table. "Come to Storrs and I'll get you to the NBA, just like Ray Allen and Caron Butler," he says now with the dollar signs to back him up.

In the spring and summer of 2005, Calhoun's pitch was in overdrive. The Husky roster was filled with seniors (4) and star underclassmen (3) who Calhoun feared could all be entering their final college season. Filling three or four scholarships is easy at a school like Connecticut. Adding seven or eight recruits was a daunting task, but one that Calhoun and assistants Tom Moore, Andre LaFleur and George Blaney saw as an achievable goal.

Before July's summer showcase camps began, the Huskies already had two verbal commitments. One came from Curtis Kelly, the top big man in New York. The other was from athletic forward Will Harris, also a New Yorker. But by that time, some of UConn's biggest targets had moved on elsewhere. Included on that long list were top 20 talents such as Spencer Hawes of Seattle, Kevin Durant of Maryland, point guard Tywon Lawson, and Philadelphia stars Wayne Ellington and Gerald Henderson.

"We were taking a lot of body blows in the spring when some of our top guys were choosing other schools," said Moore. "Duke took Henderson and Brian Zoubek and 'Carolina got Ellington and Lawson and they all seemed to happen in a row. But as I told Andre (LaFleur), Duke and 'Carolina can't take everyone."

But UConn casts a large net around the nation's prep stars. Moore takes pride in getting UConn involved, in varying degrees, with as many good players as possible. As one big fish falls off the board, he wants to make sure Calhoun has others to pick from.

"The key is finding the right ones," said Moore, the staff member who coordinates recruiting. "We can pick up the phone and talk to a kid in Dallas or L.A. and ask if they're interested and they usually say 'sure.' That's not being arrogant. It just makes you look even harder and make sure you're after the right ones. Once the assistants do that, Coach Calhoun goes in the summer before their senior year and he's just a monster in July through September. He'll fly anywhere he needs to be and go in as many homes as we need him to be in. He's relentless."

That philosophy began to bear fruit first with Kelly and Harris and then when LaFleur convinced Detroit guard Ramar Smith to come on board over the summer. In September, the Huskies grabbed Jonathan Mandeldove, a 6-10 big kid from Georgia who lacked polish but owned plenty of potential. The other key guard target was Jerome Dyson, a Proctor Academy (N.H.) star from Maryland who was also seriously looking at Boston College, Providence and Maryland. Providence had recruited Dyson hard and was in the race. Calhoun dismissed BC's chances but was right to be concerned about the Terps.

Two years earlier, Maryland and UConn had hooked up in a heated battle for Rudy Gay, then the best talent in the Baltimore-Washington, D.C. area. Gay was relatively unknown until the summer before his senior season but he became a must-get for Gary Williams, the ultra-intense Maryland coach who was just a few years removed from winning a national championship.

Getting Gay wasn't easy and not without controversy. While he was putting the finishing touches on his schedule for the 2003-04 season, Calhoun had an idea. Instead of playing an exhibition game against the New York City-based Long Island Panthers as he had in previous years, he wondered if Gay's AAU handlers would like to come to Storrs. They did, assembling a team called the Beltway Ballers that was crushed by a 102-44 score and then paid an appearance fee of roughly $25,000.

Maryland's Williams never thought of lining up the Ballers but he insinuated that UConn had delved into the sewer of dirty tricks in finding a way to get close to Gay. "We could've scheduled an AAU team and given them $25,000 dollars like some schools I know," he said after Gay picked Connecticut.

Williams calling out Calhoun's move didn't go over well in Storrs but no NCAA rules were violated. In fact, schools throughout the Big East were scheduling their favorite AAU pals for years at that point. The NCAA has since outlawed the practice. Call it the Curse of the Beltway Ballers.

Williams' recruiting losing streak grew to two when Dyson ultimately chose the Huskies after visiting the campus along with Mandeldove. That put UConn at five recruits and counting.

The jewel of the class was the toughest to pin down. Stanley Robinson, a 6-9 forward from Birmingham, Ala., liked UConn a lot. He visited Storrs in September and liked the fast-speaking coach who flashed his national championship rings and whispered sweet nothings in his ear. But he also felt a strong pull to stay home and play for the Alabama Crimson Tide, too, and when 'Bama recruits one of its own, the heat can be intense.

"We decided to give it a shot with Stanley because we really thought he would be great for us," said Moore, "but we were always ready to cut the cord if things got a little hairy. Let's just say that with some SEC schools, things happen. But with Stanley, it never happened."

Calhoun wasn't about to let it happen. Losing a kid to Kansas or 'Carolina was one thing. But Alabama? No way.

"I told him, 'you're probably good enough to be in college one or two years,'" he said. 'If you want to go to Duke, North Carolina, Kansas or Arizona, I understand. You need to be someplace where you're on TV, play for the national championship and have a great experience. Since none of those schools are recruiting you, you should come to UConn."

Shockingly, Robinson listened to the pitch and committed in early October. But nearly a month remained before the signing date. Protecting a verbal commitment is always a tricky task but making sure a top 25 recruit from the South remains true to his word is a 24-hour job. That meant Moore and LaFleur had to go into overdrive to baby-sit Robinson, making sure any Alabama coach (or booster) wouldn't change his mind.

"You can only do so much within the rules but we made sure to stay on top of that one. You hope he's strong and the family stays strong and they did," said Moore.

A few days after Robinson's verbal, the Huskies discovered Ramar Smith was in trouble. Getting him out of the Detroit public schools was a major priority if he ever hoped to academically qualify for a scholarship. UConn steered him to South Kent Prep in Kent, Conn., but he lasted just a few weeks before packing up and going home. That move effectively ended UConn's association with Smith and cut the number of commitments back to five. But some serious juggling awaited.

During a tour of New England's best prep schools in September, UConn noticed an impressive shooting forward named Ben Eaves at Worcester (Mass.)Academy. Eaves was from Manchester, England and the American colleges he saw on TV were headlined by Duke, North Carolina and Connecticut. Ed Reilly, his coach at Worcester, knew George Blaney well and called him about Eaves.

"I went up to see Ben and a big kid on his team, Chas McFarland," said Moore. "Ben played great, like fantastic. So we got him to come to campus. We weren't really recruiting his position but then Coach Calhoun went up to see him and really liked him, too."

UConn decided it wanted Eaves but was there room in this bloated class for him? The answer was no but Calhoun created room. Will Harris, the New Yorker prepping at Brewster (NH) Academy, was anxious about the size, and talent, of UConn's growing class so the UConn coaches told Harris that "his role had changed," according to Brewster coach Jason Smith. "They never said 'you can't come," Smith said, "but they took some other kids at Will's position. That's their choice, I guess, but then Will had to look at his options."

After a few conversations, Harris reluctantly looked elsewhere and ultimately latched on with one of Calhoun's coaching protégés, Dave Leaito at

Virginia. The shuffle opened up room for Ben Eaves, much to the dismay of Providence coach Tim Welsh.

By that point, Welsh had grown tired of the giant, blue and white specter that UConn had created in the neighboring state. He had chased Jeff Adrien and lost out a year before. The same with Craig Austrie, a point guard from Bridgeport who seemed set to come to Providence in April of his senior year. Although Calhoun never saw Austrie play in person for his high school team, the Huskies were squeezed a bit at point guard so Moore gave Austrie a call. For any kid from Connecticut, that's akin to E.F. Hutton inquiring about an annuity. Goodbye Providence, hello Storrs.

Providence also chased Will Harris and Jerome Dyson to no avail but Welsh thought Eaves was different. Eaves was enrolled at Worcester Academy, Welsh's prep school alma mater. He took the time to fly to England and meet with Eaves' family, something no other college coach did. Eaves and Chas McFarland visited PC and liked Welsh but, ultimately, the chance to play at Connecticut won out.

A few days after Eaves committed, Welsh and Calhoun crossed paths in New York. Welsh was still burning over losing Eaves, who he felt would be a great fit at Providence but could easily get buried under Calhoun's talent wave in Storrs.

"He told me 'we needed Ben Eaves. He's a pro.' I should've said, 'how many pros do you need?" Welsh said.

Ruffling opposing coaches' feathers is nothing new for Calhoun and the little bump-up against Providence was nothing compared to the saga of Dougie Wiggins. With Ramar Smith on the outs, the Huskies could've crossed point guard off their list of needs. After all, Dyson plays a bit of point, as does incoming freshmen Austrie and Rob Garrison. But all three of those players were unproven and when A.J. Price was slapped with a year's suspension in October for his role in Laptop Gate, the uncertainty at the critical point guard spot only grew.

With Smith out of the picture, East Hartford High's Wiggins said he began having second thoughts about the verbal commitment he gave to St. John's coach Norm Roberts the previous March. UConn had recruited Wiggins during his sophomore and junior seasons, but only lightly. After committing to St. John's, Wiggins went on to enjoy a prolific summer on the AAU circuit and clearly became Roberts' first signature recruit.

But by mid-October, Wiggins said he'd seen UConn back off Smith and began listening to friends who wouldn't stop asking him why he wasn't staying home. He and his high school coach, Anthony Menard, went to one of UConn's first preseason practices and met with Calhoun. It is not known why, or by whom, the two were asked to attend the workout although Wiggins and assistant Andre LaFleur had remained friendly, crossed paths on the summer circuit and even used the same hair stylist in Hartford.

"There were no hard feelings," Wiggins told the Scout.com recruiting service during the heat of the flip-flop. "I haven't spoken to anyone except St. John's. I just told them I was nervous and when I gave my verbal, I didn't put as much thought into it as I should have."

Roberts and Chris Casey, the St. John's assistant who did most of the leg-work recruiting Wiggins, were both said to be steamed at what they considered to be 'tampering' by the UConn staff. Neither would discuss the issue, but with three weeks to go before the signing date, Wiggins called St. John's and said he was having second thoughts. With a week to go, Wiggins held a news conference in Hartford and picked Connecticut. St. John's was again in search of a point guard.

The reaction around the league, and in the media, wasn't good for the Huskies. One national Internet columnist, Gregg Doyel of CBSSportsline, opened fire on Calhoun. He wrote a blistering, overly personal, attack on Calhoun's tactics on the recruiting trail that struck a nerve in Storrs.

"UConn coach Jim Calhoun is a Hall of Famer and a champion, but when it comes to coaching, he is not a moral beacon of light. This is not a news flash," Doyel wrote, in part. "Maybe Wiggins had grown up rooting for the Huskies. Maybe he was heartbroken not to have been recruited by UConn. Maybe it doesn't matter. St. John's offered Wiggins, Wiggins accepted, and it was up to Calhoun to honor the process. But Calhoun honors nothing but his own program....Calhoun has never conducted his business in the most morally upright way, but in recent weeks, he has abandoned all pretenses."

Several Big East coaches were privately overjoyed at the backlash but as one said, "it really doesn't matter. They got the kid and he's a good player. St. John's got nothing."

While every coach contacted agreed that it's wrong to reach out or otherwise tamper with a youngster who's verbally committed to another school, if the player calls you, the equation changes.

"That's an easy call," said Syracuse's Boeheim. "If a kid commits to a school, we don't call or go near him. Ever. If he then says I'm not going to this school, publicly, and then calls us, I would call the other school and move on."

"I know Tom Izzo very well. Eric (Devendorf) committed to them in his sophomore year. Then in his junior year he backed off, publicly. I talked to Tom and just said we're going to recruit this kid. He said fine. That happens a lot. Eric just got close to a couple guys (at Michigan State) and they told him he wouldn't like it there. If that's what happened with Wiggins, I don't see a problem with that."

Calhoun scoffs at the hubbub that boiled over the Wiggins saga. "The Doug Wiggins thing is probably one of the stupidest things I've ever been accused of," he said. "No matter what people say, we stopped recruiting him when he verballed to St. John's. We moved on to other kids.

"Then we move away from Ramar Smith and the kid calls us. I told him that I can't talk to him until he calls Norm Roberts. That happened and at that point he became a prospective student-athlete once again and we recruited him. That's what happened. That's all."

When the signing period began in the second week of November, Calhoun happily accepted signed letters-of-intent from Curtis Kelly, Jonathan Mandeldove, Jerome Dyson, Stanley Robinson, Ben Eaves and Doug Wiggins. A Super Six, a class ranked among the top three in the nation.

But UConn wasn't done. As the 2005-06 season progressed, it became clear that the prospects of keeping Josh Boone on campus for another year were dwindling. He was clashing with Calhoun, upset with his inconsistent playing time and clearly thinking about the NBA. UConn took an unheralded big forward from Arizona named Gavin Edwards in late March but a much larger prospect awaited.

In January, LaFleur was speaking with a friend in Houston who happened to mention that a 7-foot-3 player had just come to the city and enrolled at Cypress Community Christian School. LaFleur jumped on a plane and saw a tall, athletic kid with white socks pulled up high on his calves. "Andre came back and was shaking his head," said Moore. "He says, 'I haven't been doing this for a lot of years but I think he's real good. You have to go take a look.'"

"Well I saw him at a tournament in Mississippi and in the warm-ups some kids sitting behind me are laughing at the big tall kid with the long socks. I turned around and told them, 'you shouldn't laugh before you see him play.' And then he started dunking on everyone," Moore said.

UConn convinced Hasheem Thabeet to come to campus for a Senior Day game against Louisville. He liked what he saw but at that point Calhoun hadn't seen the big man play.

"The way Coach Calhoun is wired, during the season he doesn't want to be getting on a plane to go see someone play," said Moore. "That's not his release. I know Roy Williams, he loves to get out of town and go see a high school kid. (Calhoun) wants to be in the office, dealing with his team."

Some of UConn's greatest finds have come in the spring signing period. One was star forward Caron Butler. The greatest was Emeka Okafor, a center from Texas who wasn't rated in any scout's top 100 and who at one time appeared headed to play at Rice. Calhoun and UConn stepped in and three years later the Huskies were national champs and Okafor was the best big man in the country.

"Over the last 10 years, North Carolina has had 27 McDonald's All-Americans and we've had six. We've had nine (NBA) lottery picks and they've had five," Calhoun said. "That shows you can't listen to what other people say about talent."

Once the season ended in March, Calhoun flew to Houston and watched Thabeet at the Kingwood Classic in Houston, one of the spring's top AAU events. "Hasheen had like 28 points and 18 rebounds. Coach was blown away by the kid," said Moore.

That effort elevated Thabeet into the national recruiting consciousness. Soon Louisville, Cincinnati, Memphis and Miami were on him hard. Since Thabeet had already visited UConn, the Huskies could only wait and see how this one would play out. After visiting Cincinnati and enjoying a cookout at Rick Pitino's home in Louisville, Thabeet called Calhoun and picked the Huskies.

With that, the finishing touch on an eight-player recruiting class was in place. It's a class that promises to one day graduate a member or three to the NBA and a class that should keep the fans in Husky Nation very happy.

8

Dec. 13, 2005. Philadelphia

It is four hours before a Big 5 match-up with Pennsylvania and The Rev. Rob Hagan is standing in front of the Villanova basketball team talking about life.

Hagan, a 41-year old 'Nova grad, looks as if he could suit up and hit a few jumpers right about now. He's tall, slim and youthful and after reading a short bit of Scripture, he delivers a five-minute sermon that holds the attention of every player and coach in the function room at the Sheraton University Hotel a few blocks from the Palestra. At the end of the talk, the players bless themselves and file in front of two tables filled with the traditional pre-game meal of soup, salad, pasta and chicken.

There is no VCR stuffed with game film or even a scouting report hanging on a chalkboard. Instead, relaxed chatter fills the room. As each player finishes his meal, they walk from table to table and fist-bump everyone on the way out of the room, from Father Rob to each player and coach.

This is the time-honored way Villanova players prepare for games. It dates back at least as far as the mid-1970s when Rollie Massimino came to the Main Line. Massimino could be loud, incessantly nervous and more than a bit paranoid but he held tradition close to his heart. And building a Villanova basketball family was always among his prized tenets.

Family meant praying before games and at meals. It meant hugging players who needed hugs, even if it was during timeouts. It meant keeping Villanova men involved with the program well after their playing days, especially if a spot on the coaching staff became a nice fit. When 'Daddy Mass' was unceremoniously moved out of town in 1992 after 19 seasons, the concept of 'Nova's basketball family was shaken. But those shock waves were eased a bit with the hiring of Steve Lappas, one of Daddy Mass' assistants from the 1985 national championship season. When Lappas was pushed aside in 2001, another former Massimino assistant, Jay Wright, left Hofstra to take the one Big East job he always wanted.

Keeping the Villanova family alive and well is important to Wright and vitally important to the Augustinian priests who run the school. Perhaps because of its winning tradition, beautiful campus, relative wealth ($250 million endowment) and deep alumni pride, Villanova knows it can win in the modern college basketball world. In fact, it expects to win.

Unlike the other Catholic schools in the Big East, Villanova had the foresight to find room on its campus to build a first-rate basketball facility. This investment has paid off in spades. Not only does the 6,500-seat Pavilion keep Wright from fighting with pro hockey or basketball teams for practice times and game dates, it also allows Villanova to showcase itself on television. There are no empty seats at the Pavilion. Ever. The student body packs a huge bleacher section behind one basket and fills an opponent's shooting backdrop with waving arms and painted faces. This is what big-time college basketball looks like and Villanova, unlike many other Big East schools, wears the look comfortably.

With a largely white and mainly Eastern student population, Villanova is annually ranked as the top liberal arts college on an Eastern Seaboard that's filled with white, liberal arts schools. With 6,300 students, 'Nova is large enough to support a varied set of academic offerings yet small enough to carry an intimate, high school feel.

And the high school's sport of choice is clearly basketball.

" When I run into a Villanova graduate, they don't say 'Class of '83.' They say 'I was there with Pinckney and Pinone.' That's how they identify themselves," said Wright, who grew up a 'Nova fan and played basketball at Bucknell. "We want our kids to appreciate Villanova and be around kids like them from New York and New Jersey and Washington, D.C. That's our student body."

The school's president, The Rev. Edmund J. Dobbin, has steered the college for 18 years. He retired in the spring of 2006 with a rich legacy of academic and athletic achievement, as well as fundraising and new infrastructure investments that most of the nation's catholic colleges can't equal.

During the conference restructuring, Dobbin served as the leader of the Big East's President's Cabinet and earned rave reviews. He spent hours on the phone rebuilding bridges that needed mending, especially among the other catholic schools.

"Through all that, he just told me that we're committed to making it work," said Wright. "He's very worldly and sees the direction in college athletics but he sees the value of being with those (football) schools. But he wants Villanova to be a winner in our own way."

•

Winning the Villanova way isn't always easy. When Wright was hired, his star was bright after several years exciting the New York media with winning teams at Hofstra. The Pride played fast and loose and were sparked by flashy guards, most notably Craig 'Speedy' Claxton who moved on to a successful NBA career. Wright played off his warm personality to cultivate the network of high school and AAU coaches in New York, a web that can be notoriously cutthroat, if not dirty. But by the time he was leaving Hofstra some of the better city kids not only wanted to play their college ball on Long Island but were so enamored with the coach that they quickly followed Wright to his new Big East home.

Almost as soon as he arrived in Philly, Wright began making waves with some aggressive recruiting. St. John's coach Mike Jarvis had let his guard down in New York and the metropolitan area's finest talents were up for grabs. Some Catholic League coaches regarded Jarvis as aloof because he hadn't stepped in their gyms for a year or two. Jarvis may have simply disliked some of their players but in the New York basketball subculture word spreads quickly and the word on Jarvis was that he was disrespecting New York kids. That ultimately doomed Jarvis' tenure in Queens and opened the door for other Big East schools to grab New York's stars.

In the summer of 2001, Wright and Villanova warmed to the role of chief thieves. Wright was hired in March and by that summer he had secured verbal commitments from two of the top prospects in the city: forward Curtis Sumpter of Bishop Loughlin in Brooklyn and guard Allan Ray of St. Raymond's in the Bronx.

Helped by the aggressive recruiting work of top assistant Fed Hill, Wright kept rolling and added guard Randy Foye out of Newark. When he ultimately landed the biggest fish of all in 6-9 center Jason Fraser from Amityville High on Long Island, the recruiting gurus were calling Wright's first Villanova class the very best in the nation.

After a 19-13 finish with Lappas' talent in 2001-02, Wright welcomed the new kids to town and Philly was buzzing with excitement. Before they ever played a game, respect flowed the Wildcats' way. The pollsters said Villanova was a top 25 team but respect and success aren't always brothers.

Marquette beat Villanova in its season opener at Madison Square Garden, 73-61. A big win over Michigan State in the Great Alaska Shootout was trumped by a loss to the College of Charleston. A 5-0 start in Big East play elevated expectations once again but Sumpter struggled with his shooting and when Fraser developed a stress fracture in his foot late in the year, the Wildcats were cooked.

To top it off, a bizarre phone card scam came to light late in the season after players were caught making long distance calls from the basketball office. That public black eye haunted the program as several players were slapped with suspensions over the next two seasons for their sins. The year ended with Villanova lining up with five scholarship players in a Big East Tournament loss to Georgetown.

"People forget that the NCAA came in and investigated us the first year because of who we recruited," said Wright. "So they were getting pulled out of their first practices as college players. One would be in for 20 minutes and one would be in for an hour. For a whole week. That's how they started their careers. Then they end it playing Georgetown with five scholarship players."

The group's sophomore year didn't go well either. The phone card suspensions marred the start of the season and a dream trip to the Maui Classic in Hawaii turned into a nightmare when Villanova lost to the host school, Chaminade, in the first round.

"At the beginning of their sophomore year the whole team was suspended so we were moving guys in and out for eight games," Wright says. "We started that year playing Temple at midnight on Friday, flying to California the next morning for a game (vs. Redlands College) and then flew to Maui on Sunday and played Chaminade on Monday morning. We had five scholarship players and lost to Chaminade. That was (the start of) their sophomore year."

By that time Fraser's injury troubles were becoming almost comical. He missed most of the off-season after undergoing double knee surgery and then was diagnosed with a stress fracture of his left heel in early November. He missed the Maui trip and played just 10 minutes prior to January. He would score in double figures just seven times all season as his long, creaky body struggled to work up to speed.

Villanova ended 2004 with a 16-16 (6-10 Big East) record and barely squeaked into the N.I.T. Even with all the injuries and off-the-court issues, word began to spread that while Wright was a top-notch recruiter, his coaching left much to be desired.

That unfair perception ultimately changed in the fateful 2004-05 campaign. With his star recruits now juniors, Wright pushed all the healthy buttons, with the clear emphasis on healthy. While the always brittle Fraser was limited by his shaky knees and a broken hand, the Wildctas shook off a 9-4 start and thrived. The breakout game came Jan. 22 at the Wachovia Center when 'Nova rebounded from a two-game losing streak and routed No. 2 rated Kansas, 83-62. Sumpter and Ray, the two breakthrough New York City recruits, combined for nine 3-pointers in the game.

That effort jump-started Villanova's season. The 'Cats lost just two more times the rest of the regular season, to conference powers Connecticut and Syracuse. A disputed call with two seconds left in a tie game in the Big East tourney semifinals led to two free throws by West Virginia's Mike Gansey and a 78-76 loss. Villanova earned a No. 5 seed from the NCAA bosses and went out and cruised into the Sweet Sixteen with wins over New Mexico and Florida. But when Sumpter tore his ACL in the first half of the win over the Gators, the chances for a national title run were cooked.

Playing in Syracuse's Carrier Dome, Villanova made its first Sweet 16 appearance in 17 years against a powerhouse team from North Carolina. With limited options, Wright started four players 6-foot-3 or smaller. At the time, it was clear that playing Foye, Ray, Mike Nardi and precocious freshman Kyle Lowry together at once was simply a matter of necessity. No coach, let alone one two games away from the Final Four, would ever choose to roll out such a small lineup.

"What was I going to do? Those were our four best players and we had no time to regroup, really. It wasn't some cooked-up, great scheme," said Wright.

Down nine points late in the game, the team rallied behind Foye (28 points) and the gifted Lowry (18) but fell short of an upset and lost, 67-66. The Tar Heels went on to win the national championship, leaving the bruised and battered Wildcats to wonder just what might have happened if they were ever able to make a run with a full deck.

Now the heralded recruits are finally seniors but Wright is one big Ace short of a full deck yet again.

Sumpter worked with Villanova's training and conditioning staff all summer to get his knee back into shape. When he returned to school in September, the 6-foot-7 New Yorker with a big smile couldn't make his way to a class without being asked by another student about his health.

"You goin' to be able to play this year. I can't tell you how many people have asked me that," he said in the fall.

When practice began in October, Sumpter was fully cleared to play but Wright decided to proceed slowly and limit him to about 45 minutes of work a day. On Oct. 19, just a few days into practice, Sumpter drove hard to the hoop and flipped home a layup at the same time that Will Sheridan came flying at him to contest the shot. Sumpter landed a bit awkwardly, without much pain but he remained on the floor for a few minutes and could tell something was wrong.

"Curtis told me right away, 'I did it again. I can feel it,'" said Wright. "Everyone was dead silent."

Sumpter says he walked away a little stiff but when some pain and swelling persisted, the team ordered an MRI. The news was the worst possible, a ligament tear in his left knee, the same one he injured in the Florida game. Another surgery, out a minimum of three months.

The grim news reverberated not only around the Big East but around the country. Several media outlets had pegged the Wildcats as a Final Four team, if not the number-one team in the land. But that was with a healthy Sumpter.

Not surprisingly, Sumpter took the knockout news hard. He wanted to play with Foye, Ray and Fraser and compete one final time with the friends he entered college with.

"Looking back four years, we all decided to come to Villanova and compete for a national championship and graduate," Sumpter said. "To possibly not be a part of that is the hardest thing. To watch those guys compete without me is going to be real hard."

Sumpter refuses to close the book on the season. He's hoping three months means three months. If he can return to the lineup in early February, he says he'd choose that path instead of a redshirt season. After all, this is the season he's worked so hard for, especially during a rehab period over the summer that frequently reduced the strapping 225-pounder to tears."I'm not closing the book on that now," Sumpter said in early December. "We'll see how the rehab goes. I want to play this year."

Sumpter isn't Villanova's only injury concern. Fraser is still recovering from off-season micro-fracture surgery on both of his creaky knees. He's doing quite well, though, and Wright says, "Jason is actually the healthiest he's ever been since he's been at Villanova."

Frasier, a quiet, religious young man, is thrilled with his present health. "Now I can work on my game rather than concentrate on always being healthy," Fraser told the Philadelphia Inquirer on the eve of the start of practice. "That's always been my mindset: Get healthy. Get healthy. Now, I can get back to working on my post moves and jump shots."

A rotator cuff injury ended reserve big man Marcus Austin's career and backup center Chris Charles is nursing a wrist ligament injury. These challenges are just another dip in a ride that Wright says has toughened a group of tough kids more than they ever imagined. More importantly, the group owns a certain perspective that few college kids appreciate these days. The freshness and high expectations of freshman year seem like a lifetime ago. The mistakes of the phone card scam and depression brought on by untimely injuries have matured a group that's grown from wide-eyed 18-year-olds to 22-year-old young men ready for the final run at their basketball dreams.

"They've gone from being highly-touted to being kind of disgraced, really, to back now where they always thought they'd be. I think they're pretty comfortable with it," said Wright. "They've been to the mountain, to the valley, and back to the mountaintop again. Being ranked this high is how they thought it would all happen. They never thought we'd be as low as we were and now we're back. It's been a heck of a journey but I think they're stronger, more mature for their experiences."

Even without Sumpter, the Wildcats are good. Very good. They showed the country how good in a Dec. 3 showdown game with Oklahoma. Villanova came in ranked fourth in the nation; the Sooners fifth. The 4 vs. 5 sizzle accounted for the highest profile non-Big East game ever at the Pavilion. The two teams traded haymakers almost from the start with Villanova's small and quick guards matched up against a big, strong Oklahoma team led by 7-foot center Kevin Bookout and 6-8 All-American power forward Taj Gray.

The big men were upstaged, however, by the little guys. Without Sumpter, Wright has again committed to a four-guard lineup and the group feeds off each other perfectly. Against the Sooners, Foye was unstoppable, pouring in a career-high 32 points. Ray added 21 and Fraser came off the bench to battle Oklahoma's big boys for 10 points and 3 blocks. A stunning 19-for-20 free throw performance in the second half iced an 85-74 Villanova win.

Ten days later, the Wildcats are 6-0, ranked third in the country and set to play the first of their four Big 5 games against the University of Pennsylvania at the venerable Palestra. Wright knows all about the Big 5 after growing up in the Philly suburbs and rooting on Villanova in some great battles with Penn, La Salle, Saint Joseph's and Temple.

"The thing about the Big 5 games is you just never know. You never know," he said. "Something crazy always happens in these games. You can have one team that's loaded and another that's struggling and the game is an absolute dogfight. It's like that every year."

Wright is sitting at the pre-game meal, ripping through several small plates of food. He's talking about his players, Philly basketball and how much he likes his team. He's easygoing, engaging and charming, all at the same time, and doesn't appear to carry the game-day jitters that cripple so many other coaches. "I love pre-game meal. I sit and talk to whoever is around. It keeps my mind off the game so I'm usually the last one to leave," he said.

Because he grew up as a Philly hoops' nut, Wright understands the Big 5 and Villanova's fans. He describes an atmosphere where the public is both passionate and greedy, loving and unforgiving. They know the history and they expect to win.

"The Pavilion has been sold out since the day it opened and we have a six-year waiting list for season tickets," he said. " Last year, Boston College came in number 2 or 3 and Pitt came in 6 or 7 and the building was great but we were the underdog in those games. In the Oklahoma game this year, our fans came expecting us to win. That was a first since we've been here. So I think things have changed a bit this year.

"Villanova fans, if they're not old already, they were tutored by their grandparents and their fathers. They understand the history. People have had the good seats since the Jake Nevin Field House. They tell you that. They don't remember the down years. They remember the great years and expect that every year. It's kind of a cool thing. They have a great pride. When we get really good, they know how to be good fans."

Wright turns and asks Mike Sheridan, the team's publicist, how many home games the Wildcats will play at the Wachovia Center, the home of the 76ers. The answer is three and it's a key one. The Wachovia is hosting the first and second rounds of the NCAA Tournament and in order to be eligible to play there, Villanova cannot use the building more than three times. The three games – against Syracuse, Louisville and Connecticut – are sold out already.

"How many teams can sell out 22,000 this early?" Wright asks. "Villanova has done that before. When I was here with Coach Mass (1987-92), every time we played at the Spectrum we would set a record for the largest crowd to see a college basketball game in the state of Pennsylvania. Every time. They knew it would be a sellout so they'd add a few seats every game. Georgetown had (Dikembe) Mutombo and (Alonzo) Mourning. Syracuse had (Derrick) Coleman and Billy Owens, who was from Carlisle so that whole town came to the games. Pittsburgh had Charles Smith. And when we had Kerry Kittles and Tim Thomas we sold out the Wachovia Center. So Villanova fans have a great passion and know how to be good."

Wright is asked if his team can stay near the top of the polls all season without Sumpter while facing a murderous schedule.

"I don't know if we can continue top five but we can be in the top 25 all year. That's key because you're on the bottom of that ticker every night on ESPN and kids see that and they see your highlights. So you're in the mix. And I do think we can be in the mix," he said. "If you're a Big East team and you're in the mix, you can win the national championship. We've seen that before. Like West Virginia in the Elite Eight last year. I don't think that surprised anybody in our league."

With that, Wright leads the rest of the Villanova family out of the room and toward a bank of elevators. An hour later, the team reemerges in the lobby, boards a bus and rolls a few blocks toward the Palestra.

When anyone walks into the building, it's hard not to feel the history of Philadelphia basketball wash over you. In the front lobby, large murals of Big 5 legends fill the walls. For 'Nova, that means the great Paul Arizin, Bill Melchionni, Howard Porter, Rory Sparrow and Easy Ed Pinckney, now an assistant coach. This is the 50th season of Big 5 college basketball and the health of the city series is strong. Philadelphia is the best big city on the East Coast for college hoops, especially when a team like Villanova is highly ranked. The city buzzed a few years back when Saint Joseph's and its dazzling backcourt of Jameer Nelson and Delonte West raced to the top of the polls. The promise of similar success this year with Villanova keeps the sport relevant in a region where baseball and especially the NFL fill the newspapers and sports radio with a year-round ferocity.

While Wright privately knows that a good Penn team will give his kids a battle, he tells the players that a good start is important. It'll settle the crowd and make the Quakers come and defend a guard corps that's given people fits all season. But from the opening tip, things don't go well. Lowry picks up two fouls in the first four minutes and 'Nova's aggressive defense has been slapped with six fouls by the 14 minute mark. Penn is shooting 1-and-1 with 12:30 to play and at that point the team foul count is Penn 7, Villanova 0.

"Give us a chance," Wright howls at the officials. "Look at that scoreboard. 7-0. 7-0. C'mon."

The antidote to such a disparity is the Wildcats' secret weapon, 3-point shooting. The shot can be a great equalizer and Villanova has so many players who can hit it that it's never out of a game. Penn's shooting goes cold midway through the half and Villanova pulls away for a 32-23 halftime lead.

Foye and Ray are clearly superior to any player the Quakers can throw at them, even Ivy League Player of the Year candidate Ibrahim Jaaber. Villanova's lead peaks at 50-29 with 12:14 left but, almost out of nowhere, Penn claims a second wind. Jaaber handles the press a little better and his teammates convert layups in traffic. A 22-5 Penn run whips the Palestra into a frenzy, noise filling the old barn in all its glory. With two minutes left, 'Nova's lead is down to 55-51 and the game clearly is up for grabs.

But this is when guard play, and especially veteran guards like Foye and Ray, wins out. Ray is fouled fighting for a rebound and makes two free throws. Nardi steps in front of a pass and makes a great steal and Wright calls time out. He plans to isolate Foye for a wing drive but as the 'Cats break the huddle, six players take the floor. The mistake is caught by assistant coach Brett Gunning but not before the officials hand the ball to Nardi and he moves to inbound the ball. A technical foul is called, sending an embarrassed Villanova bench into shock with only 1:17 left and bringing to mind the warning that Wright uttered a few hours earlier: "Something crazy always happens in these games."

Jaaber makes the two technical shots to cut the lead to 57-53. Villanova comes up the floor and finally isolates Foye who responds with a great crossover and 12-foot jumper to push the lead back to six points. That's it for Penn.

"In the Big 5, I didn't expect anything less," a relieved Wright says in a Palestra now filled only with friends and family. "We had them a couple times and couldn't put them away. I give them credit. As long as we'll play in the Big 5, which I hope is a very long time, I know crazy things will happen in these games. We have to survive these games, which is good. It makes us stronger."

With that, Wright turns and exchanges hand shakes and hugs with a line of well-wishers. He knows friends and fans like his team and at 7-0, there is a lot to like. But he also knows getting by Connecticut and Syracuse will be a lot harder than squeezing past Pennsylvania.

"Hey, it's the seventh game. We're a work in progress," he says. "But I know no matter how good some teams are you'll always get a typical Big 5 game. We're not going to change it. We're not going to dominate the Big 5. No one ever does."

$$\textcircled{9}$$

Louisville

It doesn't take a visitor long to realize that Louisville, Ky. is a very different Big East locale.

As planes descend into the city's airport, acres of athletic venues unfold below. On one side is the Kentucky State Fairgrounds and Freedom Hall, the basketball home of the Cardinals. On the other is Papa John's Stadium, the home of Cardinal football.

In the immediate surrounding area are a host of open, green spaces that include a synthetic surface baseball park, a soccer stadium and a field hockey surface. The city's crown jewel, venerable Churchhill Downs, sits just down the street from the football stadium and a jump shot away from campus.

When you walk through the air terminal, large photos of the Cards' basketball and football teams in action grace the walls. A giant sign greets you with a slogan blaring 'Welcome to Louisville. The best college city in America."

They just might be right.

Louisville is one of the country's growing midsize cities. It's population and economy did well through the dot.com era and the relatively cheap housing and labor markets make the Kentucky-Indiana area an attractive place to do business. But unlike the Boston-Washington, D.C. pipeline that the Big

East is built on, Louisville doesn't own a professional sports franchise that isn't a horse.

That makes the Cardinals, and the University of Kentucky Wildcats down Route 75 in Lexington, the biggest show in town. This is venerable Freedom Hall's 50th year as the home of the Cards and while the building is worn on the edges, fans could care less. They pack the 18,800-seat building for every game with waves of red sweatshirts and jackets reaching into every corner of the arena. In this part of the country, people love the Cardinals (or the rival Wildcats), horses and whiskey, not necessarily in that order. That devotion is matched by few colleges in the country, if any at all.

Unlike the large, Land Grant state schools of the Midwest, Louisville enjoys the creature comforts of city living. Corporate sponsors flock to the basketball and football games and fill luxury suites that swell with cardinal red on game days. Money seems to be no object for fans that lust to see the city's adopted professional franchise. The same follows in an athletic department that's blessed with outstanding facilities and accomplished coaches.

Tom Jurich, the school's athletic director, is the man who makes the machine hum. Unlike at other schools where fans barely know who the athletic director is, Jurich is Mr. Louisville. A spot in his box for a Cardinal athletic contest is coveted. His picture hangs on a banner outside the football stadium, right alongside one depicting coach Bobby Petrino. As he tools around campus in his black sedan showing a visitor the gorgeous facilities his teams play on, Jurich wears the look of a proud father.

Thanks to Jurich and the passion of the city's fans, Louisville walked into the Big East ready to win. In every sport, not just basketball and football. He doesn't believe that the arms race that's gripped colleges from coast-to-coast should be a major concern of the NCAA's Myles Brand. In fact, he's out to win it.

"I want to be successful in everything. I know that's easy to say but in order to do that, you have to invest in it," he said. "I don't do facilities just to keep up with the Joneses because if you do that you're just going to chase your tail. What I like to do is isolate every sport. We have 21 sports now and 22 coming on board with the addition of women's lacrosse. That's a great example. They will have a state-of-the-art facility to compete in and we don't even have a team yet. We're proud of that."

Asked how difficult it is to raise private money for something like a brand new swimming center, Jurich admits "it's hard. I won't lie. But I wasn't going to stop asking until we got it done. That's what it takes."

While football has always pushed the facilities envelope with bigger and better locker rooms, weight rooms and now indoor practice fields, most elite basketball programs make do with the campus gym. Until now. Over the last few years, schools like Texas and Florida have raised money to build $15 million practice facilities exclusively for their men's and women's hoop teams. The Denton Cooley Pavilion at Texas features 44,000 square feet of luxury, including cherry wood lockers with private DVD players and XBox games for every player. It is a palace of excess and the envy of coaches everywhere.

Louisville sees itself as a national championship contender in every season, justifiably so. In order to keep moving forward, Jurich carved out a corner lot two blocks from the athletic center on campus for a purpose. That's where he sees his new basketball practice facility taking shape.

"We're doing a basketball practice facility because it's a necessity, not because someone else has it," he says. "We have one practice court on this campus for three very successful programs. Volleyball has won 30 games the last two years, women's basketball has a terrific coach and they'll make an impact even though women's basketball may have the toughest challenge in moving to a league like the Big East. The men's program speaks for itself. So you have all those demands on one building and one floor.

"We could probably make do with it, but I want to grow. Facilities are very important to me and I've always been a builder."

While seeing a new baseball stadium and soccer field take shape under his watch, Jurich's greatest coup was hiring Rick Pitino.

In 2000 both Pitino and Louisville basketball were at their lowest points ever. Pitino had resigned from his post as the coach and chief executive of the Boston Celtics. In a career marked by one exhilarating achievement after another, Pitino's four years in Boston marked his first professional failure.

It didn't begin that way, of course. After winning the 1996 national championship and lording over the kingdom that is University of Kentucky basketball, Pitino was the hottest coach in the country. He had resuscitated a Wildcat program coming off of NCAA probation and returned it to its lofty status. Kentucky fans loved 'Coach Pit-E-nah,' and with the talent he was stockpiling in Lexington, the New Yorker probably could have stayed in the Bluegrass and been happy forever.

Up in Boston, the Celtics were in a free fall nearly unmatched in their storied history. Then-owner Paul Gaston had removed the beleaguered M.L. Carr from the coach's chair and knew he needed to make a big splash. He contacted Dave Gavitt, a former G.M. of the team and the ultimate basketball insider, and brought up Pitino's name. Gavitt praised Pitino's skills so much that Gaston thought it could be worth trying to pry the coach away from Kentucky. Pitino loves to be courted and Gaston came at him hard. He knew how much he loved the state, especially once some big-money friends in the horse business convinced him to buy some yearlings.

Gaston also knew Pitino loved the NBA, especially the action of 82 games a year against the best players in the world. Gaston offered $50 million over 10 years, a whopping sum that would make Pitino the highest paid coach in the game. After plenty of heartache, Pitino ultimately said goodbye to UK and became a Celtic.

The press conference announcing his arrival was nothing short of a coronation. Family, friends and the media filled the floor of the FleetCenter and the Celtics lowered all 16 of their championship banners to make the scene complete. Franchise patriarch Red Auerbach sat back and smoked his trademark victory cigar as Pitino regaled the media with his dreams of restoring the franchise to its lofty status.

But the charmed luck that had followed Pitino on his climb up the coaching ladder didn't make the trip from Lexington to Boston. The Celts had seemingly tanked their way through the 1997 season under the bumbling Carr, winning only 21 games. But the losses were literally cheered because they gave the Celts the best shot in the Tim Duncan Sweepstakes.

Duncan, of course, didn't land in Boston. The San Antonio Spurs struck gold when lottery balls bounced their way. As expected, the Wake Forest star matured into the NBA's top center and eventually led the Spurs to three NBA titles. Those championships were supposed to be Boston's, or so Celtics fans thought. Instead, Pitino drafted Chauncey Billups and Ron Mercer with the third and sixth picks.

Without the dominant big man, Pitino frequently chased his tail with a dizzying array of trades, odd draft picks and free agent signings. The Celts did steal Paul Pierce with the 10th pick in the 1998 draft but the coach's regularly chafed with Antoine Walker, one of his stars during his Kentucky reign. Walker was a New Age hoops star from Chicago who carried himself like an all-star in his own movie. Pitino publicly praised Walker but privately moaned about his shoddy conditioning and work habits. This inevitably led to clashes and after hearing Pitino bark at him since he was an 18-year old college freshman, Walker eventually tuned the coach out.

The pressure of losing clearly got to Pitino. In one infamous post-game screed marked by its brutal honesty, Pitino told the Boston media, "Larry Bird is not walking through that door, fans. Kevin McHale is not walking through that door and Robert Parish is not walking through that door. And if you expect them to walk through that door, they're going to be gray and old. What we are is young, exciting, hard-working, and we're going to improve. People don't realize that, and as soon as they realize those three guys are not coming through that door, the better this town will be for all of us because there are young guys in that (locker) room playing their asses off."

He continued, "I wish we had $90 million under the salary cap. I wish we could buy the world. We can't. The only thing we can do is work hard, and all the negativity that's in this town sucks. I've been around when Jim Rice was booed. I've been around when (Carl) Yastrzemski was booed. And it stinks. It makes the greatest town, greatest city in the world, lousy. The only thing that will turn this around is being upbeat and positive like we are in that locker room... and if you think I'm going to succumb to negativity, you're wrong."

The Rick Pitino Era ended on Jan. 6, 2001 in Miami after a 112-86 loss to the Heat. By then the coach was physically and emotionally spent and wearing a dark, drawn look. In the final minutes of a game against the Heat, Pitino hugged young star Pierce as he exited the game but let Walker shuffle to the bench without lifting an eyelid. He announced his resignation after the game and opted to stay at a home he owned in Miami rather than resign at any type of news event back in Boston.

The Celtics were 102-146 under Pitino and never made the playoffs. The coach says the nightmarish experience made him grow.

"I think it's important that you face failure in life and that's what I needed to do after the Celtics," he said. "I'm too wise to ever think you're not going to fail in life. Failure is great if you accept it, accept ownership and do something about it. There are a lot of people out there a lot better than me who have failed and have gone on to be successful."

•

Louisville basketball hadn't fallen as far as the Celtics but the program was in serious trouble. Legendary coach Denny Crum, the man who led the Cards to national titles in 1980 and '86, had lost his touch. Once regarded as a top recruiter and strong tactician, Crum was losing the best local recruits to Pitino and Tubby Smith at Kentucky and had also fallen into trouble with the NCAA watchdogs.

To his credit, Jurich knew it was time for Crum to wrap up his career but did his best not to push too hard for a change. But when Pitino resigned in Boston, he knew a golden opportunity when he saw one.

"This was a very unique situation," Jurich said. "You had a Hall of Fame coach who had fallen on some tough times. There's no other way to put it except, to be candid, the program had really disintegrated to ashes. I don't mean that to be disrespectful to anybody. It's just the reality."

Crum's best players, including star guard Reece Gaines, were thinking of transferring. With the NCAA's 5/8 rule restricting the number of recruits a coach could sign in a single season, Jurich feared that whoever replaced Crum would be in for a serious rebuilding job. He also knew that losing wouldn't fly in Louisville, let alone multiple years of not acting like one of the sport's chosen few. With two years left on his contract, Crum resigned and was given a reported $6 million in walking money.

"We needed somebody to do much, much more than be the basketball coach. We needed somebody to resurrect a program," said Jurich. "And there was only one person. I'm not saying I'm the most brilliant guy in the world because we ultimately got Rick Pitino. That was a no-brainer. And he was available. When he became available, we knew it was time (for Crum to leave). You're not going to have that window very often. So I gave it my everything."

Jurich grew up in Los Angeles, not Louisville. He'd been in town for three years and certainly appreciated both the importance of Cardinal basketball to the city's fans and also the hatred of the Kentucky Wildcats. Or so he thought.

When he first broached the idea of Louisville hiring the former UK coach, friends laughed at him. "I remember all the people telling me I was crazy," he said. "If I had a dollar for all the people who told me I didn't know what I was doing, that I'm not from the state and I don't understand. And it was only because of the Kentucky thing. I saw that as an advantage.

Freedom Hall hosted the Conference USA tournament in March but instead of those high-stakes games, the talk of the town focused on who would replace Crum. Jurich struck first and with lightning-bolt power.

Jurich had met Pitino in passing two years before at the Kentucky Derby. The two men were not close and didn't have many common friends.

"Getting to really meet him and sit down with him and explain myself was another hurdle," he said, "so I did a press conference about him before I ever met him. We were hosting the conference tournament so there was a lot of press in town. We called everyone together and I just said that Rick is the only person I have in mind for this job and I am a one-person search committee."

Pitino was only two months removed from the Celtics and still in Miami with his wife, Joanne.

"I had met Tom one other time, I think at the Derby, and it's funny that I remember him saying 'Denny may retire soon. You'll have to come back to Kentucky.' My response to him in a very nice way was 'Tom, the Kentucky coach will never coach at Louisville. There's too much bitterness.' He just said it wasn't that big a deal," Pitino recalled.

"So when Denny resigns, I was sitting with Joanne in Miami watching TV and they ask Tom if he has a short list. He says 'I only have one person: Rick Pitino.' Joanne and I almost fell off the couch."

"I asked her, 'did you hear him say that? And she said 'I heard it, I heard it.' We couldn't believe the balls he had."

The initial reaction to Jurich's bold move was harsh, especially from UK fans over in Lexington. Jurich said he thinks now that Pitino was behind some of the backlash because he quickly told his closest confidants in the state that he wouldn't make such a move.

Jurich plugged on and got in contact with two of Pitino's advisers, Rick Avar and Brent Rice. He'd rendezvous with the two in Frankfort, a midway point between Lexington and Louisville, at an Applebees Restaurant.

"Rick Avar is a half-glass-full kind of guy and when I laid it all out to him, he never said no, never said I was nuts. He said, 'this is possible.' Brent Rice bought in, too," said Jurich. "I just believed Rick was the perfect fit here. He was the master builder of a program and he loved horses. He had so many friendships in this area so I knew I could put him in a comfort zone and not many schools could do that."

Despite his troubles in the pros, no one doubted Pitino's ability to coach. His next move clearly was back to college and Louisville wasn't the only option. Michigan had made some inquiries and was a serious player. Rumors about UCLA pushing Steve Lavin aside to make room for Pitino were hot, too. UNLV also openly began courting Pitino and Vegas really intrigued the coach. His wife, however, shot that idea down.

"My greatest ally turned out to be Rick's wife," said Jurich. "I went to Miami and stayed two days with him, in his house, so I really got to know the Pitinos. And I came away from there thinking this is perfect, it's too good to be true. We were three weeks off from his accepting the job so he had to think it through. But I felt this was too good a fit."

Pitino eventually bought into Jurich's vision and took the job. On March 21, 2001, Louisville stole the spotlight from the ongoing NCAA tourney by signing Pitino to a $12.25 million, six-year deal that included a $5 million bonus if he stayed in town for five years. The news conference was telecast live nationally on ESPN.

While Louisville fans couldn't believe their good fortune, Kentucky fans felt betrayed by their former leader. Pitino went from hero to villain overnight in every corner of a state where there are only two colors, Big Blue or Cardinal Red. You can't be both, although Pitino now had a little bit of both running through his veins.

When he coached at Rupp Arena for the first time as the U of L coach, Pitino heard boos and was branded a traitor for 40 loud minutes. His subsequent visits have gone a bit smoother but he realizes he crossed a line some of the state's basketball fans consider sacrilegious.

"It will never die down but I understand," Pitino said. "It's not directed at me now but I am the Louisville coach. It's hatred, it's bitterness. It's the worst rivalry in sports, or the best, depending on where you sit."

Pitino's coaching track record is one of remarkable rebuilding jobs. The first program he pulled from the ashes was Providence. He left a job as a New York Knick assistant in the spring of 1985 when the Friars were mired in the basement of the Big East. In his first meeting with the school's boosters, he told the fans to buy as many season tickets as they could afford because an era of future sellouts was right around the corner. "I want you to go home tonight and dream of cutting down the nets," he told a crowd that had to think its new coach was off his rocker.

Sure enough, two years later the Friars were cutting down the nets and heading to the 1987 Final Four.

Pitino left PC for the Knicks' head coaching job soon after losing to Syracuse in the national semifinals. He resuscitated life back into the franchise behind Patrick Ewing and Mark Jackson but soon left his hometown after chafing with the front office and headed back to college to take over a Kentucky program that was coming off probation. The situation proved perfect, however, for yet another rebuilding scenario and Pitino turned things around yet again. In eight years in Lexington, he led the 'Cats to three Final Fours and the national title in 1996.

The situation at Louisville fell somewhere between the losing ways of Providence and the shame felt at Kentucky.

"At Providence, I remembered Ernie DiGregorio and Marvin Barnes (in the 1973 Final Four) but I realized that was eight, nine years ago," he said. "They had been in dead last place since the inception of the Big East so the kids there didn't even remember Ernie D. It wasn't as bad at Kentucky because the only problems you had there was embarrassment and probation. That was a total different type of turn-around.

"Louisville, this was more like Providence where the brand had slipped. We were in three, four years able to get back on TV, back in the newspapers and the recruits became interested again," he said.

The Cardinals finished 12-19 in Crum's final season but Pitino's first team pressed and ran opponents hard enough to squeeze out a 19-13 record and a berth in the NIT. Helped by the recruiting of players such as Francisco Garcia, Larry O'Bannon and Ellis Myles and the leadership of veteran Reece Gaines, Pitino's second year was a stunning smash as the Cards went 25-7, won 17 games in a row and rose to No. 2 in the national polls. The rise continued and eventually peaked in 2005 when the Cardinals breezed through Conference USA and advanced to the Final Four after a stunning overtime win over West Virginia in the Elite 8. Louisville ended the season with a loss to Illinois in St. Louis but the 33-5 record matched the most victories in school history and cemented Pitino's name in the program's rich history.

"It was rewarding for the program but I was thrilled we could win for the Louisville fans," Pitino said. "They are used to winning and really love their team. To go from down in the dumps a few years earlier to the Final Four, really before I thought we could be there, that was very fulfilling."

Now Pitino is readying for the Big East. It's a challenge he hadn't prepared for but is thrilled that it materialized.

"Three years ago Tom (Jurich) said he was hearing rumblings that the Big East might break up. I said 'Tom, it's never going to happen. We're never going to the Big East," Pitino said. "I called Michael (Tranghese) and he said, 'Rick, it could happen one day but I don't think it'll happen in my tenure as commissioner or your tenure as a coach."

A year later, Miami, Virginia Tech and Boston College bolted for the Atlantic Coast Conference and Louisville rose to the top of the Big East's wish list.

"Because of Louisville's football, we became involved and it couldn't be better for us. I would've guessed five conferences before I would have thought of the Big East for Louisville," he said. "For me it'll be very exciting. I never expected it. I don't know what my window will be in coaching but this is a great window to wind down in. You get an opportunity to play in the Big East. For me it's a lot more familiar, a lot better to wind up your coaching career in the Big East."

(10)

Dec. 20 & 21; Louisville

Freedom Hall, as usual, is rapidly filling to capacity in anticipation of the first game of the Billy Minardi Classic. Louisville is 6-1 but fresh off a 73-61 loss to rival Kentucky that wasn't that close. For weeks Pitino has been telling anyone who would listen that his team isn't as good as people think and isn't worthy of its No. 11 national ranking.

Only five minutes into tonight's game against Middle Tennessee it's clear the coach isn't blowing smoke. Junior guard Taquan Dean is an obvious stud, a big-time scoring guard with a chiseled body and fierce temperament. But the rest of the Cardinals' talent is a let-down. David Padgett, a transfer big man from Kansas, is skilled but far from a monster athletically. Juan Palacios, a sophomore who Cardinal fans fear may jump to the NBA after this season, is a physical beast but slowed by a bum ankle and doesn't really know how to play.

Most of all, the highly touted Louisville freshman class is a dud. Point guard Andre McGee is slow and heavy-legged. Forward Chad Millard seems better-suited to play at his home state university (New Hampshire) than at Louisville. Terrence Williams flies around the court but lacks any feel for the game. Bryan Harvey, a wing from L.A., is in Pitino's doghouse and plays just three minutes.

Some strong second half play by Brandon Jenkins, who finishes with 20 points, helps the Cards survive for a 76-68 win. Dean, a pre-season

All-American pick in some quarters, shoots 3-of-9 and finishes with 10 points. Afterward, Pitino is concerned about his team, 7-1 record be damned.

"I was just concerned about winning out there tonight," he tells reporters sitting in a small, cramped room under the stands. "We've got to win these games right now. The freshmen have got enough experience. I can't concern myself with playing time - we've got to win. If you lose tonight, your back's to the wall. We did a decent job tonight under trying circumstances. I'm very concerned right now about double digit losses going into the Big East and just getting into the NCAA Tournament. People think I'm not serious about that but I am. This is a very young basketball team emotionally, physically. We have seven new players who don't know each other at all. We've got guys who have missed six weeks of practice. There are no mind games going on, I'm just trying to win. I think we have a rough and rocky road ahead."

Inside the Louisville locker room, a giant picture with a view of the Hoosier Dome, the site of the Final Four, hangs on the wall. Above it reads "Hard Work + Dedication = Indianapolis." The players shrug off their listless play and certainly talk the talk of a nationally ranked power.

"Coach has done this for 30 years," says Dean, "so he knows what to do with us. Once we get it together defensively, I think any concerns will go away."

With school closed for Christmas break, the rules that restrict how much time players and coaches can work together are relaxed. Pitino has the players back on the court at the Student Activities Center on Louisville's campus at 10 a.m. the next morning for a walk-through in preparation for a match up with the College of Charleston in the championship game of the tournament. Two of his sons, Richard and Christopher, are in town for the holiday and pop in and out of their dad's office.

They're also on hand to help honor the memory of their uncle Billy. On September 11, 2001, the nation watched in horror when two hijacked airliners slammed into the World Trade Center in New York. On the 104th floor of Tower 1, Billy Minardi and the other traders at Cantor Fitzgerald were preparing for another busy day of work. When the first plane tore into the North Tower, Cantor's offices only a few floors above the impact were turned into an inferno.

Back in Louisville, Pitino turned on the television and watched in horror. Minardi was both his brother-in-law and best friend. When he began dating his future wife back on Long Island in the late 1960s, Rick Pitino and Billy Minardi became so close that the coach would often kid his wife that he loved her brother more than her.

"Joanne and I were trying to laugh about stories about Billy the other night," Pitino said at a news briefing a few weeks after 9/11. "Kidding around, I said, 'You know, I always loved Billy more than I loved you.' And she said, 'I've always known you loved him more.' We had so many fun times, so many great memories. I cherish those memories. It was a good reason to marry Joanne."

As he watched the horrible replay of the crash, Pitino knew Billy worked near the top of the tower so he tried counting floors down to the impact zone. He said he called a friend who thought Billy may have moved his office to the lower third of the tower. But then Pitino called his oldest son, Michael, who was working for Deutsche Bank in lower Manhattan and regularly picked his Uncle Billy's brain on the banking business. Michael confirmed that Billy's office still sat on the 105th floor.

Minardi's death devastated a Pitino family that has had much more than its fair share of tragedy. A few months before 9/11, Don Vogt, Joanne Pitino's brother-in-law, was killed by a taxi cab in New York. And in 1987 when he coached at Providence, the Pitinos lost a son, Daniel, to congenital heart failure only a few weeks after his birth.

Coping with Minardi's loss wasn't easy and will never really end. But as the coach said back then, he had basketball and his first season as the Louisville coach to look forward to. His wife didn't share a similar sanctuary.

"I'm emotionally spent," he said then. "The only solace I get is when I'm on that court for four hours a day. What I have to do is to immerse myself in it, day and night, so I don't think as much. The only thing you have to do is go overboard and immerse yourself in your work and your family and just pass out at night."

Minardi was a huge Pitino supporter who regularly sat behind the team bench at Providence, the Knicks, Kentucky and the Celtics. His friends were Pitino's friends and the two shared golf trips and horse racing jaunts all over the world. There was no question in Pitino's mind that he'd do something to honor Minardi's legacy and he wanted it to revolve around the sports he loved.

"I learned from my wife, who is part Irish, how to mourn," Pitino said. "When you go to an Italian wake, it's so sad. They're throwing themselves on the coffin, it's so miserable. When it's over you feel distraught and abandoned. You go to an Irish wake, you feel great about the person who just passed.

"After losing my son Daniel, I didn't know what to do, how to react. So we set up a Homeless Shelter in Owensboro, Kentucky named in his honor and started a foundation in his name that's helped so many people. When Billy passed, I didn't know what to do. My life, as I knew it, was basically over. But I wanted to celebrate his life like the Irish would. We had 15 of his friends come together and we bought the naming rights for $1.5 million to a dormitory here on campus that the team lives in, Minardi Hall. And we started this tournament."

The Billy Minardi Classic began in 2003 as a single game. In the first year, the Cardinals upset a No. 1 ranked Florida coached by one of Pitino's former players, Billy Donovan. The event is now a traditional, four-team affair where Louisville packs Freedom Hall and is all but assured of two wins. But Pitino knows no game is easy for his team right now. He purposely lined up wins early in the season against the likes of Bellarmine, Southern Indiana and Prairie View, part of a non-league schedule ranked 331st in the country by one service. But he knew this team needed time to grow and mature. The Cards flunked their first test at Kentucky but with a stretch of at Miami, home against Villanova and at Providence only two weeks away, the coach is clearly concerned. Even if the masses aren't buying it.

"It's not a concern what the people think but their mindset has to change," he said. "They're more concerned about whom you're playing non-conference than how you're playing and I've told them that last year we played a tough non-conference schedule but this is a much easier schedule because we need it to be much easier.

"They don't quite understand what they're in for. They think that at Rutgers is like at Tulane. At Providence is very tough. They don't understand that. They know Conference USA. We played Southern Miss, there were 500 people in the stands. Here, you go on the road and it will be very tough to win."

Asked if last year's Final Four run spoiled the fans, Pitino says, "we are so painfully young. I'm trying to be realistic but no one else is. I don't know why we were ranked so high. When you lose Garcia, O'Bannon, Myles and George, you've lost 60 percent of your points and rebounds. We have Palacios back but he was the fifth, sixth guy last year and he was good because he had Garcia, O'Bannon, Myles and George around him.

"I would've ranked us 17,18,19 if I was optimistic, saying if they reach their potential and come on well," he said. "Where they ranked us, I thought that was crazy."

Pitino is sitting in a large office that's filled with activity. His secretary and personal assistant dot in and out and Christmas presents set to hit the mail litter the floor. He may be a one-man corporation, complete with his own Web site (rickpitino.com), but the 53 year old still loves to coach. The fact that he became the first man to ever lead three different schools to the Final Four last spring hasn't dampened his spirit. In fact, the move to the Big East has reinvigorated him and set up a new challenge that he knows will be tough to conquer.

The conference switch has already paid big dividends on the recruiting trail. The Cards signed one of the nation's top classes in the fall and three of the four players (Derrick Caracter, Edgar Sosa, Earl Clark) hail from the New York City area. Pitino expects to beat a path to his recruiting roots on a yearly basis.

"It wasn't that difficult, really," he said. "Caracter and Sosa were relatively easy. We had to battle Villanova pretty good for Clark. It's funny because we were going to recruit a little more out West but then we go into the Big East so we said, 'ok, let's hit the metropolitan area hard.'

"We're so lucky here because there really is no region for us recruiting-wise. Louisville is a national school. Pretty soon we'll have a new arena being built, a new practice facility, 19,000 fans every night. That's season ticket holders. You have a great dorm, a city that's infatuated with basketball, and a great tradition. Everybody right now is so proud of what the University of Louisville has to offer. The Big East has enabled that to take off. You don't get that in a lot of cities."

Now that the Big East games are around the corner, Pitino sounds like a coach who's standing in front of an oncoming train. Sure, it's nice to go back to Providence and New York City and see some old friends, but at what cost?

"I came back to Kentucky because it's a place I wanted to live. I also had never experienced the places we'd play at in Conference USA and so it would be something new," he said. "So when this whole thing came full cycle back to the Big East, I was in shock a little bit. When Tom (Jurich) first approached me about it, there was a part of me that wasn't for it. We were playing Memphis and Cincinnati, DePaul and Marquette and then you have 4-5 games where you have to play well to win but that's manageable. Now, it's like 'what's this all about.'

"The thing people don't appreciate about a league like this is how it helps everyone," he continued. "In 1986, Seton Hall and Providence were in the bottom of the Big East since its inception. Two years later, we were in the Final Four at Providence and P.J. (Carlesimo) takes Seton Hall to the championship game (in '89). That's the way it is in a conference like this. Everybody may look at a Syracuse, Connecticut, Villanova as being very strong but before you know it St. John's, Marquette and Seton Hall can turn it around. In college basketball, it only takes three great players to turn it around. For me at Kentucky, it took one great player, Jamal Mashburn, to turn things around.

You get one, two big-time players you can go from the bottom to the top in a hurry. Unlike football."

Before Pitino can worry about Connecticut and Villanova, he has to find a way past the College of Charleston. While the tourney's consolation game plays out, fans gradually fill Freedom Hall and circulate through the corridors of one of basketball's oldest jewels. The building has hosted six Final Fours and played host to Louisville basketball since 1956. It is tired and worn, but historic. Plaques honoring members of the Kentucky Athletic Hall of Fame ring the arena's walls and tell the stories of Frank Ramsay, Paul Hornung, Muhammad Ali and Steve Cauthen. In one corner sits the Louisville Hall of Fame room where the history of Cardinal basketball is told.

The 'Ville has journeyed to eight Final Fours; only six schools have played in more. A large picture of a young Denny Crum as the 1973 Missouri Valley Coach of the Year catches your eye, as does one of Pitino which sits under a banner proclaiming, "Louisville: Rick Pitino's New Kentucky Home." Life-size pictures of the greats dot the room and a Dream Team exhibit featuring Wes Unseld, Rodney McCray, Pervis Ellison, Derek Smith and Darrell Griffith, as well as those honoring the 1980 and 1986 national championship teams, attract plenty of fans.

Louisville is 610-126 (.827) in its 50 years at Freedom Hall and rarely plays in front of an empty seat. The school has ranked in the top five in attendance nationally in each of the last 23 years, including a record 19,590 average in 1997. A crowd of 18,884 settles into the stands for this game and from the start the Cards look pretty good. Palacios, Padgett and Dean spark some early offense that sends Charleston back on its heels. Louisville is up 17-7 after seven minutes and builds a 26-11 lead at the 7:30 mark.

Some sloppy turnovers and four missed free throws open the door for the visitors who race back into the contest and cut the lead to six points. Louisville leads at the half, 34-23, and is only ahead by eight points with 8:32 to play when an explosiveness that's been missing all season finally shows up.

Two McGee 3-pointers and one by Dean spark a 15-2 run that blows the game open. The Cards cruise to a 78-63 win that sends everyone home happy and even makes Pitino smile during a post-game ceremony on the court that he shares with Billy Minardi's widow, Stephanie, and her three children.

"We are getting better, just not better for 40 minutes," Pitino said, "but we are getting better. We're starting to learn what to do defensively. We're stepping up and rotating a little better and that's what I want to see. I think we could be a good offensive team, we just have to become a good defensive team, that's how you win on the road. It's going to take some time, we are a work in progress, but I think we're making headway in that area."

Jenkins earns the tournament's MVP award but Dean, who is bothered by a balky ankle, hits just 5-of-20 shots in the two games. Both players need to be stars for the Cardinals, especially with Palacios (13 points in the two games) struggling with a ankle injury suffered last summer that's limited his conditioning for the season.

"He's not playing particularly well," Pitino says on his post-game radio show, carried on WHAS-840, one of the nation's strongest AM signals. "Check out his ankle when it doesn't have ice on it. It's huge. It's not that Tello doesn't want to do it, but five and a half months without playing, it doesn't come back right away. That's tough to do if you miss a month, but you miss five months, it's tough to do. He's nowhere near back. I don't know if he'll get it back this year - back to where he was."

Palacios is a subject on many caller's minds, for good reason. He's easily the most talented player in the program and he'll almost certainly one day have a chance to play in the NBA but right now he's struggling. When a fan calls in and wonders if this will be the sophomore's final college season, the hosts all but laugh. That's when you realize that the expectations Pitino has talked about are indeed a little out of wack.

"I think we can be good but the veterans have to play well for us and right now Tello is hurt, Padgett isn't where he needs to be and Taquan has a bad ankle. Brandon Jenkins is the only guy playing right now," he says. "We'll see what happens. All I know is the games are about to get a whole lot tougher."

The biggest night in the first month of a new era for Big East basketball actually took place at a football stadium. West Virginia won the league's football championship and the right to play in the Bowl Championship Series on Jan. 2 against Georgia. The Bulldogs, the Southeast Conference champ, were nearly a touchdown favorite and enjoyed a home town advantage with the Sugar Bowl game moving to Atlanta after Hurricane Katrina ravaged the New Orleans Superdome.

What made the night so big? Besides the legs of Steve Slaton and the arm of Pat White, the most important ingredient that came out of the Mountaineers' 38-35 win was a flood of respect for Big East football. After all, the SEC is widely ranked as the nation's premier football conference. The SEC champion, playing in its home state, certainly isn't supposed to fall behind 28-0 and lose to a team from the lowly Big East.

"I've been part of six men's basketball championships, six women's and national football titles with Miami, but West Virginia's win in the Sugar Bowl was as significant a night as we've had in the Big East in the last 28 years," said Mike Tranghese. "That was the start of hearing people begin to say, 'Maybe they can play. Maybe they belong.'"

The nation's sports media may have been thirsting for the men's basketball league to tap off but securing football's future was still Tranghese's number-one concern with his giant, new league. Only a year before, Pittsburgh represented the Big East in the BCS. The Panthers went to the Fiesta Bowl and were smacked around by the Utah Utes, 35-7. That loss only intensified criticism of the Big East and its right to an automatic BCS bid. But with the conference playing without Miami and Virginia Tech for the first time, Tranghese knew he was being unfairly graded.

"We had five teams. That's not a league," he said. "And Boston College was a lame duck team for us that year. It was an unfortunate situation for Tom O'Brien's team to be in. We needed to move on and I knew what Louisville was going to bring. We needed to move ahead and that's what we did this year."

The potential loss of the BCS' money hovered over the Big East/ACC showdown of 2003 but the relationships Tranghese fostered over the years with other big-league conference commissioners ultimately gave the Big East a chance. With Louisville coming into the league in 2005, the BCS partners agreed to credit Louisville's strong 11-1 season in 2004 to the Big East. The Cards finished 10th in the BCS poll, an important factor since future inclusion in the BCS system would be awarded to conferences that average a top-12 finish in the final BCS standings over a revolving four-year period.

West Virginia's top 10 BCS finish only served to further solidify the football league's future and prop up everyone's spirits heading into the start of the basketball season. As Tranghese left the Georgia Dome that night, he knew things were falling into place.

"We had so much positive momentum with the basketball season set to begin but football needed a big win and West Virginia gave us that. It really was a big night for everyone," he said.

Jan. 3; Milwaukee

It is opening night in the Big East, the night fans have craved and coaches have dreaded. Connecticut, the league's dominant force, is in Milwaukee to play at one of the new schools, Marquette.

Jim Calhoun has caught some heat from The Horde in recent days about a run of cream puffs during a seven-game home stand that's included 30-point blowout wins over New Hampshire, Morehead State, Stony Brook and Quinnipiac. All of those wins came without Marcus Williams but the lefty point guard began practice two weeks ago and is finally set to make his season debut at the Bradley Center.

A few days before, UConn lets Williams face the media for stories on his controversial return.

"The thing I did is over," he told the Hartford Courant. "I think I'm wiser. You make sure you think twice before you act. Plus the opportunity, I think about that. It has been a struggle but it could have been a lot worse. I thought I may never play here again, never go to school here again. It's a blessing."

Williams stayed in shape during his suspension by frequently working out on his own at a high school one block from campus. He also served a chunk of the 400 hours of community service he owes the state by helping nuns with assorted household chores at the Franciscan Life Center in Meriden, Conn., one of Jim Calhoun's favorite charities.

Craig Austrie, a freshman, has started every game in Williams' absence and helped the 11-0 Huskies to wins over Arkansas, Arizona and Gonzaga in the Maui Classic and a series of easy home victories. But everyone has waited for the return of Marcus Williams, most of all Calhoun.

"He's looked good in practice but he needs to get his legs under him," he said before the trip to Marquette. "It'll take him time but he's already making unbelievable passes. He's the best passer we've ever had here, easily the best."

Heading to Marquette, the Huskies are ranked second in the polls and sparking plenty of arguments around the country as to who owns the best team in the nation, UConn or Duke. Ten minutes into the game, those high hopes are quickly deflated. The Marquette crowd has waited two years for its first taste of the Big East and the 15, 831 fans quickly rattle the Huskies.

Even with buddy LeBron James in the stands, Rudy Gay can't get in the flow. While Husky Nation waits for Gay and the boys to shift their game into gear, Marquette comes out firing and shreds the UConn defense for a 39-33 halftime lead. The Golden Eagles keep rolling and enjoy a truly special night in a 94-79 victory. The best player on the floor is not Gay, Josh Boone or any of the other NBA-ready talents on UConn's roster. It's Marquette senior Steve Novak. He torches every defender Calhoun sends at him and rolls to 41 points, the greatest scoring debut in Big East history.

The ultimate indignity comes in the final few minutes when UConn legend Donyell Marshall, in town with LeBron and the Cavaliers, gets up from his courtside seat and leaves the building in disgust.

"Donyell Marshall left with four minutes to go. That's never happened before," said a disgusted Calhoun. "Guys don't leave with four minutes to go. We've built up too much over the last 20 years for that to happen."

Marcus Williams' return is only spotty, at best. He has seven assists in 23 minutes but makes just 1-of-5 shots and hears plenty of hoots from the Marquette crowd, including 'Where's My Laptop' and 'Can I get a printer with that?' Afterward, Williams laughed off the taunts but more importantly voices what many UConn fans had feared about the team's schedule.

"We may have needed this loss to get us back to being focused," Williams said. "Playing those six or seven games (at home after Maui), we weren't ready. I think we had a loss of focus."

Calhoun is clearly shocked by the lopsided loss and chooses to zero in on Gay's relatively inconsequential showing (3-of-12, 8 points, 7 rebounds, 5 turnovers) in a revealing 15 minute post-game news conference where he takes a few rips at his star forward. "I don't think Rudy Gay did anything other than report for the starting lineup," Calhoun said.

Calhoun keeps rolling, wondering aloud whether Gay is playing like everybody's All-American. "We don't have, right now, anybody on our team ... that plays like an all-star in our league and a top 15 player. For the first time, I'm wondering for a couple of our kids if they are as good as they are supposed to be. They were in Maui, and they aren't now. Marquette had a lot to do with that, but the teams over there - Arkansas, Arizona, Gonzaga - were pretty good, too."

Calhoun is clearly piqued by Gay's reliance on his jump shot. "I think Rudy was lousy. L-O-U....If you want to play at 23 feet at 6-foot-9...That's the way Novak plays. [Gay] is our three man and we don't play him that way. We play him as a slasher. We play him as a post-up player. We play him as one of our better rebounders. He had a lousy game."

With the Wisconsin reporters stunned in their seats, Calhoun never takes a breath and keeps ripping his team.

"We got completely taken out of our offense and were just casting prayers," he said. "We were well-prepared. We were living on our 11-0 record, which means absolutely nothing because you have to play the next game. I'd have liked my team to have put forth the effort that Marquette did. That's what I would have liked. It's always easy to fix effort. We'll do that tomorrow afternoon at one o'clock. There won't be a lot of talking."

Before he vacates the podium, Calhoun gets a twinkle in his eye and warns the celebrating Marquette fans that every night in the Big East won't end in revelry.

"Don't get too carried away. You've got a lot of games to play. A lot of places to go," he said. "It's a great beginning for Marquette, certainly. I'd relish it to

11 o'clock tonight, which I'm sure Tom (Crean) will. I've said this is going to be the greatest college basketball conference ever. It looks like one of the 16 teams is struggling. Everyone else is good. Nobody is shocked that you can go to Marquette and lose. Get on the road in this league and see some of the friendly faces. They won't be so friendly. Maybe see us at another time, in March sometime."

Jan. 4; Pittsburgh

If the opening night shocker in Milwaukee could be topped, it happened just one night later. Two thrilling overtime games shook the Big East, one in Pittsburgh and the other at the Meadowlands in New Jersey.

Pitt came into the Big East season as a true paper tiger. The Panthers left their home city once (beat South Carolina) and rolled to an 11-0 record. The combination of point guard Carl Krauser and 7-foot center Aaron Gray pushed the Panthers into the top 10 but you couldn't be sure just how good the team really was.

Notre Dame entered conference play 9-2 but faced plenty of iron. The questions surrounding the Irish centered on the talent in the program more than anything else. The two teams hooked up for an exhilarating game with Pitt hanging on for a 100-97, double overtime win.

Pitt looked like it had the game won several times but Chris Quinn, a fresh-faced Irish kid from Dublin (Ohio), kept making staggering 3-point shots. He and Colin Falls sank two 3-pointers apiece in the final 45 seconds to erase a 9-point Pitt lead and force overtime. In the o.t., Pitt led 90-83 with 1:08 remaining but Quinn made a 3-pointer with a minute left and another with 14 seconds remaining to cut the lead to two, 93-91. Notre Dame fouled Antonio Graves but he missed both free throws, and the Irish quickly got the ball to Quinn again. This time he drove to the basket and made a layup with six seconds left to send the game into double overtime.

The Irish held a slim one-point lead with 16 seconds left but Pitt's Ronald Ramon drained a 3-pointer for the lead and Quinn, who finished with six of Notre Dame's 14 threes and 37 points overall, missed in the final seconds.

Meanwhile in New Jersey, two fierce rivals were playing out a flip-flop of historic proportions. St. John's appeared well on its way to its first road win in more than two years as it raced to a 32-15 halftime lead and a 47-27 advantage with 12 minutes to go. But Seton Hall closed like an enraged thoroughbred and caught St. John's at the buzzer on a wild runner by freshman Paul Gause. In overtime, the Pirates took care of business and won, 69-61.

Jan. 5; Louisville

While Marquette and Cincinnati successfully navigated their first Big East games, Louisville wasn't so lucky.

Rick Pitino's team was coming off an impressive road win over Miami but the coach knew his 11-1 record and national No. 8 ranking were about to be tested. The Big East's schedule maker welcomed Louisville into the league with home games against Villanova and Pittsburgh sandwiched around a trip to Providence, the birthplace of Pitino's basketball legend.

The Villanova game came with all the trappings of a big night. Freedom Hall was filled with its sea of Cardinal red and black and everyone couldn't wait for a look-see at the third-ranked Wildcats.

"I guess you could say it's on now," 'Nova coach Jay Wright said before his conference opener. "There are no easy games. It's similar to when we had nine teams (in the 1980s) and it seemed like every night you were playing a top 25 team. We play Louisville, West Virginia and I can't remember who after that, but I'm sure it's going to be a great team. When you play in a league like that and you make the NCAA tournament, you have a chance to win a national championship because you're used to playing great teams every night. Playing teams like that back-to-back-to-back prepares you for the NCAA Tournament."

Pitino wore a ready-or-not feel into the opener. He knew his team wasn't the eighth best in the nation but he wasn't quite sure how they'd match up against the iron. He would soon find out.

With Taquan Dean still slowed a bit by a bad ankle, the Cardinals had no prayer defending Villanova's ultra-quick, four guard lineup. Randy Foye scored 24 points and grabbed 9 rebounds and Allan Ray added 17 points as the Wildcats went up 21-9 out of the gate and were never seriously threatened in a 76-67 victory. Center David Padgett led Louisville with 17 points but Juan Palacios shot 1-of-9 and the painfully young Cards clearly didn't have enough firepower.

"Villanova is certainly deserving of their ranking," Pitino said afterwards. "They are a great basketball team that's difficult to guard on both ends of court and they have experience and great tenacity. They were probably a travel violation away from being national champions last year. Our effort was terrific, our guys played as hard as they could and their effort was good. Villanova was just a better basketball team."

If U of L fans hadn't figured it out by the end of the game, Pitino continued to remind them that Francisco Garcia and Ellis Myles and Larry O'Bannon were now long gone. In their place were too many youngsters who weren't ready for prime time.

"With seven new players, we're never going to have an experienced lineup. This is who we are, we're a very young and inexperienced basketball team," he said. "Our young guys did a good job. The key is six weeks from now. How good can we become?"

The morning after the loss, Pitino packed his bags and prepared to fly to one of his favorite places.

Rick Pitino and Providence, Rhode Island own very rich roots. From 1985-87, a youthful Pitino pumped basketball life back into a city that had forgotten what it felt like to win big. Providence was one of the East's powerhouse teams through the 1960s and '70s under legendary coaches Joe Mullaney and Dave Gavitt but the dawn of the Big East propped other schools up to that national level and the Friars faltered.

This was not what Providence fans had come to expect, however. Providence College is run by the Dominican Fathers, a small sect of priests who've always lived on campus, taught many of the classes and rooted like heck for their basketball teams. The school was founded in 1917 as an all-male, mostly commuter school for Rhode Island's working class but athletics were always a priority. They received a needed boost in the mid-1950s when the school hired Mullaney, a New Yorker who played with Bob Cousy and won the national championship at Holy Cross.

Only a few years into his tenure, Mullaney had developed a knack for finding sleeper recruits and his teams began knocking off one giant after another thanks to a defense he called the "combination," a precursor to the match-up zone. One of his first good teams included Lenny Wilkens, a future Hall of Famer, and blazingly quick guard Johnny Egan, who also went on to star in the NBA. When Mullaney's Friars first played at Madison Square Garden and posted upsets in the National Invitation Tournament, the New York City tabloids embraced the small school with the underdog pedigree.

The sudden notoriety made The Rev. Robert Slavin, the school's president, remark that, "Seven hundred years of Dominican scholarship and nobody ever heard of us until we put five kids on the floor at Madison Square Garden."

Mullaney kept the program rolling through the 1960s with great players such as Jimmy Walker, Mike Riordan and future Georgetown coach John Thompson. Mullaney left to coach Wilt Chamberlain and the Lakers in 1968 and Gavitt was hired as his replacement. The City of Providence built one of the East's first downtown arenas, the Providence Civic Center, in 1972 and the Friars fit the new scene like a well-worn glove. Two homegrown heroes, Ernie DiGregorio and Marvin Barnes, led teams that raced to the top 10 in the polls and all the way to the 1973 Final Four. As that decade ended, however, Gavitt moved on to run the Big East and Providence wasn't quite ready for the jump.

In the Big East's first six seasons, Providence finished last or next-to-last. Then the good Dominican Fathers hired Pitino. As a proud Italian in a city known as a mafia haven, Pitino was an instant hit. When he guided his first team to a 17-14 record and the NIT, Friar fans started to believe again.

In 1987, Pitino took things a step further and made a run at the top of the Big East. It was the first year of the 3-point line and Pitino embraced the bonus shot and freed Billy Donovan, Delray Brooks and Pop Lewis to fire from all angles. When the Friars earned their first NCAA Tournament bid in nine years, experts pegged them as a team to watch. Two weeks later, Pitino's band of 3-point shooting over-achievers were cutting down the nets at Freedom Hall and headed to the Final Four.

The Friars lost to Big East rival Syracuse in the Final Four in New Orleans but still returned home as conquering heroes. After first agreeing to a contract extension and getting the Friars involved with high schools stars such as Malik Sealy and Bobby Hurley, Pitino left Providence to return to his hometown and coach the New York Knicks. His loss shocked the PC fans but as the years passed, mostly everyone realized he had accomplished the impossible. More importantly, he showed tiny Providence College (enrollment, 3,800) that it could win big playing with the Big Boys.

"It was a glorious time. The greatest year of my coaching career," Pitino says. "Providence will always be dear to me. I only spent two years here but I learned to believe in fairy tales and Cinderella."

An hour or so after Pitino and his Louisville team flew into Providence, a few of his former players called on him at the Westin Hotel next to the Dunkin' Donuts Center. A local cable TV channel celebrated his return by replaying a huge win against Georgetown from that magical 1987 season. "It was so funny, the player's shorts were so short and I was laughing at how I looked, the hairstyles," he said.

More former Friars showed up for Louisville's shoot-around on Saturday morning. So did Gavitt and John Marinatto, the Big East's Associate

Commissioner who became Pitino's lifelong friend when he served as PC's sports publicity officer during the Boy Wonder's two-year reign. Afterwards, Pitino grabbed a quick Italian lunch on Federal Hilll and went to a local cemetery and prayed at the grave of his son, Daniel, who died as an infant just after the Big East Tournament in 1987.

When Pitino entered the Dunkin' Donuts Center on game night, he wasn't thinking about the past. His Cardinals may have been nationally ranked but were 0-1 in the Big East and facing a hungry Providence team. The Friars are coached by Tim Welsh, a native of Upstate New York who grew up a big Syracuse fan. In fact, when Welsh was honored as Massena High's Athlete of the Year in the 1970's, Jim Boeheim was the guest speaker at the banquet.

Welsh went on to coach at Syracuse under Boeheim before succeeding his father, Jerry, and leading Iona College to three 20-win seasons from 1995-98. After wavering a bit at first to see if the St. John's job would open (it eventually did and Mike Jarvis replaced Fran Fraschilla), Welsh jumped at the chance to coach in the Big East and succeeded Pete Gillen at Providence. Within three years, Welsh's Friars won a school-record 11 conference games and made the NCAA's.

PC was back in the Big Dance in 2004 behind All-American Ryan Gomes but a first round upset at the hands of Pacific stained a 20-9 season. Now it's nearly two years later and the Friars are rebuilding with six freshmen or sophomores in their top eight players. Under Welsh and long-time assistants Steve DeMeo and Vince Cautero, the Friars have carved out a niche as a program that unearths hidden gems. The prime example was Gomes, a pudgy high school star in Connecticut who chose PC over Creighton and then matured into a star.

But some other potential finds went bust. A slew of transfers plagued the program, including two in the last month that's left the team with only eight scholarship players. Guard Dwight Brewington, the team's leading returning scorer, left in a huff in the pre-season because Welsh wouldn't let him play point guard. DeSean White, a talented big forward from Philadelphia, was beaten out for a starting spot and he never returned to campus after going home for Christmas.

With just one senior and as many as three freshmen starters, Welsh was walking into the best basketball conference in the country with his hands tied.

"The guys who are here want to be here and I like them a lot," he said. "How many games we win, no one knows. But I do know we have some good, young players and we're headed in the right direction. There are no more malcontents here now."

Providence let a halftime lead at Georgetown slip away in its first Big East game, a 72-62 Hoya win. The Friars came out firing again against Pitino's troops and led at the half, 34-30. PC still led, 67-66, with 1:43 to play but one of Louisville's struggling freshman, Andre McGee, scored on a strong drive through the lane with 1:22 left. At the other end, Providence's star freshman guard Sharaud Curry appeared to get whacked on a drive to the basket but there was no call and the ball fell off the rim.

McGee came off the same high screen and scored again in the lane to put the Cards up, 70-67. When Friar senior Donnie McGrath missed a 3-pointer to tie with 16 seconds left, Pitino had his first Big East win, 72-67.

"I told Andre to look for Chad Millard in the corner, look for Taquan (Dean) or look to score. He liked the third option the best," Pitino said afterwards. "We're so painfully young that we don't have a lot of offensive confidence. We're struggling for an identity. We needed to get a win tonight to get our confidence going."

Pitino received a hearty pre-game welcome from the Providence fans. It was quite a difference from the heavy boos and catcalls he heard when he took his Louisville team back to his other former college, Kentucky.

"I hardly get emotional about crowds or anything like that but I had tears of joy inside tonight," Pitino said. "I've had so many tears of sorrow in my life that you learn to go back and think of great things that have happened. That's really happened in the last day coming back here and seeing so many great friends but I just assumed coming back I was going to get booed. I spent six years at Kentucky and we went to two Final Fours, two Elite Eight's and won a national championship and I went back there and 24,000 people were booing me. So I just assumed that you go on the road, you get booed. But I guess more than anything else this restored my belief in people, fans and friendships.

"I don't think you ever leave. I was very, very happy here," he continued. "It was only two years that I spent here but Providence will be very dear to me. I still believe in fairy tales and Cinderella because of it. I watch that team and the emotion of the town and how they got behind us. I remember the stories of the people in Cranston and how they went outside and were banging their pots and pans when we won to go to the Final Four. It really was a special time."

Jan. 8; Philadelphia

The big game in the Big East is at Villanova this Sunday afternoon. The third-ranked Wildcats are off to their best start (a perfect 10-0) in 44 years but are stepping into the meat of their schedule. Today the West Virginia Mountaineers are in town; later in the week come trips to Rutgers and Texas.

Although he seemingly is riding a wave every coach craves, Jay Wright is worried sick about this stretch of games. First off, he doesn't like playing West Virginia. Then again, no one in the Big East does.

The Mountaineers play with five seniors and a junior but it's how they play that confounds and frustrates opposing coaches. Coach John Beilein has assembled a group of players than no one else of note really recruited and mixed them into a national power. As juniors a year ago, the Mountaineers shocked the nation and nearly made the Final Four. WVU shot the lights out from downtown with a blizzard of 3-pointers and built a 20-point lead over Louisville in an Elite Eight game. The Cardinals responded with a 3-point flurry of their own in the second half and stormed back to win in overtime.

Beilein's teams are a throwback, a group that cuts backdoor, makes the extra pass, covers each other's backs on defense and shoots the lights out. They're fun and explosive, the college version of the Phoenix Suns. "I'd pay to see West Virginia play. I just don't like playing against them," is how UConn's Jim Calhoun sums up the Mountaineers.

Calhoun followed Beilein's career at LeMoyne and Richmond and was always a big booster of his style.

"John Beilein was friendly with a few coaching friends of mine and I remember he came to me when he went to West Virginia and asked me 'what should I do, how should I play,'" Calhoun said. "'I said 'John, coach like you always have because people can't stop your stuff. And as you get better players, that'll get even harder.'"

"They play Princeton (style) but faster," Calhoun added. "The team they remind me of, a little bit, is the (New Jersey) Nets when Byron Scott first got there. They ran that Princeton stuff but with a 24-second shot clock. At 35 (seconds), it's perfect if you go full speed. They're looking to score 80 every night unless you defend them."

This year, WVU began the season ranked 14th in the nation and in the top 10 in some experts' eyes. Neutral court losses to Texas and Kentucky in November and a home loss to LSU knocked the team from the polls but WVU is clicking now. It has won seven games in a row as it gets ready for Villanova, including a 92-68 blowout of then No. 7 Oklahoma Dec. 22 at the All-College Classic in Oklahoma City.

West Virginia-Villanova is an intriguing matchup on many levels. First off, WVU knocked Villanova out of 2005 Big East Tournament in a 78-76 thriller. Both teams fire 3-pointers at a dizzying rate but also play smart and aggressively.

"Their whole offense is based on you making a mistake and them being prepared to read it and take advantage of it," Wright said. "A big part of it for us is not to get frustrated. We're going to make mistakes and they're going to make us look bad. They're going to get some dunks. They're going to get some backdoor cuts and they're going to get some threes. The thing we can't do is get frustrated and lose our concentration."

The Villanova-West Virginia game is played opposite the NFL playoffs so the nation's TV's are tuned in elsewhere even though this game deserved plenty of eyes. 'Nova posted some unbelievable statistics, yet somehow still lost, 91-87. The Wildcats shot 71 percent in the first half - 77 percent from the 3-point line (10-of-13) – to race out to a 46-37 halftime lead and built a 15-point lead early in the second half. Villanova made 15 threes, including 7-of-8 by Mike Nardi.

West Virginia's numbers were more startling. The Mountaineers sliced and diced the Wildscats in the second half with 54 points on 56 percent shooting. In typical West Virginia fashion, the offense took care of the ball (9 turnovers) and registered 27 assists on their 33 baskets. Joe Herber led the Mountaineers with 23 points, Kevin Pittsnogle added 22 and Mike Gansey continued to make his case as perhaps the best all-around player in the Big East with 21 points, 5 assists and 4 rebounds.

"There were games in the past where we had beaten a team and everybody thought it was a fluke," Beilein said. "Then you go and beat them again. We wanted to prove that we can play with people, that those games weren't flukes. We're going to be god-awful some nights, but we're also going to play like this some nights."

The Mountaineers certainly look to be rolling. Pittsnogle, who's connected on 64 percent of his shots over the last four games, put it this way. "They were hitting tremendous shots but we can shoot with anybody," he said.

A week into the Big East season and any dreams of going unbeaten were dead for Villanova. They may have been pipe dreams, of course, but the 'Cats don't like to lose at any point. A tough, overtime win at Rutgers a few days later was followed by another defeat, this one a 58-55 stinger at Texas on national TV. At 11-2, Villanova saw its ranking slip from third to eighth, but plenty more wins were on the way.

Jan. 9; Hartford

After one week of Big East games, Connecticut finds itself in last place. This does not concern Jim Calhoun very much but it may be the only thing that's not sending the Husky coach into orbit these days.

Two days earlier, UConn struggled mightily but rallied for a huge 67-66 win over LSU at the Hartford Civic Center. The game served as a coming out of sorts for the Tigers' human pogo stick, Tyrus Thomas, but the most bizarre moves of the day came courtesy of Calhoun.

With his team trailing 33-19 after an alley-oop jam by Thomas, Calhoun called a 30-second timeout. When the fans began booing, Calhoun looked into the crowd and motioned for more. The fans responded with even heartier boos and the coach couldn't believe it. As he walked off the floor at halftime, Calhoun pointed at one fan in particular before disappearing under the stands.

"I said, 'Go ahead, keep coming,'" Calhoun said, mocking the boo birds. "We're 11-1. What are you doing? That's what I was saying. What are you doing? You love these kids. You love this program. Why would you do that? That's what I was saying."

Calhoun said the idea of booing college kids irks him but why his national power would ever deserve that treatment puzzled him.

"We're at Marquette, they call a timeout and they go back on the court and you couldn't hear yourself think. We go out there and they're booing us," he said. "I just don't think it's appropriate. It's not what these fans have done over the years. These fans, for my 20 years here, have been very good, terrific.

"Maybe they need to understand this team a little better. We keep saying superstars. There's not one yet. I don't see a [Adam] Morrison [of Gonzaga] yet. I don't see anyone yet. Do I think Rudy [Gay] can get there? Yeah I do. But we're not there yet, clearly. You watch this game or the Marquette game, we're not there yet. And when we're not there, we need you. We need you for 40 minutes. And our fans have a great deal of loyalty. They continue to show up, sellout crowds. They've got to be with us for 40 minutes and understand that."

Tonight, Cincinnati is in Hartford and the boo birds have reason to stretch their vocal cords once again. The Bearcats are physical, strong and athletic but not very deep. Thanks to the outside shooting of Armein Kirkland (14 first half points), the Bearcats go right at Connecticut but with 7:49 left in the half, Kirkland drives the lane and lands awkwardly on his left knee. He quickly limps into the locker room and UConn leads at the break, 37-33.

It's later revealed that Kirkland tore his ACL and is out for the season. His college career is now over and his loss is an absolute killer for Cincy. The Bearcats have a load inside in burly Eric Hicks but he's only about 6-foot-7. Interim coach Andy Kennedy has no legitimate, proven big men among his nine scholarship players so the 6-8 Kirkland is vitally important. After losing Kirkland, the Bearcats struggle.

"Did you see our bench," asked Kennedy. "It's comical. We were drawing up plays in the dirt trying to fool them a little bit."

No team in the country can overwhelm a smaller squad like UConn can. The Huskies have a bevy of shot swatters and no one is playing better than Hilton Armstrong right now. A project recruit coming out of Peekskill High, Armstrong was knocked around early in his career by Emeka Okafor and Boone but now he's fighting back. He put on 20 pounds of muscle in the off-season and is now a 245-pound force and the Huskies' most effective inside scorer. Against Cincy, he makes 7-for-10 shots for 14 points and also blocks six shots, alters even more and grabs 11 rebounds in 33 minutes. He also made the move of the night when he flipped in an acrobatic reverse layup that gave the Huskies a 56-46 lead with 9:42 left in the game.

Cincinnati wouldn't back down and with 4:46 referee Pat Driscoll runs by the UConn bench, hears something he doesn't like and stops and whistles Calhoun for a technical foul. The coach is stunned and while the Bearcats shoot their free throws, Calhoun stands in front of his team and yells across the court at Driscoll asking what he did to deserve such treatment. It is a priceless Jim Calhoun moment, the scorned coach wondering just what he did wrong.

The Bearcats keep clawing and close to 65-59 with 3:44 left but Marcus Williams drains a deep corner 3-pointer with two seconds on the shots clock, drawing an explosion of noise from the Hartford crowd. The Huskies go on to a 70-59 win and afterward, Calhoun is happy and it's easy to understand why. His team may have dropped to fourth in the polls but that's irrelevant. This is the night the REAL Huskies showed up, the one without a patchwork lineup and freshman point guards. He finally has his point guard in place and Williams delivers with 11 points, 7 assists and 6 steals. UConn's big men are instantly turned into offensive forces because of Williams' passes and they respond by overwhelming Cincy's frontline with 11 blocked shots and a whopping 52-32 rebounding advantage.

"This is encouraging," Calhoun says later, "because we're coming together, at last. It's a funny team. I like them all but they're not ferocious. They like each other too much. The other day, Marcus and Jeff Adrien almost had a fight. I like that. Our '99 team had that. Kevin Freeman was one tough sucker. Khalid El-Amin, Edmund Saunders, even Jake (Voskuhl), they were all tough.

"These kids, you ask them about the game and they say, 'did you see Vince (Carter) dunk last night?' They want to win and all but it's tougher to get kids to focus today. Tonight, we had a little bit of everything. Marcus isn't there yet. He'll make a great play and then slack off a bit but if we can get that type of rebounding and shot blocking and improve our offense, which we'll work hard on, then we can be very good."

The Cincy-UConn game was featured as part of ESPN's Big Monday package. Everyone in the conference was watching, maybe everyone in the country. They had their first glimpse at the nation's premier team in its coming-out party of sorts and if you happened to be on the Huskies' schedule, it wasn't a very comforting sight.

$$\textbf{(12)}$$

Jan.14; Cincinnati

It's just after two o'clock at the Kingsgate Marriott Hotel which sits around the corner from the University of Cincinnati campus. Jim Boeheim and his Syracuse Orangemen are in town preparing for a stiff test from the injury-ravaged Bearcats. As the players tear through a buffet of salads, chicken and pasta, the coaching staff relaxes and talks about their team.

The Orange have been on the road for five days now. First came a trip to South Bend where a Gerry McNamara (7 threes, 25 points) explosion helped SU pull away to an important, 88-82, road win. Now comes another test. Cincinnati is reeling from the knee injury to key senior Armein Kirkland but Andy Kennedy's team remains dangerous, especially at home where the Bearcats are expecting their first sellout crowd of the season.

While assistants Bernie Fine, Mike Hopkins and Rob Murphy discuss Cincy's attack, Boeheim is holding a much broader issue firmly in his craw. He's dealing with a five-game stretch that is nothing short of brutal. After tonight's game, the Orange board their charter jet for home where none other than the Connecticut Huskies await the next night for a Big Monday showdown in the Carrier Dome. The next Saturday brings another test, this one at Villanova, also on ESPN. Then the Orange play at Pittsburgh two nights later in another national TV game.

So in a span of 16 days, Boeheim will bring his team to South Bend, Cincinnati, Philadelphia and Pittsburgh with the biggest home game of the season (UConn) plopped in the middle. Four of the five games are on national TV.

"This is a joke. What kind of schedule is that?" Boeheim asks. "We're waiting to play tonight for God knows what reason and Connecticut is playing right now (at home vs. Georgetown). That's ridiculous. All the coaches told Mike (Tranghese) that this isn't the right way to schedule. It's no way to run a league. Why should the best teams all beat each other up? I know they said it's the contract we have but I would've left the money on the table. This is bullshit."

The Big East's unbalanced schedule is an issue on many fronts. Thanks to existing contracts with ESPN and CBS, the networks are owed a certain number of marquee matchups. CBS gets first crack at the best games, like Villanova at Connecticut, but ESPN asks for, and receives, the rematch in Philadelphia. It's a system that rewards the elite programs and patently discriminates against the ones in need of a publicity boost. Connecticut (14 national TV games), Syracuse (12) and Villanova (11) will dominate the league's TV windows all winter while other programs fight to see any national TV time.

"Where's my ESPN game. I'll take ESPN2," said Providence coach Tim Welsh. "I tell Jim (Boeheim) that this country doesn't need to see his old face every week anymore."

Welsh's Friars are the only Big East team not scheduled for a single ESPN/ESPN2 appearance. The conference office saw fit to throw a bone to newcomer South Florida so when it hosted Michigan in December the nation's hoop crazies could watch on ESPN2. Providence played both Florida and Memphis in December but Welsh can't figure out why the conference office couldn't get either game on TV.

"We played the toughest non-league schedule in the league and we can't get any of the games on TV. I must be crazy," Welsh said.

Yet the coaches who are getting the extra TV games aren't happy either. Boeheim and Calhoun, not to mention Rick Pitino and Jay Wright, view the unbalanced schedule as too daunting a challenge in a world where piling up wins is every coach's dream.

Besides the coach's whining, the more important fallout from the unbalanced schedule will come in March. That's when the NCAA Tournament selectors will sift through the qualifications of the country's best teams and decide which ones merit a berth in the national tournament. When they look at the Big East, they'll be confused thanks to a system where teams don't play two conference brothers at all but face three teams twice. Syracuse, for example, doesn't play Marquette or Providence. Cincinnati doesn't match up with Notre Dame or St. John's. Seton Hall won't see Louisville or Georgetown. All three teams will be in contention for an NCAA bid but have little in common except their Big East pedigree.

The conference's TV contracts expire after the 2006-07 season so Tranghese says the unbalanced schedule will remain in effect for one more season. "Then we'll make sure everyone plays one another at least once. The way we're scheduling now is not what we want but we have a contract that we will honor. I've never walked out of a contract and we're not about to now," he said.

Despite their personnel limitations, it's clear that Cincinnati is prepared to battle every team in the Big East. That's a direct reflection on the legacy of former Bearcats' coach Bob Huggins, one of the winningest and most controversial coaches in the country. Huggins was forced out of Cincy over the summer after losing a power struggle with school president Nancy Zimpher. Huggins assistant Andy Kennedy has taken over on an interim basis and while he's doing a good job, it's a long-shot that Zimpher would ever approve the hiring of anyone associated with Huggins.

The team Kennedy is putting through the Big East owns a Huggins feel. Center Eric Hicks may be undersized but no big man in the league plays harder. Athletic forwards James 'Flight' White and Cedric McGowan place a lot of pressure on a defense and electric freshman point guard Devan Downey is the most surprising newcomer in the league, if not the country.

Downey gets the Bearcats off to a solid start as Syracuse's big men struggle with the game's speed. Boeheim has always lit into his big guys over the years and his whipping boy this season is often 6-11 junior Darryl Watkins. Cincinnati's White is making all sorts of shots early on and finishes with 14 points in the first half but Syracuse's Demetris Nichols bangs home a 3-pointer at the buzzer that ties the game at the half, 34-34.

The second half belongs to Gerry McNamara. He pours in 22 of his 29 points over the final 20 minutes and SU's zone defense slows the Cincy offense to 29 percent shooting and only 24 second half points. Syracuse wins going away, 77-58. McNamara makes five more 3-pointers to go along with six assists and four rebounds in what was an overdue breakout shooting game.

"I don't think Gerry missed in the second half except for one to beat the shot clock. That's as well as I've seen him play all year," Boeheim said.

Those are words the coach has wanted to put together for weeks now. McNamara has struggled with his shot most of the season, mainly because he's lacked a competent running mate. While his deadeye shooting receives more acclaim, McNamara is also a fine playmaker and passer, especially on the fast break. But the Orange is thin at point guard. Sophomore Josh Wright doesn't play with confidence, junior Louie McCroskey is always battling with the coaching staff over playing time and freshman Eric Devendorf is just a hair short of nuts.

Devendorf is the Big East's Eminem, a white kid from Bay City, Mich., who plays hoops like a rapper. He wears tattoos from his neck to his ankle, walks with an exaggerated strut, is always barking at teammates and the opposition and wears his toughness on his sleeve. It's a rare package, one that's difficult to like, really. Except if he's on your team.

While Boeheim rolls his eyes at Devendorf's histrionics, he loves his competitiveness. As the season progresses, he and McNamara begin to play off each other better. But the freshman isn't a top ballhandler and neither is small forward Nichols so McNamara has to run the team, defend guards who are quicker and faster than him and try to knock down one long jumper after another. It's a lot to ask but on this night the senior is running at full speed.

"When Gerry gets going like that, you can ask anybody who plays against him, he's difficult to stop. It's disheartening. He can pull up and make it from anywhere inside half court," Boeheim said.

"He's really struggled shooting the ball this year, except for the Davidson game. He's about 30 percent from the three. He just hasn't gotten a good rhythm. But I felt he had it a little more at Notre Dame and Gerry likes to play on the road. I don't keep stats but he might be a better road player than he is at home. The more people yell at him the better he plays."

With that, Boeheim grabs his trenchcoat and heads for the team bus that's sitting just outside Fifth Third Arena. Most of the players are already on board, filling the rear of the cabin and chatting quietly. Boeheim, like every other high school and college coach in the country, sits in the first seat, just behind the driver.

"Let's go. We're ready," he says, as the bus pulls away.

While the SU radio team of Matt Park and color man Gene Waldron always travel with the team, Boeheim doesn't allow other media to make the trips. Because of Syracuse's remote location and the lack of extensive air service in and out of Hancock International Airport, the Orange fly a chartered Continental Express jet to virtually every road game. It's a sleek, 40-seater that is short on frills but long on convenience for trips up and down the East Coast.

The same pilot and one flight attendant work the majority of the team's flights. A box lunch filled with a sandwich, chips, grapes and a Milky Way sits on each seat and even though it's just after 11 p.m., the players tear through their meals before they fall asleep. Boeheim settles into the first row of seats, opens a Ken Follett fiction book and is alone with his thoughts for the next hour and a half.

The plane lands in Syracuse at 12:40 in the morning. A bus pulls onto the tarmac and the driver begins pulling everyone's baggage from the plane. As the party leaves the plane and walks 10 steps to a waiting bus, the biting Central New York wind grips everyone's bones. A light snow, as usual, is falling.

On the half hour ride back to campus, team managers dial their cell phones and chat up friends who are still out celebrating the team's win. Bars in Syracuse are open until 2 a.m., so last call is rapidly approaching. Unfortunately for the Orange, so is a date with the third-ranked Huskies of Connecticut.

Jan. 15; Syracuse

An empty Carrier Dome is a sight unlike any other in college basketball. While the nation's TV fans know the Dome as a raucous, orange and blue-colored madhouse, you need to step into the giant bubble to appreciate that Syracuse's flagship sport actually plays on a court that's tucked into a corner of a football stadium.

Although the ESPN generation doesn't know any better, it wasn't always this way. When a skinny, bespectacled Boeheim played Robin to All-American Dave Bing's Batman in the mid-1960s, the Manley Field House became one of the East's premier home courts. Boeheim stayed at SU after graduation as an assistant coach and helped recruit a team that rolled to the school's first Final Four in 1975. The head coach was a man named Roy Danforth, a good coach who for some unknown reason considered Syracuse a way station and not a destination.

After the 1976 season, Danforth left Syracuse for a job at Tulane. You could make a case that this was the single dumbest job switch in college basketball history. In six seasons at Tulane, Danforth never led a team into the NCAA Tournament and his coaching star fizzled.

After a little hemming and hawing, the school gave Danforth's job to his longtime assistant. One of his first moves was hiring a local high school coach, Bernie Fine, to his staff. Fine was a student manager during his undergraduate years but the Brooklyn native was always a coach-in-training. Also on Boeheim's first few staffs were hot, young coaches who'd cut their teeth at Howard Garfinkel's Five-Star Camps: Rick Pitino and Brendan Malone. Both went on to be head coaches in the NBA. During his first four years, Boeheim's SU teams won 85 percent of their games (100-18) and advanced to the NCAA Tournament each season.

The stars of those teams were Roosevelt Bouie and Louis Orr, two big men who highlighted Boeheim's first recruiting class. Helped by talented veterans such as Marty Byrnes and Dale Shackelford, the Louie and Bouie Show quickly grew from an Upstate New York hit to a national phenomenon. Tickets to games at 8,900 seat Manley Field House were all but impossible to procure as the beloved Orangemen rose to number two in the national rankings in 1980.

While Syracuse's basketball program was firmly entrenched as an Eastern power, its football team had sunk to unthinkable depths. In the 1960s, Syracuse owned the premier football program in the East thanks to a conveyor belt of star running backs that began with Jimmy Brown in the late-1950s and rolled into the next decade on the shoulders of Heisman Trophy winner Ernie Davis, Floyd Little and Larry Csonka.

But by the 1970s, old Archbold Stadium was crumbling under its own weight. Recruits stayed away and fans tired of both the losing and the biting November winds stayed home as well. In order to compete with Eastern Indy powers Penn State and Pittsburgh, Syracuse needed an answer to its football stadium problem and school leaders dreamt big. The Carrier Dome, a 50,000-seat football palace, would keep Orange fans forever comfortable and provide recruits with a palatable option to chase their pigskin dreams.

"You had to see Archbold then. It was truly falling apart," Boeheim said. "Football had no choice but to do something or risk becoming irrelevant."

While the Dome was a slam dunk for football's future stability, bringing basketball along under the Bubble wasn't an automatic decision. Boeheim owned one of the best home court advantages in the country and he was going to give that all up to move his games to a corner of a football stadium?

"I didn't want it at all. I liked Manley and we had great success there," said Boeheim. "We thought if we'd get 15,000 (fans) once in a while, we were doing great. Of course I had no idea what 15,000 fans would look like in the Dome and no one ever imagined 30,000."

The Dome's first major highlight came when the Big East played its second post-season tournament in Syracuse in March 1981. The Orange upset favored Georgetown in the semifinals and then outlasted Villanova in a three overtime thriller in the finals that ended with a Leo Rautins tip-in in the final seconds.

As the Dome opened, a perfect storm of success enveloped the Orange. Boeheim had Syracuse routinely in the national top 20, he had a new, exciting conference to sell and the dawn of ESPN and its far-reaching satellite signal made the Carrier Dome in snowy Syracuse, N.Y., one of college basketball's hot spots.

Not surprisingly, SU's recruiting profile soared. While the Orange still secured most of Upstate New York's best players (with the notable exception of Albany's Sam Perkins, who starred at North Carolina), Boeheim, Fine, Malone and Wayne Morgan significantly elevated the program's recruiting profile. Thanks in large part to the New York City connections of Malone, SU fought its way into the final two for the most exciting prospect in the country in the class of 1983. At halftime of a national TV broadcast, Dwayne 'Pearl' Washington told Al McGuire that after weighing his choices, he wanted to play at Syracuse.

The Pearl's impact on Syracuse cannot be overstated. With a flashy style suited perfectly for a fast-breaking game (not to mention TV cameras), the Brooklyn native became the Orange's maestro, a player who literally brought the Dome crowds to their feet every team he snuck out to lead a breakaway. Syracuse T-shirt merchants even created a hot selling product that read 'On the Eighth Day God Created The Pearl."

"Pearl gave us a footing with the better players in the country but more importantly our teams were good once he got here," said Fine. "People might forget we had other good players around him who weren't highly recruited like Rafael Addison, Wendell Alexis, Andre Hawkins, Howard Triche and Greg Monroe. He was just the guard that we needed."

Boeheim is fiercely loyal to his players but none more than The Pearl.

"Pearl really was the guy that was not only important to the program, but I think, along with Patrick (Ewing) and Chrissy Mullin, they're the guys that founded and built the Big East. Those three guys, we rode on their shoulders," Boeheim said at the 2003 Final Four. "I remember before Pearl came to Syracuse, I went to recruit in Los Angeles and went to a good high school and the kids looked at me and said, "Where are you from again? Where is that?" After Pearl played, when I got off the airplane at LAX, the bell guy said, "Coach, how you doing? You coach Pearl, don't you?" He didn't know who I was, but he knew I coached Pearl."

In subsequent years, Syracuse added hotly recruited future stars Derrick Coleman, Stevie Thompson and Billy Owens but also mined some greats that few recruiters took notice of. That group was headlined by Greek center Rony Seikaly and Washington, D.C. point guard Sherman Douglas, both of whom went on to enjoy 10-year NBA careers. From 1984-1992, Syracuse finished the season ranked in the top 20 and advanced past the second round of the NCAA's four times but that era was ultimately defined by one game.

On March 30, 1987, Syracuse led Indiana, 73-72, with 27 seconds left in the national championship game. Coleman, a left-handed freshman from Detroit, went to the foul line and missed the front end of a one-and-one. With the Hoosiers holding for one shot and looking for star shooter Steve Alford, Keith Smart shook free on the baseline and arched in a 16-footer that rose over the corner of the backboard and swished through the basket with three seconds left. Stunned, Syracuse barely got off a desperation shot at the buzzer.

A disconsolate Boeheim walked off the Louisiana Superdome floor that night in a fog and 15 years later said he still had never watched a replay of the entire game. Instead he kept mixing top recruits and hidden gems into a perennial winning team in one of the nation's toughest conferences. It's an achievement that won him more than 700 games and paved the way for his induction into Basketball's Hall of Fame in 2005 but also earned him the unfair label of a coach who always had great talent but couldn't win the big one.

In reality, the Orange's talent was certainly good enough to win in 1987 and a few years after when Coleman, Douglas and Owens played together. But once Owens left in 1991, Syracuse kept finding its way to 20 or so wins every season without a single All-American. From 1992-2002, the Orange averaged 23 wins but had just three first-round NBA picks (David Johnson, John Wallace, Etan Thomas). Boeheim, Fine and the rest of the recruiters found plenty of very good college players such as Lawrence Moten, Otis Hill, Preston Shumpert and Jason Hart but landing the superstars didn't come easily.

That all changed with the arrival of Carmelo Anthony in 2002 but his recruitment wasn't exactly high stakes poker.

When Anthony committed to SU as a high school senior out of Baltimore, he was known as a good scorer but he weighed 175 pounds and needed to firm up his academic credentials. He moved on to prep school for a year at Oak Hill Academy in Virginia and when he showed up at Syracuse, he weighed 220 and was one of the top five recruits in the land.

"We knew Carmelo was good but the kid who showed up here as a freshman wasn't the same player we recruited," said assistant Mike Hopkins. "No way did we think he'd be a one-and-out for the NBA kind of player."

The mix Boeheim fit around Anthony in the 2002-03 season turned out just right as Syracuse returned to its fourth Final Four, this one again in New Orleans. Besides Anthony, the team's other stars were junior Hakim Warrick and freshman Gerry McNamara. Warrick was an under-recruited, skinny pogo stick from Philadelphia who nearly signed with Providence out of high school. McNamara was a gym rat from Scranton, Pa., who Hopkins fell in love with when he was just a deep-shooting prep sophomore.

That SU team lost its first game to Memphis but would lose only four more times all season. With Anthony maturing by the week into a scoring machine, Syracuse rolled into the national championship game against Kansas. Led by six first half 3-pointers from cold-blooded shooter McNamara, Syracuse built a big lead but a good Jayhawk team charged back. With time winding down, Warrick blocked a corner 3-point try by Michael Lee and Orange Nation celebrated a 81-78 victory and the school's elusive first national championship.

•

As the Syracuse players wipe sleep from their eyes and the Cincinnati win from their heads for an afternoon practice in the empty Dome, Bernie Fine settles into a chair and starts talking about Orange basketball. Fine and Boeheim have coached together for so long that the two have become synonymous. When you see Boeheim on TV bellowing at referees or sitting stoically on the bench, Fine is the burly man seated to his left. It's been that way since 1976 and after falling short a few times trying to land his own head job, Fine and Boeheim will probably be linked until they retire.

More than anyone, Fine protects Boeheim's legacy because, in effect, it's his as well. So when he's asked about the perception that Syracuse should have more national titles with its legion of great players, he scoffs.

"Besides Pearl Washington, in the '80s the only other high school All-American really was Derrick Coleman," he said. "Sherman (Douglas) wasn't anything and no one knew about Rony Seikaly. Rony never played basketball until he got over here. And we red-shirted Rony in his first year. Now that is true for Duke and 'Carolina. They get all the All-Americans. We haven't had a whole lot. The big thing about our program, and Jim's been really good about it, is he wants to see the players get better. We do a lot of individual stuff throughout the year and the players improve."

"I think Jim's a great coach and that's a big part of it. We have a system in place. It's fairly simple and we try to get the players to understand what we want to do. They have to play unselfish and play together and you can win. Look at this team. Who are the All-Americans? Eric Devendorf. That's it."

Fine also shakes his head at the idea that Syracuse simply rolls the ball out and watches its players go.

"I believe that Jimmy's one of the two or three best offensive coaches in the country," he said. "We keep it simple and we run what we're supposed to run, which is a big thing. If we're going to play zone we're going to recruit long players. The way we play, we want guys who can shoot the ball. This is one of our better shooting teams. Gerry shoots it. Eric shoots it. Demetris shoots it. Andy Rautins shoots it."

Fine is also a great ambassador for his alma mater. Before road games, he's the coach who's besieged by alumns and fans looking to catch up on the program and the University. After all, he's the kid who came to Syracuse from Brooklyn in 1964 and has never left. The fact that he's run Boeheim's summer camp and sold insurance, sporting goods and who knows what else in the city through the years makes him as connected as any person in Central New York.

"I've seen where we came from so I don't take our success for granted but a lot of people do up here," Fine said. "They say 'well, we only had 15,000 people tonight.' Somebody said that this year because one game (versus Texas-El Paso) we had 15-something, which was the smallest crowd of the year. I said 'do you know how many schools would kill to have 15,000 fans once in a season?' We're complaining about that? Our fans have been great. Super. They just keep coming. We have people that buy those front row seats now that live on Long Island, Connecticut, Florida. They use the ones they want and give away the others. We have a guy that lives on Long Island who comes to every game, home and away. We have a lot of very loyal alumns."

As the practice ends, Boeheim walks off the court with a heavy sniffle in his voice. He settles into a small locker room deep inside the Dome and flicks on an NFL playoff game. An avid sports fan, he calmly answers questions as the Steelers and Colts go down to the wire. As Indianapolis kicker Mike Vanderjagt misses a game-tying field goal, Boeheim is locked into the action.

The same can be said for every big city in the East, in fact. The NFL has that type of hold on the country, especially come playoff time. But in the city of

Syracuse, the Orange trump the NFL and every other pro sports league and that dynamic exists principally because of Jim Boeheim.

In his 29 years as coach, Syracuse has won 20 or more games 27 times. Twenty-four of his teams have played in the NCAA Tournament and three moved on to the national championship game. When the 2003 team won it all, Boeheim punched his admit card into the Hall of Fame.

As good coaches such as Lou Carnesecca, John Chaney, Bob Huggins and Rick Majerus found out, winning big and winning it all are two different things. That they all don't own a national title doesn't make them less of a coach but it does keep them out of an exclusive club that anyone who toots a whistle would love to be in.

"The thing about the '80s in the Big East is a lot of the teams back then had great players. Georgetown, certainly," he said. "We had good results during those years, for sure, but I don't think about why we didn't win more games. We won a lot. I think some of those teams that didn't win had weaknesses, for sure. I don't pay attention to any of that shit talk anymore. I just coach. I don't think about it. In '96 we got to the Final Four and that changed a lot of things about us but then we had Carmelo and we won the national championship with our two best players being freshmen. That wasn't our best team or the most talent but it won. That's basketball."

While the NBA scouts still flock to the Carrier Dome, their eyes see potential fringe players these days, not the next Coleman or Carmelo. But that's not by design, of course.

"It's hard to get great players," Boeheim says. "We haven't gone after some for the last couple years, guys like Al Harrington, Sebastian Telfair. We could've gotten those guys but I knew they were going pro. Carmelo wasn't supposed to be a one-year guy. He weighed 180 pounds when we recruited him. He would've been here at least two years if he didn't put so much weight on so quickly, which is unusual. But in Hakim, Gerry, we have good four-year players and that's who we want to recruit.

"We'll try to get a great player if we can but we have to pick our spots. Paul Harris (a top recruit out of Buffalo) is a great player and we recruited him hard. A lot of times a great player is from the South or out West and they're a hard get. We'll try to get a player at that level if we can but we also want to make sure we have a good nucleus of guys who we think will be here for four years."

Besides the winning, of course, the crowds that flock to the Dome see an exciting style. Boeheim has lived off the zone defense for about 10 years now but his offenses always push the ball and look to score quickly.

"We play a finesse game," he says. "As a zone team, we don't grab and hold as much as some other teams do. We push it on offense and are a quick shot team. We don't try to run a whole lot off the shot clock. We try to pick at things where we can be successful and get a shot, if not in transition, then a good shot in a short amount of time."

As the Steelers celebrate their upset win over Indianapolis, Boeheim starts talking about this year's Big East. This is when the real Boeheim comes out, the one who is keenly intelligent, strongly opinionated and can squeal in a whiny voice like few other men. He's been on Connecticut's bandwagon since the start of the season and considers the Huskies "easily the best team in the country. If anything, they have too many players."

He goes down the roster, pointing out one NBA-draftee after another. "I say they have four first rounders – Gay, Armstrong, Boone and Marcus Williams. We have none, I know that. But we have to play them twice, of course."

Connecticut has replaced Georgetown as Syracuse's biggest rival. Tomorrow night's invasion from the Huskies is big but UConn-Villanova is the game people really want to see this year. Then again, there is a great game seemingly every other night in the conference these days.

"This is a big game for the fans and the league but all the games are just too hard.

We have Connecticut and they're as good as anybody in the country. I've said that all year long," he says, ramping up his voice. "Then we go to Villanova and they're as good as anybody in the country. Then you go to Pittsburgh and they're undefeated. They gave us that stretch, wow. There's going to be some bitching when I go to the league meetings in the spring. Some out and out screaming. This has to change. If they go to 18 games, that's fine but the three extra games don't have to be against the three toughest teams. That's just not fair. Any way you add it up we're just going to be beating ourselves up. Louisville could be 0-3 right now. They were on the ropes at Providence. They don't even know how much trouble they're looking at with their schedule."

With that, Boeheim pulls on a Syracuse sweatshirt and a blue Syracuse overcoat and heads out into what is a typical January Sunday afternoon: overcast with snow flurries filling the sky, the wind whipping and 25 degree temperatures chilling the bones. He jumps into his white SUV and as he pulls the truck towards home, he's asked about the phenomenon that is the attention Syracuse basketball receives from Central New York's fans.

"It amazes me every game," he says. "Sometimes I look up into the corners and can barely see the fans and I know they can barely see the game and they're still there, all the time. It's amazing to me. You know that about five, six years ago they were actually worried that we might not get 30,000 in here again. The economy was bad, Carrier laid off a lot of people, the military up here really took a hit. We were struggling. Then we won it all and people just fell in love with Carmelo and Gerry. They love Gerry McNamara up here. Just love him. It's unbelievable. Pearl was the most exciting player we ever had but Gerry is the most popular. By far. We set records, 32-33,000, and they all want to see this kid play. It's unbelievable."

•

The second game of the NFL's playoff doubleheader is winding down but very few patrons are watching the TV's at the Embassy Suites Hotel in Carrier Circle. Instead, young adults, teenagers and a few 12-year olds – male and female – mill around the lobby area with pictures, posters and yearbooks under their arms.

Instead of orange, the operative color of the memorabilia is Husky Blue & White. UConn is staying at the hotel but the Huskies' fans have beaten the team into town. While the 30 or so lobby lizards made the six hour drive up the New York State Thruway, the team sat back in Hartford waiting for its charter flight to arrive. It seems the plane was the same one flying St. John's back from its game at South Florida on Saturday and is a bit late.

And it also seems that Jim Calhoun firmly struck his foot in his mouth when the team finally arrived in town and he was asked by members of The Horde what the travel snafu was all about. Calhoun, who later said he was kidding, relayed a story that claimed the plane was ready to take off in Tampa when St. John's suddenly realized it was missing a player in the travel party.

"He was literally at the hotel," Calhoun said. "It took well over an hour and a half to go through the screening process. They had to call the Feds. This kid, who apparently wasn't very upset, was just watching basketball at the hotel."

Then he said, at the end of a long travel day, "St. John's paid us back, I think," in no doubt a friendly, thinly veiled reference to the Doug Wiggins recruiting saga.

The fact that Calhoun's words were voraciously scribbled down and patched back to the Nutmeg State in rapid fashion shouldn't surprise anyone. That Calhoun's facts were blatantly incorrect shouldn't either. It seems the St. John's party was boarding the plane in Tampa when it realized that academic advisor Eric Rienecker had missed the team bus from the airport hotel. A call was placed and Rienecker arrived less than 10 minutes later, coach Norm Roberts told the New York Daily News.

Apprised of Calhoun's remarks, Roberts clearly wasn't laughing and even fired a shot back. "It was stupid. You shouldn't make comments like that," he told the Daily News. "(Calhoun) knows just like I know - and I'm a young coach - that when you're dealing with the media, people write what you say. So he should know something like that is not funny. Just like somebody making comments about computers with his program are not funny. I just think he didn't use good judgment. That's what I think."

When the Huskies finally wander into the hotel at around 7:30, their fans eagerly pounce on the players. Rudy Gay and Marcus Williams linger the longest, signing posters, yearbooks, hats. It's a scene played out in lobbies where virtually every NBA team travels. But this is a college team, or at least that's what the system tells us, and as the college basketball nation is about to find out, sometimes this University of Connecticut team plays an awful lot like professionals.

Jan. 16; Syracuse

It's game night inside the Carrier Dome but this is no ordinary game. Gone are the warm-ups against Cornell and Colgate. Tonight it's 15-2 Syracuse against UConn, the third-ranked team in the country and owner of a sparkling 14-1 record.

The Huskies are a big-time opponent and the entire city of Syracuse is abuzz. ESPN has bumped its regular Big Monday crew of Sean McDonough-Bill Raftery-Jay Bilas in favor of the network's top crew: Dan Shulman, Doris Burke and the omni-present Dick Vitale. "We got Dicked," is how one producer with the McDonough-Raftery crew puts it.

The bull crew that turns the Dome into college basketball's biggest block party is ready, too. While the basketball court and grandstands for 30,000 fans are tucked into one end of the giant bubble, the other 80 yards of the football field are filled with concession stands, T-shirt outlets and vendors pushing games you'd normally play at a country fair. Long lines snake up to two regulation-size basketball hoops where fans pay $2 to hoist three shots to benefit Coaches vs. Cancer. Other fans dressed in orange from head to toe pose for pictures in front of a NASCAR automobile.

With 90 minutes to go before tip off, the student section behind one basket is filled. Beer dubbed 'Dome Foam,' is flowing freely. When UConn's players come out for their pre-game shoot, the students have Marcus Williams in their crosshairs.

"Convict, convict,' and 'Where's your laptop?' are the top refrains that echo through the air. Another sign reads 'I Wish I was Gay.'

Along the sideline opposite the team benches sit two rows of plush, black chairs. Syracuse has joined other schools around the Big East, and the country, who've chosen to create an NBA-like feel to their arenas and sell courtside seats. The media, not to mention the students, are pushed farther away from the action so well-heeled boosters can fork over big cash and see the sweat pour off their heroes. That this decision could one day provoke a Ron Artest-type confrontation between players and fans apparently isn't an issue. The fact that revenue from the seats is more than $500,000 and 30 different game sponsors bring in close to an additional $1 million more is much more important than preserving some type of collegiate feel in arenas that look more and more like the NBA with each passing season.

When the 9 o'clock tip-off time finally rolls around, college basketball's biggest stage is ready. But then Syracuse's players forget to show up.

UConn's Gay nails a catch-and-shoot 3-pointer on the second pass of the game. After a quick-shoot miss by Nichols, Josh Boone sticks back an offensive rebound. A Darryl Watkins travel is followed by Williams penetrating and feeding Boone for a dunk. Another turnover leads to a Husky fast break that ends with Williams lofting an alley-oop pass that Gay rises into the sky, catches with one hand and slams through the hoop.

Gay then blocks a shot and Syracuse fouls the weak-shooting Craig Austrie as he tries a wild 3-pointer. Austrie's three free throws make it 12-0. UConn blocks shots by Terrence Roberts and McNamara, capping an 0-for-6 with three turnovers nightmare start for the Orange. Roberts ends the scoreless skid at the 15:39 mark to make it 12-2 and a few McNamara jumpers help Syracuse cut the lead to 21-17 but Rashad Anderson catches fire a few minutes later and his two 3-pointers spark a dizzying 19-0 Connecticut run that drains all of the air out of the Dome.

"That's as good as we've played this year and maybe for the last five years," UConn associate head coach George Blaney says later. "We had everything going."

UConn leads 45-25 at the half. The Orange has 10 field goals while the Huskies have blocked 11 shots. That stat alone speaks to how dominant the visitors have played.

Syracuse uses its press to cut Connecticut's lead down to a dozen but can't get any further. The rest of the game is reduced to organized garbage time. In fact, Calhoun serves as the best entertainment of the half. After a hard foul by Watkins on Boone, Calhoun walks 15 feet onto the floor and howls at veteran officials Reggie Greenwood and John Cahill. Although up 19 points, the coach is protesting every whistle. Cahill, who's worked several Final Fours, turns and shakes his head after one explosion over a meaningless traveling call.

When Calhoun isn't berating the refs, he's screaming at Blaney and his bench about a mistake his players just made. He even targets Dan Gavitt and John Paquette, two of the Big East's associate commissioners who are sitting next to UConn's bench, after an official's call goes against his squad. With three minutes left and his team up by 11, Calhoun and the team's trainer leave the bench. Despite a commanding lead for more than three-quarters of the game, the coach had worked himself into such a tizzy that he's become dehydrated. UConn wins, 88-80.

Tom Moore steps in for Calhoun for the post-game media dance and as he scans the stat sheet, plenty of numbers jump out. Rapidly improving Hilton Armstrong swatted 8 of his team's 16 blocked shots. Anderson drained five 3-pointers and finished with a team-high 21 points. Boone posted a solid 18-point, 10-rebound double-double. But UConn needs Marcus Williams to be good and tonight he was great. He finishes with 14 points but his 11 assists, four steals and loads of leadership tells more of the story.

"He's getting better exponentially every game," Moore said. "He was like the walking dead with strep throat going into the Marquette game. ... Not only has he gradually gotten better physically, but he feels like he's got a hold of the team. He's starting to take more freedom and liberty, barking at guys, telling guys what to do. That's what we need."

In the Connecticut locker room, Williams sits with diamond studs in his ears, surrounded by reporters. Then he clearly dissects his fifth game of the year.

"I know I have some room to improve my stamina, especially. I couldn't simulate 5-on-5 when I was out but playing the last couple weeks has helped my feel a lot," he says. "I try to get my teammates the ball early and get our confidence rolling. If the confidence gets up, they'll play for you."

He's asked about the crowd of 26,805, many of whom yelled obscenities at him for the last two hours.

"I think it's getting old and it's getting lame now to say, 'Where's my laptop?'" Williams said "I mean, you hear older people, guys who are like 30. They should be ashamed of themselves. I look at them, smile, do whatever I got to do. I can taker that. I hear Coach (Calhoun) every day."

Things aren't as cheery over in the Syracuse dressing room. McNamara, maybe more than any other Big East player, is an excellent interview who sounds an awful lot like a coach-in-training. He made just 5-of-16 shots and finished with 14 points and five turnovers.

"I didn't get a lot of good looks. They play as good a team defense as you're going to see. It was difficult for me to get a shot off," he said. "I'm just disappointed the way we played. To come out flat on Big Monday is not good. It's disappointing. It's a difficult league. Every night you're going to get tested. You can't hang your head too long because you have another tough one coming right back at you. Perhaps the impatience was because of how excited we were to play in a game like this, Big Monday on ESPN against UConn. You have to pride yourself in what you do. If you don't have pride, you shouldn't play."

The defeat is a stunner for Boeheim. He knew Connecticut was coming in with a loaded deck but he's disappointed that his team played scared out of the gate. The moment, the intensity, clearly rattled everyone on his team except McNamara.

"This team has gotten better. We played really well on the road at Cincinnati and at Notre Dame when we needed to but we still have a lot to do," Boeheim told the media. "Our big guys have to play better. Our perimeter guys are giving us great effort. Demetris (Nichols) struggled shooting in the first half but he bounced back. Louie (McCroskey) is doing a good job. It just depends on those two inside guys (Terrence Roberts and Darryl Watkins). I thought Mookie (Watkins) showed some signs in the second half of doing some things, but we're going to go as those two guys go, especially against certain teams. If they continue to work hard, continue to improve, we're going to be a good team. If they struggle, we're going to struggle. Our juniors have never been in a position where they had to play in a big game. This was kind of a big game, but they weren't ready for it. We have a lot of games left to get them there."

Boeheim then sings the praises of UConn, which certainly deserves the kind words. "Hey, Connecticut is a veteran basketball team. It took them a little while to get Marcus back in there but this is a team that can beat anybody, any night, anyplace. I still think they're the best team in our league and I think they're the best team in the country.

Then, almost in midsentence, Boeheim shifts into high gear. The only thing that stings as much as the night's beating in the coach's eyes is a look at the Orange's schedule. Paquette, the Big East's long-time publicity manager, is standing off to the side and Boeheim's words are clearly meant for his ears.

"Scheduling is too much in this league for television and not enough for the players. It's very disheartening to look at scheduling and see that," he says. "Granted TV is important but it shouldn't run the league, which it is. Something needs to be done about that. Now we have six days off and we have to play the two best teams in the conference besides Connecticut (Villanova, Pittsburgh), back-to-back and on the road. Which is again for television. I think that's crazy to have to do that.

"I'm glad we've won a few games already because I would've said this tonight anyways. People would've thought I was upset just because we lost a few games, which we could have. It's foolish. The way we're scheduling is just not going to work. That's my opinion. Jim and I talked about this before the game. There's too many good teams, it's too difficult to stack the decks against people. But, hey, we'll play anyways. Take that message back, John."

Sure enough, Boeheim is a prophet. The Orange go on the road and get smacked by Villanova, 80-65. Then they stumble at Pittsburgh, 80-67. A 3-0 start has turned into a 3-3 record for a team that has a load of tough games left to go. No wonder the old coach isn't smiling very much.

$$\left(13 \right)$$

Perhaps more than any other school in the Big East, life in West Virginia revolves around the state university's athletic teams.

Life dealt the state's citizens a cruel fate early in January when a horrific mining accident in the small town of Saco cost 12 men their lives. An explosion rocked the mine and trapped the men in a shaft two miles deep. After reports that several survivors may be inside the mine were broadcast nationally by the army of TV trucks camped out in the small town, a wave of euphoria enveloped the state. However, that news was quickly reversed and ultimately only one survivor clung to life and eventually left the hospital.

The accident shined a spotlight into West Virginia's hills where life in many corners of the state isn't easy. Poverty and low wages are a way of life. Generations of families worked in coal mines and they considered the jobs good ones. The danger was simply a part of life.

Sports, and especially sports at West Virginia University, help brighten life in those gloomy hills. The Mountaineer football team will always be number one in the people's hearts and the fact that the fantastic Sugar Bowl win over Georgia took place just days after the Saco mine tragedy served as a salve for the entire state. And now the basketball team is rolling again. After stumbling early, John Beilein's veteran group has ripped off 10 wins in a row and sits atop the Big East with a 4-0 record.

Tonight, the Providence Friars invade the WVU Coliseum but the game turns into a mismatch quickly. The Mountaineers are an anomaly in today's college hoops world. Beilein recruited a pack of unheralded players three and four years ago and sent them out to take their lumps. But now Kevin Pittsnogle, Mike Gansey, Joe Herber and the coach's son, Patrick, are giving the lumps. As juniors, the group roared to a 24-11 record and became one of the season's startling stories when they nearly beat Louisville in an NCAA regional final before losing a wild shootout.

This season, no one is sleeping on WVU. For the first time in his tenure in Morgantown, Beilein has a target on his back but he also has plenty of players to help him fight his battles. The Friars start strong but West Virginia answers and closes the half on a sweet run to take a 33-21 halftime lead. Another strong run early in the second half ends any doubt and the Mountaineers coast to a 64-48 win.

Providence coach Tim Welsh knows Beilein as well as any Big East coach. The two locked horns when he coached at Iona and Beilein led Canisius and both own extensive Upstate New York ties.

"They are a well-oiled machine. They have all the pieces and are a true team. It's all been written," Welsh said. "I remember we played this group as freshmen in the Big East Tournament and got them pretty good (73-50). They've grown together for four years and now they're a very, very good basketball team. John's teams always make you battle and play their game. They take care of the ball as good as any team I've ever seen."

West Virginia posts numbers that are rarely seen in basketball anymore. The team is so unselfish and passes and cuts so well that they value every possession. Against Providence, the Mountaineers finish with 17 assists on 26 baskets and commit just seven turnovers.

"They're good people and good people are not selfish," Beilein says of his players. "There is a sincere love of your teammate on this team."

More than any other coach in the conference, Beilein comes across as a teacher and with good reason. He was not a great player and didn't break into coaching easily. In fact, he began his career in his twenties as a teacher-coach on the high school level. Then he did the same at Erie (Pa.) Community College and at Nazareth College in Rochester, N.Y. He moved on to LeMoyne College in Syracuse and after 14 years as a winning head coach he finally got a shot in Division I at Canisius. More winning punched his ticket to Richmond and then he moved on to West Virginia. No one in the history of basketball has won 20 games at four different college levels (junior college, NAIA, Div. II, Div. I) until Beilein and he's enjoyed crafting the discipline and style each of those teams shared. When he's relaxed, his thoughts on team basketball sound like Norman Dale in the movie Hoosiers.

"On the court we value the ball. We try to take good shots, not necessarily the first shot, but the best shot. If it takes five seconds to get that shot or 34 seconds," he said. "When you turn the ball over you get run over, you give up easy baskets. Rebounding is very important but we may value lack of turnovers more than rebounding.

"You're not a good coach if you don't continually examine and reexamine what you do. In that first year here, we were down 40 to Pitt and Syracuse. At Providence one night, we're sitting there wondering 'what have we gotten ourselves into.' But what we have found is that the experience of senior players has helped make our style work.

Good players are worth nothing if you don't have good chemistry. That's how you measure good players, if he's a good teammate. People don't connect the two. If he's not a good teammate, he's not a good player. That's the nature of the game. You have to have players who are willing to play together. If not they should go out for an individual sport and excel in track or tennis."

As first and second year players, fans questioned whether Pittsnogle, Joe Herber and Patrick Beilein could ever be Big East players. Not any longer.

"Hakim Warrick (at Syracuse) was a great example," Beilein says. "Coach Boeheim always has some freshman who doesn't play much and in a few years they're tremendous. I always bring those things up. We try to tell them that this is not like a microwave. It doesn't happen in two minutes. It takes a long time to become a good college player.

"We play with a two-guard style but also have a shooting center in Kevin (Pittsnogle)," he said. "Kevin helps open the floor for us and we have four other shooters out there with him. We've had a shooting center before at Richmond and Canisius but never anybody like Kevin. It's something we try to feed off of. He essentially has a green light and he'll discipline himself when he takes a bad one. He certainly opens up the floor and takes a shot blocker away from the basket. This system came from years of learning from my uncle, Tommy Niland, who was a great coach at LeMoyne College. He played with a two- guard style that opened up the floor. But you have to have the players that fit. We recruit to our system. Sometimes nothing works and we're bad. But if we're shooting well, we're a tough out."

West Virginia remains a tough out and goes on the road and wins at UCLA to cap a 12-game win streak. The Mountaineers keep rolling right into

February and start league play 8-0. That makes for a pretty good winter in the hills of West Virginia.

•

On the same night that WVU improves to 13-3, Louisville looks like it's in a full-fledged swoon.

First came a tough, 61-57 loss to Pittsburgh at Freedom Hall on Sunday. The Panthers can play like a football team in shorts and Rick Pitino's players haven't learned yet that pushing the bully back is the only way to earn respect. The Cards miss five layups and 15 of the 22 shots they attempt in the lane.

"This is not Conference USA," Pitino said. "That was a finesse, fast-break type league. This is a football league in a basketball league. We let them push us around on the glass. You've got to put pads on and get ready to go."

Pitino knows the impact of losses to Villanova and now Pitt in Freedom Hall more than anyone. Good teams can afford to lose at home but young ones like his won't see many road victories. That makes losing at home tough to swallow, even if star guard Taquan Dean is still hobbled with a balky ankle.

"I'm really not interested in his health. Right now we can't be concerned with that," he says after the Pitt game. "If we keep losing at home, we're going to be an NIT team. So we can't be concerned with injuries, whether a guy's mouth is wired or his ankle is hurt. We can't make any excuses. I don't care if we're young. I don't care if we're seven years old, we've got to win, simple as that."

Two nights later, Pitino returns home to New York to face St. John's at Madison Square Garden but things go from bad to worse for the Cardinals. Dean does not play and St. John's pushes the young Cards around to the tune of 68-56. Louisville is now 1-3 in the Big East with a date against Connecticut up next. If Louisville's fans weren't listening to Pitino's warnings a month ago, they certainly are now.

"Our inexperience showed in a lot of areas," Pitino said after the game. "Missed free throws, missed wide-open shots. We had a lot of wide-open shots that didn't go down. Our guys give great effort, they want to win. They have strong desire but don't have the ability right now. We struggled with Bellarmine and Southern Indiana.

"Don't get carried away with beating Louisville," he added. "We've never been a top-20 team yet. It's nice that they rate us so high, but I've said it from the first day that we're not a top-20 team. I don't understand how we lost to Pitt at home and stayed 15th (in the coaches' poll). I don't see any reason to put us in the top 20. I never have."

Jan. 24; South Bend, Ind.

Unlike football or baseball, basketball is a game that's too often decided by a bounce of the ball. A last second shot that falls or bounces away. A rebound that tips off a finger and out of bounds. A loose ball secured amid a wave of fallen bodies.

Over the course of a season, these bounces balance out. At least that's what every God-fearing coach is hoping for. So far this season, God has not sat on Notre Dame's bench very often. After starting 9-2, the Irish entered Big East play with hopes of ending a two-year streak of bids to the NIT but then strange bounces began falling against Mike Brey's team.

First came the double overtime thriller in Pittsburgh. Six-point losses to DePaul and Syracuse stung but nothing like a two-point loss at Marquette or another double o.t. defeat at home tonight against Georgetown. The Irish went on to end January with a two-point loss at the Joyce Center to Villanova when the Wildcats' point guard, Kyle Lowry, snuck inside the trees in the lane and tipped in a rebound at the buzzer. The 72-70 loss dropped the Irish to 1-6 with each defeat coming by six points or less.

"We've had some tough ones," said Brey. "I love the fact we've been in all these but we have to find a way to finish them. All I can ask is that we keep laying it on the line like this. We've continually given ourselves chances to win but we haven't made the key play or the key stop. You can't feel sorry for yourself. You have to get back on the horse. I told our guys we're trying to claw our way to New York. That's all we have in front of ourselves right now."

Notre Dame's start illustrates how difficult the Big East is right now. While South Florida has endured a few blowout losses, every other team in the league is very competitive. That the Irish are a game out of the basement and just took sixth-ranked Villanova to the buzzer tells you all you need to know.

Notre Dame has six more weeks of games to play but the specter of missing out on the Big East Tournament is very real. The biggest downside in the creation of the 16-team conference is a decision to bar four teams from the league's post-season tournament in New York. Mike Tranghese overruled the coaches and athletic directors who pushed for every team to be included in some fashion. The commissioner insisted that altering the tournament would require games to begin on Tuesday and run through Saturday, and make the elite teams play four days in a row.

"That's no way to run a tournament and I just said we're not going to do it," Tranghese said. "I know some coaches are upset with me but I just feel that's not the way to go."

As Brey watches his team lose one nail-biter after another, he sees his team's chances of being one of the ones that stays home in March increase. That's not a pleasant thought. As one head coach in a rival league says, "that will be a coach killer. Every year a coach who doesn't go to New York will get fired. It's horrible pressure to be under."

Brey is just hoping the bounces start falling his way. If so, the Irish can recover some confidence and look ahead again. "We're not thinking about a bracket of 65. We're thinking about a bracket of 12 and getting to New York. This is murder, for sure," he says.

Another coach who says he's only focused on getting to New York is John Thompson III. The Hoyas' win in South Bend is the third straight in a streak that will grow to seven and place the team back in the top 25 for the remainder of the season. The biggest win in the streak came on Jan. 21 at home when the Hoyas shocked Duke, then the undefeated and No. 1 ranked team in the land. Two days later, Connecticut replaced the Blue Devils atop the polls.

"Our whole focus through the last part of the season is to make the Big East Tournament. That's the truth. We have to make the Big East Tournament first," Thompson said. "It's more scary because you know going into it that the bottom four teams aren't going to make the Big East Tournament. That is pressure."

"I remember I got the job at Georgetown and I go to the first meeting in Ponte Vedra and they say, 'ok, starting next year the bottom four teams don't go to New York.' And I'm like, "wo,wo. Can we re-vote. Can we talk about this?"

Thompson is nothing if not refreshing. While nearly every question he faces from a reporter has to do with something regarding his famous father, young John is a very different cat. He's not intimidating or forceful but does share his dad's intellect and polish. He's also more than a bit shy, perhaps one of the ancillary traits you acquire growing up as the son of one of the most famous black coaches in history.

"I'd say when I was in high school, around 1983 and '84, that's when it hit me how things were different," Thompson, 39, says. "Really the glory years. Georgetown was just so big then but he was still just my father. I'd play my high school games (at Gonzaga High) and the people in the stands would yell at me about Georgetown and St. John's. It's just the way it was. It is what it is."

Thompson was an All-City high school player who dreamed of playing at North Carolina. His father knew his son wasn't that good and recommended the Ivy League. The younger Thompson went on a recruiting visit to Princeton and met Pete Carrill, a man who would change his life.

"I went to visit Princeton and, I'll never forget it, it was the opposite of what I thought it would be," said Thompson. "Coach Carrill picked me up in a van and Billy Ryan (and assistant coach) put me through a workout. And for 45 minutes, Coach Carrill proceeded to tell me how awful I was and how I was going to be a jayvee player if I didn't improve on this and that. I remember thinking, 'man, he is just like my dad.' There was no bullshit."

When Thompson arrived at Princeton, he was listed in the media guide as John Thompson III. After a season, he was listed as 'John Thompson.'

"I don't know what happened but then some guy writes 'now he's more comfortable being just John Thompson.' I didn't do anything. It doesn't matter to me. I don't correct people."

Thompson enjoyed a nice career with the Tigers but the time spent in Carrill's basketball laboratory only spurred his interest in coaching. "Pops told me I was a fool. He said he paid too much money for me to go to Princeton for me to become a coach," Thompson said.

After serving as an assistant at Princeton under both Carrill and Bill Carmody, Thompson took over and in four seasons the Tigers won three Ivy League titles. When Thompson replaced Craig Esherick at Georgetown after the 2004 season, a spotlight of a different sort came his way. Now he was John Thompson coaching at Georgetown and using Pete Carrill's Princeton offense to boot.

Thompson can feel the double-barrel questions coming about either his father or his college coach. He'd clearly rather talk about Roy Hibbert, Jeff Green or Brandon Bowman, the stars of his current team. More than anyone, the Georgetown coach knows all about the power of perception.

"I happened to be in town in the last few years Pops was still coaching and we were sitting one time watching a game and the announcer was talking about 'the suffocating Georgetown defense.' He looked at me and said, 'we haven't been a good defensive team for a couple years.' But because it said Georgetown across the chest that's the image that people have and the image that people will always have.

"This is the same thing with the way we play at Georgetown now. The way we play will be different than the way Princeton plays or Bill Carmody plays at Northwestern. But because we all pass and cut, they say 'it's the Princeton offense.' The beauty of the way Coach Carrill taught me, and all of us, to see the game is that I just see it as motion. Motion and sharing the basketball and being able to have unselfish players."

While the stress of the first season in the New Big East is overwhelming most coaches, Thompson is coping with a much more important issue. His wife, Monica, was diagnosed with breast cancer in November and had surgery a day after fixing Thanksgiving dinner for her three young children and several Georgetown players. Thompson's father pushed his son to take a leave of absence for a few weeks but JT III decided against that. Instead, he's the one who takes his wife for treatments in the mornings and runs his high-profile basketball program in the afternoon. If he has to carry a laptop along to the doctor, that's fine.

"I still believe [he should take a leave], which is why I watch him closely," the elder Thompson told the Washington Post in February. "If he is strong, his family will be ok. It's like when you're on an airplane, and you've got to put the [oxygen] mask on your face before you put the mask on your baby's face. If he goes down, his family's got a major problem. So I watch him as closely as I can. The irony is he thinks he's taking care of me, too."

College basketball insiders know about Thompson's wife and the respect most everyone in the business has for him has only increased. After losing to Georgetown, Duke coach Mike Krzyzewski made sure to pull the Hoya coach aside under the stands at the Verizon Center for a hug and some comforting words.

"His nature is he keeps a lot in. He's not a complainer in that way; he hasn't done it," Thompson's father told The Post. "He has not had any less pressure because of what's going on in his personal life. That job, by nature, is loaded with pressure. He hasn't been given any slack, and he hasn't asked for it."

$$\left(14\right)$$

Jan. 28; Providence

It's a little after nine in the morning at the Westin Hotel in downtown Providence and Jim Calhoun is awake and rearing to go. His top-ranked Huskies (17-1) invade the Dunkin' Donuts Center and take on the Providence Friars at high noon but the time for strategy and film sessions is over. Now Calhoun has reserved a little time for his greatest passion: to talk.

The most obvious topic for Calhoun to opine about is himself and, by extension, the glorious program he lords over. In a few hours, he'll be wearing a gray suit and a tie that loses its tight knot only seconds after the ball is tossed in the air. Now he looks like he's ready to play 18 holes, dressed in a relaxed pair of khaki's and a blue UConn golf shirt. He walks out of an elevator and as he passes through a hallway, the Husky fans milling in the lobby wave and call out his name. One even stops him and asks for his picture with a friend. He obliges and then ducks into a conference room.

Getting Jim Calhoun to stay on subject is a never-ending quest that seasoned reporters in the state of Connecticut realize is a lost cause. His 63 year-old mind races from one anecdote, one topic, to the next and his recall seems encyclopedic. He's always on the attack, defensive and most often wildly entertaining. If there's a better interview in college basketball, bring him on.

He's first asked about his image, both nationally and among Big East coaches who would just as soon rip his lungs out than invite him to a corner bar for a beer.

"I'd disagree nationally," he said while sipping a spot of coffee. "With the Wooden Award and the Jimmy V award and the Metropolitan Award in New York and all that stuff, I've been received very well nationally. But the rest of it is typical. There is no doubt that I heard more things about Dean Smith back when. That the game had past him by, that he can't win the big game, all that stuff building up until he left. As you continue to beat people, whether it's the games or in recruiting, the natural inclination of all of us, all of us, is to go after the targets."

"When I first started out in the Big East it was probably John (Thompson) and Jimmy (Boeheim). They were everyone's targets. For my first 10 years, Jimmy couldn't coach a lick. Then he became a good coach. It's the stupidest thing I've ever heard. The culture of basketball and the culture of all the head and assistant coaches is we sit around a lot. Think of all the time between practices and between games. We gossip, tell stories, all sorts of things. And the business is such a public business we all know each other's issues.

"When guys go on the road, we're all together and we talk about each other. Now you don't talk about the last place guy in your league. So as you work the way up the ladder, there is natural animosity. They say, 'they didn't get their players the right way.' All I know is 35 years and I've never had an NCAA violation. I've self-reported two kids, Kirk King and Eric Hayward. I hear all sorts of stuff about us but you can't get me there.

"Someone said once that if you're sitting at the top, your butt and everything about you is exposed pretty good. It'll always be that way. It's the Yankees, the Lakers, the guys on top. That's what happens," he concluded.

The new, 16-team Big East has only spiked the competition that Calhoun and UConn have thrived in and everyone involved knows many aspects of that fight aren't healthy. The fight for the top of the league, or to stay out of the bottom, is played out in public. The ones for recruits, sponsors, media coverage and so many other behind-the-scenes battles can be even more intense.

"When I first came in the league, we were all closer. We've certainly lost a lot of that," he said. "I remember Alonzo Mourning had a problem with Nadav Henefeld one year. John (Thompson) and I talked that night and settled it. We had a problem with St. John's and Louie (Carnesecca) said to me, 'Irish, coach your own team. One is hard enough. Two is a bitch.'"

"That's how it used to be. Even Rick (Pitino). I'll never forget how he embraced me when I came into the Big East. I've always appreciated that. We just said that we'd better put our battles away because this is a hell of a bigger fight. And you get all the publicity you want. Rick came to see me before our game in Louisville last week. He's had a lot of things happen to him and we've both changed an awful lot since our time in Boston. By the way, have the Celtics changed very much since he's left? Not that I can see.

"Anytime you're at the top, you're going to find the arrows slung at you. That's the nature of our business, especially because you have to beat out people in recruiting and recruiting is a very personal thing. To a coach, winning and losing is more than personal. So it's hard sitting up at the top. Anyone who's sat on top of anything knows that. I'd much rather come out on top and know we're going to get everyone's best shot. That's what you aspire to be. That's what you work for when you're going like crazy in October and November."

No one knows Calhoun's plight in the spotlight quite like he does. He knew about The Horde, the Connecticut press corps, when he accepted the job but no one could've imagined how the success of the Huskies would feed that monster and create an environment with an insatiable appetite. Perhaps because he's readily accessible and enjoys the media tango, Calhoun and UConn have created an atmosphere where what the state's sporting press write and say truly matters.

Almost daily, the coach's son, Jeffrey, surfs the Internet and scoffs up any news about the team and reports it to his father. Kyle Muncy, the team's publicist, is paid to do the same and he owns the near-impossible job of playing referee between reporters and columnists around the state and a coach who seemingly reads and hears everything. Combine that barrage of information with a coach who, as one long-time beat writer puts it, "can have diarrhea of the mouth at times," and you get an environment that is filled with one brush fire after another.

"I'm an aware person but I am a private guy. The newspaper guys in Connecticut, they don't know me," he said. "You guys in Providence might know me better. Sometimes the atmosphere is unhealthy and I have to be aware of that for my players. They take shots at me and if that keeps them away from the players, that's fine with me. I can take it. But I won't take unfair shots or ignorant people.

"In some cities, like in Providence, you have one newspaper that frames what people think about Providence basketball. In our state, we have 14 papers, plus Jay Bilas, plus Dick Vitale, plus CBS, really everyone in the country, that has an opinion about us. That's an incredible amount of talk and stuff written about one team. It's unheard of, really."

Covering Calhoun can be like walking in a field filled with grenades. You never know what'll set him off. Consider the second exhibition game of the season against Concordia of Canada. Randy Smith, a columnist with the Manchester Journal-Inquirer who frequently locks horns with Calhoun, happened to write something that day asking if Rudy Gay deserved the flood of pre-season accolades that came his way. It was no bash of Gay, but more of a does-he-deserve-it-yet piece.

In the first half, Gay looks great against the overmatched Canadians, scoring 15 points with 3 steals, 2 blocks, 2 assists and 3 rebounds. No doubt fully briefed on Smith's column, Calhoun strides off the floor at the half and makes sure to brush up against the press table. "He's pretty fucking good, isn't he? He's pretty fucking good," Calhoun says in Smith's direction.

Smith wandered back into the press room at the half, more than a bit dumbfounded.

Lately, however, the blowups have become more personal. Maybe that's the age of the Internet chatrooms and all-sports radio and cable TV but more likely it's just how much of a lightning rod figure Calhoun can be. First it was CBS Sportsline's Gregg Doyel openly questioning Calhoun's ethics after the Doug Wiggins affair. That was followed by another highly personal and point-ed column by Jeff Jacobs, the talented columnist at the Hartford Courant.

Jacobs took exception to an early December remark Calhoun made while speaking with a small pack of reporters in Storrs. In a column in the Courant, Jacobs relayed a nugget from a book on Jerry Tarkanian written by Dan Wetzel of Yahoo Sports where Tark claimed a UConn coach told then-recruit Souleymane Wane that he shouldn't play for him at Frenso State because he was dying of cancer.

Jacobs, who was barely recovered from heart bypass surgery, wrote that there was no room in college sports for such a 'malignant recruiting trick.' Calhoun rebutted the Wane story and had a real problem with Jacobs' choice of words. "Jerry Tarkanian. Malignant cancer. I really think that for a cancer survivor, that's a real nice thing to say," a clearly peeved Calhoun told The Horde. "Don't worry. You don't have to print that because I'll tell (Jacobs) when I see him tomorrow. If he has enough balls to come up here, he better come up with a couple armed guards, talking about malignant cancer."

When he found out about the bitter exchange (a month after it occurred), Jacobs seethed. He and Calhoun exchanged letters on the issue but in January, he typed a missive in the Courant that fired back, reading in part that "making not-so-veiled threats is Jim being Jim."

Asked about the tête-à-tête, Calhoun shrugged. "We get a lot of things written about us. I appreciate when people aren't ignorant. That's all."

After his issues with The Horde are dismissed, Calhoun is asked about his health. Perhaps more than ever before, watching Calhoun on the sidelines has become a sport in itself. If he's not berating a player, he's turning to assistant coach George Blaney and yelling at him about a bad play, referee's call or who knows what else. It just seems that with Calhoun, the sideline spins never stop.

"I've asked Timmy Higgins who the hardest guys to referee are," he says. "Timmy said, 'Boeheim wants most every play and a good whistle for him. You and (Mike) Krzyzewski want every call. Every damn one.' He had no problem identifying the two toughest guys to do a game with. It isn't like you want a good whistle and things going your way. You want every call. So we're both driven by competitiveness. It's something in our makeup. Does that fuel the flame a little bit? Sure. If you're down on the other bench and you think that I'm going to get preferential treatment, you won't like me. But that's just the way I operate, I guess."

Calhoun said he regularly receives letters from concerned fans, mostly older women, who fear for his health. He says he makes sure to write them back and tells them "I don't plan on dying on the bench."

"I've had people want to put heart monitors on me to make sure I'm healthy. Well, I have a cholesterol issue but I've lost about 13 pounds since the season started and I work out every day. The best way to say it is I'm in control but I'm in a tizzy at the same time. I think tone setting is very important. If you start out and you let a team think 'they're not ready for us, we can play these guys,' you set a bad tone.

"I get on the kids because they need it. I was all over Marcus Williams the other night in the St. John's game. He came to the bench and I stayed all over him. Are there things I wished I didn't say? Of course there are. But I had Marcus in the next day and explained to him why I was all over his stuff. I care about him too much. I said 'you're too good. If you're thinking about the NBA, well the only thing they knock you for is you can be too lazy. I told him that I care more about his game than he does.'"

The conversation quickly veers to this year's team and how it's blessed with more talent than anyone in the nation. This is a lightning rod subject for the coach and he quickly corrects the term.

"This year, we don't have McDonald's All-Americans all loaded up. The word talent isn't good. It's having the right components. I'd rather have two great players sometimes than six good ones. This group is certainly very talented but we need to play a certain way. We just can't show up."

As an illustration, Calhoun says that while the NBA scouts may flock to this team's practices and games, their business isn't grading which team meshed together best or won the most games like his is all about.

"The best team I've ever had in coaching, far and away, was a starting team of Doron Sheffer, Ray Allen, Kirk King, Rudy Johnson, Travis Knight. We brought off the bench Eric Hayward, Rashamel Jones and Ricky Moore. That team was 32-3 (in 1996 and lost to Mississippi State in the Sweet 16.) That was the best team I ever had but it wasn't the most talent I ever had. Right before then I had Donyell (Marshall), Ray (Allen) and all those guys playing together.

"So I think there are some misnomers about talent and a great team. I would pay money right now to watch West Virginia and they're not the most talented team in the league. Are we talented? Of course we are. Do we have experience? Of course we do. Do we have a terrific point guard? Sure. You could break down the components and ask 'what else do you want?' I would like to have a team that would be more flexible when a team pressures us. Just have guys go by their man. We don't have that with the exception of Marcus."

No one, however, is buying it. Gay has enjoyed some great games, Rashad Anderson has shot the lights out, Hilton Armstrong has doubled his statistics from the year before and given UConn yet another future NBA first rounder. No one is crying for Jim Calhoun. "Charles Barkley said on TNT the other night that the Celtics can't beat UConn. I guess that feeds the monster a bit," he said.

It's a problem every coach in the country would gladly try on for size. Too much talent. Too much media. Too much pressure.

"George Blaney tells me almost every day 'you asked for this. All this stuff, you made all this happen," said Calhoun. "That may be true but you still have to live it. No job in this business is easy."

When Calhoun arrives at the Dunkin' Donuts Center in time for the noon start, he hears boos at every corner. No matter. His team is ready and after some early problems and a very average (38 percent) shooting day, the Huskies wear out Providence with some dominating rebounding (52-34) and pull away for a 76-62 win.

Providence's Donnie McGrath, one of the Big East's most dangerous jump shooters, is asked afterward what it's like to play against a team with NBA size up front, several good shooters and a pinpoint passer running the show. "It can be overwhelming," McGrath says. "They're the biggest team I've ever played against. We had some transition baskets in the first half but once they got on the boards, they shut us down. They have a lot of answers."

Calhoun praises Providence's young players and says he made sure to pull McGrath over at the end of the game. "I told him at the end of the line (that) 'you're having a heck of a senior year. Keep it up."

As his press conference ends, Calhoun is clearly happy. His team is now 18-1 and clearly coming together. "We played much better today than we did against Louisville or St. John's. They got the loose balls and scrapped today. That's what we need. I'm going home thinking we're getting better."

With that, Calhoun turns and leaves his team behind. A few minutes later they'll roll home in a large bus painted in Husky blue. The coach chooses to drive his car, a Bentley, back to his home in the tiny town of Pomfret. Bigger tests await his team but for this moment anyway, the UConn coach is a happy man.

(15)

Feb. 1; Providence

It's easy to lose track of a team's progress in a 16-team conference filled with marquee talent and that certainly is the case at Seton Hall. The Pirates began the season with two problems: a supposed lack of talent and the presence of a target on the back of coach Louis Orr.

Orr led the Pirates to the NCAA Tournament in 2004 but a 4-12 Big East record in '05 and the presence of too few marquee recruits from the talent-rich New Jersey high school scene has Hall fans expressing grave concerns whether Orr is the right man for the job. When the Pirates were embarrassed in a 53-point loss at Duke in November, more red flags were raised. When the team began Big East play 1-3, it was certainly easy to write off both Orr and his team.

But something clicked with the Pirates a few weeks later. In back-to-back games in late-January, Seton Hall won easily at North Carolina State and then upset Syracuse at the Carrier Dome. Guards Donald Copeland and Jamar Nutter, both local Jersey kids, played with that city toughness that defines the Big East and whenever big man Kelly Whitney decided to play, the Hall was dangerous.

Tonight, Orr has his surging team in Providence to face the Friars for a third straight road game. The road isn't where most teams go to get healthy but considering that the Pirates haven't played a home game with more than 50 percent capacity at the 20,000-seat Meadowlands, it's not like they know what a home court advantage is anyway.

What the players have learned is the power of one. Individually, Seton Hall doesn't have a top 15-20 player in the conference. Together, they're pretty good. That's definitely the case defensively and shines through again in the Dunkin' Donuts Center as the Pirates hold Providence scoreless over the final 1:55 and win, 77-74. Geoff McDermott missed two free throws with 46 seconds left that could've given the Friars the lead and Sharaud Curry's floater in the lane popped in and out with eight ticks left. A final, long 3-pointer by Curry with one second left missed, securing Seton Hall's fourth win in a row.

"We're showing a lot of grit, a lot of character and a lot of poise," said Orr. "Those are intangibles that are invaluable."

When The Hall finally goes home, it keeps on winning and knocks off Rutgers. Another win at South Florida makes it six in a row and puts Orr in great shape heading down the stretch.

While he's doing fine, the coach at Jersey rival Rutgers is in hot water. Gary Waters, a solid coach with Midwestern roots who never really fit in Central Jersey, planned to be honored by the Kent State Hall of Fame on a Saturday night and return home for a game against Marquette the next day. But a big snowstorm gripped the East Coast and closed Newark Airport. On Sunday morning, the airfield was still closed so Waters altered his plans for a flight to Philadelphia. The move didn't work and after six hours of waiting, Waters abandoned hope and called back to Jersey to tell associate head coach Fred Hill, Jr., he had to take over.

Before a few thousand hardy souls who braved the big storm, the Knights won their first game in two weeks in a 91-84 upset. When Waters finally returned home, he faced a firestorm. First off, the Knights returned to form and lost a winnable game to St. John's, 54-51. Then the Newark Star-Ledger reported that the coach's travel snafu came without permission from athletic director Bob Mulcahy and that the school was considering firing Waters with four years left on his contract.

The embarrassing gaffe only stoked the fire of Waters' critics even more. In some circles it almost seemed as if Rutgers was looking for an excuse to escape the coach's contract. A 25-inch snowstorm may have just turned the trick.

Feb. 13; Philadelphia

Since the Big East season tipped off in January, two dates stood out among the rest. Tonight is the first of two showdowns between Villanova and Connecticut, the two heavyweights in the East and perhaps the two best teams in the country. ESPN snagged the rights to round one. CBS gets the rematch two weeks later in Storrs, Conn.

ESPN's Big Monday crew of Sean McDonough, Bill Raftery and Jay Bilas couldn't have asked for a better scenario. UConn is 22-1 and ranked first in the country. Fourth-ranked Villanova has won eight games in a row and is 19-2. Both teams own identical 9-1 Big East records. The crowd of 20,859 at the Wachovia Center is the largest to ever attend a college basketball game in the history of the state of Pennsylvania.

Luckily, the game meets everyone's expectations. Villanova receives performances from two unlikely players and wins in comeback fashion, 69-64. Kyle Lowry, the supposed playmaking guard, goes berserk in the first half with 16 points on 6-of-6 shooting. His drive through the teeth of the UConn defense to close the half gives the Wildcats a 33-32 lead at the break.

Randy Foye and Allan Ray shoot a combined 5-for-15 in the first half and Connecticut's dominant size advantage is clearly causing Jay Wright to juggle his four-guard set. Even so, Villanova more than holds its own in the lane with 13 offensive rebounds and 26 points in the paint. Jim Calhoun's substitution pattern is especially bizarre all night. For one, he starts Craig Austrie instead of seasoned vets Denham Brown or Rashad Anderson.

The Huskies come out of the halftime break with Anderson in for Austrie but after only 12 seconds of action, the whistle blows. Jeff Adrien checks in for Josh Boone, who comes to the bench with a shocked look in his eyes. The puzzling move has little to do with a sparkling start to the half for UConn which puts up the first 13 points and takes a 45-33 lead. Rudy Gay is playing like an All-American, draining two long 3-pointers and causing Villanova major match-up headaches.

But just as quickly as UConn grabs control, Villanova fights back. This time it's Ray who starts dialing in long-range shots, one deeper than the next. He drains four threes in a row to slice UConn's lead to 47-45 and when Mike Nardi bangs home a trey, the Wildcats are back in the lead with 12 minutes left. The sprint to the finish is a doozy and Villanova's hero is Will Sheridan. Playing against a slew of NBA-sized big men, the junior forward knocks down several big baseline jumpers and finishes with 13 points and 10 rebounds. "I feel like everybody doubles our guards. They were backing off a little bit so I felt like I had good looks tonight," he says.

A Sheridan free throw with 1:52 left gives Villanova a 67-60 lead but UConn isn't done. Marcus Williams hits a quick driving layup and then scores again in the lane to make it 67-64 with 31 seconds left. Villanova is blessed with excellent foul shooters and UConn puts one of the best, Nardi, at the line with 15 seconds left. But he misses the front end of a one-and-one, giving UConn a final chance to tie.

Williams sets everyone up and UConn runs a play for a handoff to Anderson and a 3-pointer. As the two veterans meet, they muff the pass and Ray swoops in for the steal with 5.9 seconds left. He makes two free throws to ice the game and at the final buzzer, the stands empty and Villanova is atop the Big East.

"It was a big test for us," said Ray, the game's high scorer with 25 points. "We needed to see where we're at. We'll probably see them two more times but now we know we can play with them."

Asked about his second-half shooting explosion, Ray shrugged and said, "UConn was giving me open shots and Coach Wright was running plays for me. Once I got it going, I felt like I couldn't miss."

Like every team they've faced, Villanova's quickness bothered UConn. Lowry was too quick in the first half. Ray's quick-trigger shooting hurt the Huskies in the second.

"It was a battle of could they keep us away from the paint and could we deal with their quickness," said Calhoun. "They were able to keep us on the outside offensively and we had trouble getting the ball in the paint."

For the first time this season, fans finally saw UConn's clear-cut weakness: making someone, anyone, other than Marcus Williams beat them.

"We had one guard tonight," Calhoun said. "It's difficult for us but Marcus was going to be the one to deliver the ball. For 40 minutes they did such a good job of putting ball pressure on us that we had a tough time running our offense."

After the arena clears out, Wright and several friends including Hofstra coach Tom Pecora and the patriarch of the Villanova family, Rollie Massimino, head into the city for a late-night Italian dinner. Wright is praised as the conquering hero, accepting hugs and handshakes from friends from New York and Philly.

"Hey, that's a magical night for our kids," he says in a hoarse voice. "To have everything in place for a big night and them come through like that. Wow, that's huge. That was a lot of fun."

Feb. 15; Philadelphia

Two days after Villanova's biggest win since beating Georgetown in the 1985 national championship game, Jay Wright hits the jackpot.

For much of the past year, Wright and 'Nova had talked about an extension to his contract. After a strong NCAA tourney showing in 2005, Wright certainly enjoyed some leverage in the talks but as time wore on, he was in no mood to play hardball. He liked the school he was at, loved the conference he coached in and was convinced he could satisfy all of his dreams at Villanova.

With the foggy glee of the UConn win still in his head, Wright signed a seven-year extension. No terms were released but it's clear that Villanova was "stepping up" like none of the other Catholic schools in the Big East is capable of.

"People might ask me 'How could you not be interested in this huge state school or that huge state school," Wright said. "Well, unless you're not a part of Villanova you wouldn't understand. That's why I think it is the best job in America. You very rarely get a chance to coach in your home town or at the school you were a fan of growing up. That's why it is a dream."

Wright took part in negotiations that have come to symbolize the public-private split the Big East deals with daily. While Connecticut and Louisville rarely spare an expense trying to win, smaller schools watch every penny. DePaul, for example, reports expenditures of $13.5 million while Louisville counters at nearly $35 million in figures supplied to the U.S. Department of Education.

Coaches salaries vary widely in the league. The biggest names such as Calhoun, Pitino and Boeheim draw enough ancillary money from show companies and media obligations that their packages range from $1-$2.5 million. St. John's, meanwhile, pays $600,000 for Norm Roberts. And not all of the Big East's public schools throw around the dollars, either. Rutgers, for example, chooses to pay its football coach Greg Schiano close to $800,000 while hoops coach Gary Waters earns $525,000.

Wright wants to stay at Villanova but only if it was committed to play with the Big Boys. When it announced the coach's new deal, Villanova also said that the school's board of trustees met the day before and signed off on the construction of a $15 million basketball practice facility and improvements to the Pavilion on campus.

Commitments like that not only say you want to compete with anyone; they also serve to scare off would-be suitors. After no doubt assuming that a Catholic school lacked the resources to keep someone as good as Wright, rumors began to spread about him filling a marquee opening at Indiana or maybe Missouri.

"When there were rumors, we had to respond," Wright said. "This is where I want to coach. We didn't want to deal with any of those questions because it is a distraction to our players and our recruits. This is important because we can say I have a long-term contract."

Feb. 18; Syracuse

With five games to go and an uncharacteristic 5-6 Big East record, time is ticking on the Syracuse Orangemen.

The team's season will likely boil down to the next three days. Tonight Louisville is at the Carrier Dome. West Virginia comes in for Big Monday two nights later. Win both games and the Orange (17-8 overall) are back on the right track for an NCAA bid since getting to at least 8-8 in the conference looks like a necessity. Lose one, or both, games and Syracuse will need a minor miracle to find its way into the field of 64 on Selection Sunday.

The stakes are even higher for a Louisville team that's 16-8 overall but limping along in the conference with a 4-7 mark. The Cards have won two of their last three games, however, and the backcourt of Taquan Dean and Brandon Jenkins is playing as well as it has all season.

Both games are ESPN national broadcasts. Most coaches would roll out the welcome mat for such coverage but Syracuse and Louisville almost expect their games to be telecast coast-to-coast. Told he'd have a chance to impress the country with two good showings, SU coach Jim Boeheim sniffed and said TV owns too much say in the Big East.

"You cannot allow TV or anybody else to dictate your schedule," Boeheim said. "If you're going to play 16 games, it's 15 and one (repeat opponent). You have one rival game. If it's a little less money, it's a little less money. Who cares? Instead of getting $2 million at the end of the year, you get $1.9 or $1.8? The budget at Syracuse is like $400 million, so $100,000 is going to matter? The budget at UConn is what, $600 million, $800 million? And $100,000 is going to matter? Please. You can't let that happen."

Boeheim actually catches a break by playing Louisville and West Virginia at home instead of at Freedom Hall or WVU's Coliseum but that's irrelevant to him. He's correct when he says TV's control over scheduling is too broad. But the Big East signed contracts with ESPN and CBS that guaranteed both networks requested glamour games and the millions involved in those deals make the scheduling decisions easy.

Syracuse's fans certainly haven't given up on their team. The Louisville game draws 31,190, the largest crowd of the season thus far. The big crowd sees its team play well from the start and no one is as sharp as Gerry McNamara. He fires in 14 first-half points and the Orange shoot 54 percent but still trail at the break, 36-35. The officiating crew of Curtis Shaw, Reggie Greenwood and Will Bush is calling everything in sight, slowing the game to a crawl. They whistle 32 fouls in the first half alone and the Cards take advantage by sinking 13-of-15 free throws. Syracuse is the direct opposite, making just seven of 20 tries.

The second half is a different story. The teams keep fouling one another but not before the Orangemen open the half with a 20-6 blitz over the first 6:45. Louisville makes just 1-of-7 shots against the Syracuse zone defense while the Orange backcourt tandem of McNamara and Eric Devendorf combines for 18 of the 20 points on the way to a 55-40 lead.

Syracuse's offense continues to shred the Cardinals and shoots 14-of-22 in the second half and 59 percent for the game. McNamara pours in 30 points, his high in a Big East game this season, and is ecstatic with his team's play. The only glaring weakness was a head-shaking 19-of-46 rate from the foul line.

"Hopefully this gets us going," he says to a large throng of reporters in Syracuse's locker room. "We had to come out strong. It's all about intensity. If we bring our A game, we'll be tough to beat. That's what we did. We stepped it up on the defensive end."

A frustrated Rick Pitino leaves the podium after his news conference and walks back toward his locker room and a bus that'll take the Cardinals to their waiting charter plane. The Cards have needed a game like this one to jump-start their season but just don't have the offensive firepower to get things rolling. With two weeks to play, Louisville is clearly in danger of missing the Big East Tournament.

"We had to win tonight, they had to win tonight," he says. "Now we have to win three of our next four games to have a shot at this. We'll have a couple easy games when we go on the road at West Virginia and Connecticut. Right now we're painfully young. It's excruciating at times. They play hard but they don't play well. We just have to keep getting better."

Feb. 20; Syracuse

Quick turnarounds are commonplace in the Big East with its many scheduling quirks. With one day to prepare for 14th-ranked West Virginia, Mike Hopkins is under the gun. Hopkins is a former Syracuse guard who found his way to the tundra of Central New York from Orange County, Calif. and famed Mater Dei High. He played on some powerhouse teams and loved everything about Syracuse basketball.

Now he's in his 11th season as an assistant coach with Boeheim and few coaches in the country work harder. Hopkins is credited with landing many of Syracuse's current stars on the recruiting trail and helping corral a slew of good players in the next two classes. SU has a signed letter-of-intent from Buffalo's Paul Harris, a senior regarded as one of the top 15 players in the country. It also owns verbal commitments from five of the top juniors in the country, including Donte Green, a 6-9 forward who grew up idolizing Carmelo Anthony in Baltimore.

What makes Hopkins unique is he also handles the scouting of each opponent. Other staffs in the conference divide those duties among the four assistant coaches the NCAA allows on the bench or a coach who's not allowed to recruit away from campus.

"I started scouting when I was the third assistant and I did them all for a few years and then when I started recruiting more, I just stayed with the duties," he said. "It's more demanding but when people say 'wow, I can't believe you do all the scouting,' well that's how you stay fresh and see what all the other coaches are doing. I'm studying more basketball while other guys are just working on recruiting.

"We've been real fortunate that we've completed most of our recruiting for the next year," he continued. "During the season, I've become a smarter recruiter because we have to be. I've gone out four or five times since our season started. I don't like to go out and miss practice. You have to get your guys better and you have to win. That helps recruiting more than anything."

Hopkins is standing in a runway off the court while the Syracuse and West Virginia players warm up. He's asked if any of the Orange players can one day play in the NBA and told that this team doesn't have the Derrick Coleman-Billy Owens type of stars that he played with.

"This team has a few 'could be' pros," he says. "The scouts actually like Demetris (Nichols) because he shoots the ball so well. But we need Terrence (Roberts) and Darryl Watkins to be good. Hey, if your top guys don't pan out, you can be hurting. A couple years ago Charlie Villanueva called us and said he wanted to come to Syracuse. Coach (Boeheim) was like, 'No. We already have Terrence and Demetris at that spot.' So Connecticut took him even though they had a lot of good forwards. That's their philosophy. We've never had a lot of McDonald's All-Americans. We've had a lot of guys develop, like a Hakim Warrick. I don't think many teams in the country would've thought Hilton Armstrong (of Connecticut) would be a sure-fire pro. You never know. They always say that big guys take longer to develop. Have our guys exceeded expectations? No. Do they still have the potential? Yes."

Asked what the keys are for Syracuse to grab a second win in a row for the first time since Jan. 14 and Hopkins answers defending West Virginia's shooters and getting easy chances off the transition game.

"Obviously you have to guard the three-point line against these guys," he says. "(Kevin) Pittsnogle and (Mike) Gansey, they make winning plays, hit daggers. We have to play defense to get into transition. We don't have a Sherman Douglas or a Pearl (Washington), guys who are one-man fast breaks. We have no inside scoring so if we have to play half-court offense, we're in trouble. Against Louisville at the start of the second half, Eric Devendorf got a 3-pointer and three layups, all off the defense. That's where Gerry is great, too, because he can pull up off the break and shoot it from anywhere."

West Virginia comes into the Dome in a mini-skid, losing at Pitt and Seton Hall and at home to UConn. Some coaches around the league have noted that the Mountaineers received the 'easy' schedule from the conference office. John Beilein laughs at that suggestion and points out that his repeat opponents - Pittsburgh, Cincinnati and Georgetown – could all play in the NCAA's and he doesn't get to face either Rutgers or DePaul. "Anyone who says that doesn't know what they're talking about," Beilein says. "I'd like to see an easy schedule, that's for sure."

From the opening tip, this game is a good, old fashioned, Big East rock fight. Syracuse's zone does a great job extending to WVU's array of jump shooters but the magic that McNamara played with 48 hours earlier is gone. He makes just 2-of-14 shots and doesn't score a single point in the second half. That puts even more stress on the Syracuse defense and makes the game a race to score 60 points.

West Virginia is shooting poorly from the 3-point line, making just 12-of-33 shots. But the Mountaineers are bottling up McNamara and doing a solid job off the boards. No more than five points separate the teams in a tense second half. Patrick Beilein hits the last of his six 3-pointers to give WVU a 51-49 lead with 7:35 left but Devendorf (17 points) answers with a 3-ball of his own to put the Orange back up by one. Layups by Devendorf and Roberts push SU's lead to 56-51 before Johannes Herber makes two layups in traffic to cut the lead to one point with five minutes left.

That's when the defenses really stiffen. West Virginia has trouble cracking Syracuse's zone and resorts to long bombs late in the shot clock. Smooth-shooting big man Kevin Pittsnogle makes a three with four minutes remaining that ties the score at 58-58 but the Mountaineers fail to score another point.

Syracuse's Roberts flips in a jump hook for a 60-58 lead. Pittsnogle misses two long 3-pointers and then throws the ball away. McNamara turns the ball over with 37 seconds left, setting up a finish that hads the Dome crowd standing and roaring. Beilein misses a deep 3-pointer with seven seconds left and Roberts chases down the rebound, his 10th of the game. Unlike the Louisville foul fest, the teams are called for 17 fouls total. West Virginia doesn't attempt a single free throw, while Syracuse is only 4-of-7. The final try comes by McNamara with two seconds left. A 90 percent free throw shooter, he misses the front end of a one-and-one but hustles and chases down his own rebound and the game is over.

"I told Gerry 'you're probably going to miss so you better go and get it (rebound). He was having the kind of game where nothing is falling," said Boeheim. "It shows you what kind of heart he's got. They might have had four or even all five guys in the lane and he just goes and gets the ball. The kid's got some heart. The biggest I've ever seen. I thought Sherman Douglas had the biggest but if it's not a tie, then it's this kid."

John Beilein is asked about his team's execution in the final minutes when rare turnovers proved costly. "We were running a certain pattern and it takes just one person to get confused to throw us off. Then we ended up throwing the ball away. On the last one we ran a different pattern and the same thing happened. It's just the way it goes.

We'll learn from it. It's hard to do in that situation," he says.

The Mountaineer coach, like his team, is getting worn down by the weight of the conference schedule. He also takes it as a huge compliment when the Syracuse students rush the floor after the win. "I didn't think that would ever happen. It happened at Seton Hall the other day, too. It shows where we are, I guess."

When one questioner asks if he thinks his team is playing well, Beilein insists he's happy. He's just working in the deepest league in the country.

"Look at our schedule. And on the horizon is three more," he says. "I think we're playing pretty well, actually. When you're on the road, whether you're playing South Florida or Syracuse or anybody, it's going to be a last minute game. We're not going to blow people away. We always need to have confidence and that's my job to know where they erred and to tell them they are good players. We're a good team. We're just playing a monstrous schedule and it's three of four on the road against teams that have been ranked or have beaten highly ranked teams. So we've lost three of those four."

Feb. 25; Pittsburgh

It's a Saturday morning along Forbes Avenue, the main drag through the heart of the University of Pittsburgh campus. Fifty years ago, the Pirates won the World Series a few blocks away when Bill Mazerowski hit a majestic home run to beat the Yankees. Now the street is filled with pizza shops, bars and bookstores catering to the collegiate set.

Barry Rohrssen likes the scene. The Pittsburgh assistant coach is sitting in a coffee shop and about to dig into a stack of blueberry pancakes. He's also busy talking basketball. Rohrssen is one of the characters in the Big East. He's a big, burly man who was born and raised in Brooklyn and played college ball at St. Francis of New York. Everyone calls him 'Slice,' and like many nicknames of basketball people with Eastern roots, the moniker came courtesy of Howard Garfinkel at the renowned Five-Star summer camp.

"Being from New York the backboards are always cracked, the rims are bent and I wasn't a shooter," he says. "In the counselor games, I'd always slash to the basket. Mr. Garfinkel would call me Slice."

Slice caught the coaching bug in high school and began working at some of the best summer camps in the East. One of his first stops was at Holy Cross where George Blaney was the coach and hopeful of getting his Crusaders in a new league one day. "George told me about the Big East before it even began. I thought it was ingenious. It was like I had a hot stock tip, insider trading," he says.

To pay the bills out of college, Rohrssen helped open a hip New York City night club called The Limelight in the mid-80s. He met the rich and famous in New York but couldn't shake the urge to coach. His Five-Star connections eventually landed him a job with Ron Ganulin at St. Francis and then Bill Bayno at Nevada-Las Vegas. When California native Ben Howland landed the Pittsburgh job, he asked friends for tips on Eastern recruiters and Rohrssen's name kept coming up.

Howland hired Rohrssen in 1999 and he stayed on when Jaime Dixon replaced Howland, who jumped to UCLA. Howland and Dixon have taken Pitt basketball to historic heights over the last six years and the recruiting of Rohrssen has had a lot to do with that. When St. John's let its guard down on the New York recruiting scene, Pitt and Rohrsson jumped in. Good city players like Brandin Knight, Chris Taft and Carl Krauser have led the Panther resurgence and the current team has five key players with deep New York City roots.

Not surprisingly, some opposing recruiters aren't fond of Slice. They whisper rumors that the Golden Panther days must be up and running again, a reference to the 1980s when Pitt boosters were overly involved in the recruitment of stars like Charles Smith and Jerome Lane. Rohrssen sniffs at the suggestion of impropriety.

"Look at the guys we have. No big-timers," he said. "Carl Krauser, it was us and Hofstra. Chevy Troutman was Pitt, Duquesne and UMass. Levance Fields was St. John's and Pitt. Ronald Ramon was Pitt and Providence. It's not like we're getting highly touted recruits."

Both Howland and Dixon have used that New York City flash and dash and combined it with tough, physical defense and rebounding. The mix has worked well. In the previous five seasons, the Panthers have won 19 or more games and played in four NCAA Tournaments. In 2003, '04 and '05, the Panthers won 29, 28 and 31 games and were as good as any team in the Big East. Upset losses in the NCAA's have dogged the program but Pitt is now firmly entrenched among the best programs in the country.

Tonight, the ninth-ranked Panthers improve to 21-4 by running away from Providence, 81-68. An impressive first half built a 41-27 lead with Krauser, guard Antonio Graves and 7-foot big man Aaron Gray all playing well.

Krauser thought about jumping to the NBA after last season but his market is limited. Now he's 24 years old and filled with toughness and savvy. Gray played behind Taft for the last two years and used the time to reshape his plump body and go to work on his game. The results are staggering. Now the Emmaus, Pa., native is a strong 280 pounds who handles the ball well, is a crafty passer and has NBA scouts more than interested in him leaving school a year early this spring.

"We've worked an awful lot on individual improvement with our players and I think that's showed up for a couple years now," said Dixon. "We really stress that."

The Panthers are now 10-3 in the Big East and in position to make a run at a top four seed in the NCAA's. Up next is a Big Monday game at West Virginia, always the school's biggest rival.

Feb. 26; Storrs

It's been 13 days since Villanova upset Connecticut at the Wachovia Center and passed the Huskies in the polls. Today is pay back.

If there was any way for the hoopla surrounding the game in Philly to grow any larger, it has today in Eastern Connecticut. The CBS eye is in the house with Billy Packer and Jim Nantz calling the shots. Writers from newspapers in the East and the national Web sites are in town, too.

Villanova is ranked second in the country. UConn is third. As the season has progressed, the number of NBA scouts flocking to Big East games has been impressive. UConn, of course, leads the way. But Villanova's season has helped the NBA stock of its players immensely and no one has risen as sharply as Randy Foye.

While Big East coaches grew to fear his game over the last three years, Foye did not have a large national profile until the NCAA Tournament last March. Now he's a favorite for All-America honors, quite an achievement considering just how far he's traveled to get to this point in his life.

Raised mainly by his grandmother, Ruth Martin, in the mean streets of Newark, N.J., Foye is one of the great stories in college basketball. He's the best defensive guard in the Big East because he insists that no one will score on him, demands it even. He'll check point guards, shooters or even power forwards who'd better watch out or he'll pick their pockets like a watch thief in Grand Central Station.

Refining that toughness to fit the Villanova structure has been a challenge for Wright but with good reason. Before he was three years old, Foye was an orphan. His father, Tony Zigelo, was killed in a motorcycle accident. His mother, Regina Foye, walked out on him and his younger brother a few weeks after Foye finished kindergarten. His grandmothers, Ruth Martin and Betty Foye, shuttled the two boys between their houses in Newark. "When I got tired of one neighborhood, I would go to the other one and make new friends. I kept going back and forth," Foye said.

Foye was fortunate to grow up under the wing not only of strong grandmothers but also a few key mentors. One was Zegale Kelliehan, an older man from Foye's project. He played Division III college ball and would work with Foye on his game and take him to his college contests. Kelliehan also made sure to tell the tough guys in the neighborhood to stay away from Foye and protect his talent. The same lessons were taught by Bryant Garvin, Foye's coach at East Side High in Newark.

Leary of his Newark public school academic background, recruiters weren't sold on Foye right away. Wright, however, was close with his AAU coach and he risked any academic issues and pressed him for a commitment. "Coach was the most loyal guy. Simple as that," Foye said.

Through his first three years, Foye took a back seat at times to Ray and Curtis Sumpter. He'd enjoy his moments, for sure, but as juniors the Big East coaches picked Foye third team all-league while his buddies made the second team. He thought about jumping to the NBA but his stock wasn't high enough.

Wright thinks a trip to Turkey for the World University Games last summer helped Foye realize just how good he could be. He starred alongside Gerry McNamara (Syracuse), Vincent Grier (Minnesota), Craig Smith (BC) and Shelden Williams (Duke), guarded the opposition's top backcourt player and emerged as a team leader.

"Each of the United States teams picked a captain and our team picked Randy. Then all the captains got together and voted on who should carry the flag and they picked Randy," said Wright. "So he carried the flag and led the U.S. delegation into a stadium of like 70,000 people in Turkey. It was really cool."

Wright speaks with a glow in his eye when he talks about Foye. He knows how far his senior star has come, appreciates the roots and the fact that he's in position for a slice of the NBA's multimillion dollar pie.

"Randy came out of the (Games) feeling very wordly," Wright said. "He's from Newark, really tough. He wasn't a big AAU guy, traveling all over. But we went to the Ephesus over there, where Saint Paul spoke. Our priest did a reading from Saint Paul a few weeks ago and Randy comes over and says 'Coach, Father Rob talked about where we were in Ephesus.' I think that trip opened a whole world up for him. He's on another level now. It's really a great story. He came from no mom and dad and now he's ahead of schedule to graduate. He could've left after last year but he came to me and said 'I want to be the first person in my family to graduate and I want to win a national championship with these guys.'"

His Villanova experience may have polished Foye's rough edges but the best part of his Newark toughness shines through when he takes the floor. He's not afraid to take the big shot or carry his team and he'll guard the 6-8 forwards when Wright uses the four-guard lineup.

"Our toughness comes from our background," Foye said. "No one can give you physical or mental toughness. That comes from your background. It comes from where we grew up. We're all city players. We all know what it takes to survive and we transfer that to the basketball court."

Foye said he likes to see bigger teams take the floor and think they're ready to sweep the backboards when they see himself, Ray, Lowry and Nardi take the floor together. "I think people underestimate our toughness," he said. "If you look at us on film, you can see our quickness, but you can't measure the other things we do. You might not see how we box out a 6-8 guy or do those little things and that's the reason we're able to out-rebound teams. We know we have to outwork the other team."

Taking a lead from Foye, the Wildcats' exude toughness and Wright says "people who come to our practices are surprised at how hard we compete. My biggest problem in practice is I have to tell them 'don't run these drills to try to beat each other. Run them so we can get better.' It's actually a struggle.

"I don't know a lot about a lot but when we recruit we really try to get competitive kids. We want kids that love to play," Wright says. "We're so into it, 12 months a year that we don't want anyone who we have to tell, 'you have to work out,' or 'you have to want to play hard.' If we think that's going to be a question, we won't recruit them. We want ball players, kids who just love to play. Randy and Allan, they'll go all day."

Foye is a load for any defender and a major source of conversation among the Connecticut coaching staff. UConn chooses to counteract Villanova's four-guard starting five with an exact opposite look that emphasizes its great size. George Blaney thinks that starting 6-11 Hilton Armstrong on Foye and 6-9 Rudy Gay on Ray could cause the shooters to pause a bit before they fire away.

The move works early as UConn races to a 12-6 lead. But Foye swishes a 3-pointer and then lucks out by banging one in off the glass to give 'Nova a 15-14 lead. Later in the half, Foye takes Gay off the dribble for a strong layup and then out-battles Gay and Denham Brown for a loose ball. He finishes with 10 points in the half but the 'Cats make just 35 percent of their shots and trail at the break, 36-33.

The second half is more of the same. UConn makes sure to fight over every ball screen and its size bothers the Villanova jump shooters. The 'Cats make 9-of-30 shots from the 3-point line and shoot just 33 percent for the game. Foye (18) and Ray (19) get their points but need 34 shots to do so.

UConn needs one of its best games of the season to win and comes through. Several players step up and the team's great balance (and 54 percent shooting) wears down Villanova. Marcus Williams choreographs the show with 12 assists and 10 points. Denham Brown scores 16 of his game-high 23 points in the second half, Hilton Armstrong blocks 8 shots and Rashad Anderson comes off the bench to pop in 5-of-7 threes for 17 points.

An Anderson 3-pointer and Brown hoop and foul with 5:15 left caps an 18-3 run that swings the game in UConn's favor. Down 71-57, Villanova slaps on a full-court press and showcases its speed and quickness. But with three minutes left, Ray falls to the floor and grabs his knee. He leaves the game and Villanova's comeback chances go with him as the Huskies nail down a 89-75 win.

"I thought Connecticut was on top of every aspect of their game," said Wright. "They executed better, they handled our press better and rebounded better."

Calhoun is all but giddy when he meets the media. He privately feared his team wouldn't match Villanova's intensity and again fall victim to the 'Cats speed and quickness. Instead, his team showed up with all of its guns firing.

"A lot of times games are built up and don't fulfill their promise," he says. "That game from a competitive standpoint and a toughness standpoint more than fulfilled its promise. I'll tell you, Villanova may be pound for pound the toughest team we've played in a long while. We had to increase our toughness if we were going to compete with them."

The game had a Round Two feeling to it and anyone at Gampel Pavilion certainly longed for a Round Three. It could easily come in two weeks at Madison Square Garden in the Big East title game.

"I think both of these games were great advertisements for college basketball and our league," Calhoun said. "Villanova will be a tough out for anybody. They'll be an awfully tough team to beat before the Final Four."

Wright has seen enough of UConn. While his team miraculously grabbed 24 offensive rebounds and barely edged the Huskies off the boards (43-38), their overall team size bothers his group of mighty-mights. Then again, any team outside of the NBA will have a problem with UConn's front line.

"It would be great because if we see them again, it would be in a big game. I don't particularly want to see them again but at least it would be in a big game," Wright said.

The Big East finals certainly qualify as a big game. But chances are Calhoun and Wright would gladly settle for a showdown about five weeks away in a bigger locale. Like the RCA Dome in Indianapolis.

March 1; Providence

This week marks the final home games for several outstanding seniors in the Big East. Villanova saluted Foye, Ray, Jason Fraser and Curtis Sumpter tonight at the Pavilion before a win over St. John's. Syracuse is bracing for a record-setting Carrier Dome crowd on the weekend for Gerry McNamara's final home game.

Tonight at the Dunkin' Donuts Center, Providence honors its senior guard Donnie McGrath. The shooter from Katonah, N.Y. owns the school's all-time 3-point shooting records and has anchored Tim Welsh's backcourt for four years but after the pre-game pictures and standing ovation subsides, the Big East's first playoff game taps off.

With two games to play, the jockeying for spots in the Big East Tournament is intense. South Florida, which needs to beat either UConn or Georgetown to avoid going winless in its first trip around the conference, won't be coming to New York. But the identity of the other three teams who'll stay home is a mystery. Six teams are in the mix for the three spots and two face off in Providence where the Friars host Notre Dame. PC (5-9) can all but clinch a spot with a win. Notre Dame (4-10) can't afford another loss.

"Hey, the Big East Tournament starts tomorrow for us," Irish coach Mike Brey said the day before. "I can't lie to my players about what's on the line. We've played well and certainly had some excruciating losses but at some point you have to deliver."

Notre Dame is coming off an eight-point loss at home to Marquette, its largest margin of defeat in a Big East game all year. The other nine losses have each come by six points or less. Seven of the losses came by a combined 15 points, including a 75-74 overtime loss at Connecticut 10 days ago.

Facing intense pressure to finally win a close one, the Irish lost at home to Marquette in its last game, 80-72. "The weight of the world was on their shoulders. It showed up in their play and in body language," Brey said.

Providence was in the thick of the race at 4-6 a few weeks back but three defeats in its last four games has put Tim Welsh's team into the hopper. "Time is running out and this is our last home opportunity," said Welsh.

As the game prepares to start, Mike Tranghese files into the midcourt seat he's frequently used for the last 25 years in Providence. He's praised the intensity of the race to New York, calling it an unintended bonus of the 16-team league. Now he'll watch two teams play a game fearing the consequences of a loss more than the euphoria of a win.

To the delight of a big home crowd, the Friars race out to a 10-2 lead. But no deficit is too great for Notre Dame's army of 3-point shooters. Colin Falls, Chris Quinn and Russell Carter have shot the ball well all year and tonight they're joined by freshman Kyle McAlarney's three 3-pointers. The Irish make six threes in the first half and shoot 57 percent to take a 42-38 lead into the half.

Providence's season-long issue has focused on a porous defense. That's the problem again with the season hanging in the balance. Superb freshman point guard Sharaud Curry (25 points) is doing all he can to push the Friars over the top and his 3-pointer with two minutes left cuts Notre Dame's lead to 70-66. But the Friars cannot get the defensive stop they need. Quinn makes all the big plays, including a quick drive past McGrath for a tough score to make it 72-66.

After PC makes one of two free throws with 1:29 left, the Irish get a huge offensive rebound by Torin Francis and the Friars have to start fouling. No doubt steeled by so many close games, Notre Dame's shooters make 9-of-12 shots in the final 48 seconds to close the deal in a 82-75 win.

"It's a heck of a win for us and a long time coming," a happy Brey said. "I thought our seniors helped us with a poised demeanor. They were the rocks that the other guys could rely on."

The feeling in the Providence locker room was funereal. McGrath (3-for-13) went out firing but couldn't find the range on his shot. "We were looking at this as our biggest game. It's as disappointing as it gets," he said.

While all of Providence didn't like the Friars' odds of beating Marquette in the season finale, Welsh wasn't ready to throw in the towel just yet.

"The Big East Tournament did not begin tonight," Welsh said. "We have another game Saturday. We'll get on the plane and go play."

March 5; Syracuse

This is the final day of the regular season and the race to New York isn't over yet. Notre Dame and Louisville (both 6-10) have punched their tickets with wins in the last week. Providence loses at Marquette and will join DePaul on the sidelines. The last spot comes down to St. John's or Rutgers but Quincy Douby makes sure it's no contest. Rutgers' outstanding shooter and the Big East's leading scorer (25.1) fired in 36 points to lead a 82-70 win.

The other game of the day has attracted CBS and a record 33,633 fans to the Carrier Dome. It's not unfair to say everyone has come to see one player. This is Gerry McNamara's day.

"He's a hero here and a hero in Scranton," said teammate Matt Gorman. "He'll be a hero around here forever."

This isn't a good day for G-Mac. As he said after the West Virginia win a week ago, "I'm not happy about it. I'm not thrilled about leaving Syracuse but that's life. It's going to be a tough day for me and my family."

When McNamara signed with Syracuse out of Scranton, Pa., four years ago, no one knew what a phenomenon he would become. It's not that he's the best player Syracuse has ever had. He clearly isn't in the top 10. But the fans of Syracuse, just like the good people of Scranton, fell in love with his gritty game and deep-shooting talents.

After a national championship, a Big East Tournament title last season and countless heroics in the biggest of games, it's time for the ride to end. No one has enjoyed playing at Syracuse more than Gerry McNamara.

"He's a great kid who goes out and gives you everything he's got every time he steps on the floor," said longtime SU assistant Bernie Fine. "He's the little, everyday guy. There's nothing ostentatious about him. He's very down-to-earth. If somebody comes over and asks for an autograph, he signs every one. That's the kind of kid he is."

Scranton lies two hours south of Syracuse and the two cities have bonded through Orange basketball and one special player. Gerry and Joyce McNamara have piled into their Ford Windstar, pointed it north on I-81, and driven through rain, snow and ice so often the car could probably drive itself.

"Gerry's thrilled by the way his four years turned out," said Gerry, Sr. "It's been a ride that unless you've experienced it, it's hard to explain. I don't know if anybody's taken a ride quite like this."

While winning the national title as a freshman, becoming a national star and scoring more than 2,000 points under the Syracuse spotlight would make any father proud, what's truly stunning is the reaction McNamara's career received back home. He was obviously a major high school star and his prep games were almost always sold out but Scranton has lived their favorite son's career every step of the way. McNamara's uncle, Jimmy Connors, is a former mayor. He's helped organize bus trips to SU games that morphed into the hottest ticket in town. For today's game against Villanova, 64 busses carrying nearly 3,000 people made it to the Dome.

"I've lived in Scranton all my life and I know a lot of people there because my brother-in-law was the mayor for 12 years but I see more people at the Dome in one night than I see in a week back home. It's just incredible," McNamara said. "We played down at the Garden (vs. St. John's) and there was 26 inches of snow and there were three bus loads there that day."

McNamara has a unique relationship with Boeheim, who clearly savors every moment young Gerry is under his watch. Losing him will hurt the coach as much as it will the father who won't be able to jump in his car and watch his son play out his childhood dreams anymore.

"The first time I met Coach Boeheim, he told me that when Gerry comes to Syracuse he would play 30 minutes a game because he's that good," said McNamara. "He said 'I'm a man of my word.' So I said 'I'm a man of my word, too, so I'll hold you to yours.' He laughed and said 'no problem.' He's done that and more, from day one.

"I think the relationship between the two of them is so good because they think alike. When Gerry's out there running the team, he knows what Boeheim wants. It's like two eyes at the same time. They're amazing to watch together. After a game, they can win by 20 points but they talk to each other and they know what the other is thinking. It's what every coach always hopes for. He also knows that the toughest critic that Gerry has is Gerry himself. I think that their personalities are very much alike."

The game is also difficult for young Gerry McNamara because his Syracuse team needs a win to creep closer to an elusive NCAA bid. The Orange is 7-8 and a win over a top five team like Villanova would all but clinch a berth. Before the action starts, a children's chorus sings 'McNamara's Band' and Boeheim and school Chancellor Nancy Cantor present the star of the day with his jersey. McNamara wipes away tears and says later "the whole day was emotional for me."

Once the action starts, the fans' favorite is struggling a bit. By the second half, Syracuse is down 81-69 with just over four minutes remaining. Then, almost on cue, McNamara hits back-to-back 3-pointers. He drains another three with three minutes left to make it 83-78 as the crowd is standing and chanting "Ger-ry, Ger-ry."

But the storybook finish is extinguished by Randy Foye, Kyle Lowry and the rest of the Wildcats who hold on for a 92-82 win. McNamara scores 29 points but has no bullets left and with 46 seconds left, Boeheim pulls him from the game and a curtain call for the ages fills the Dome. As he comes off the floor, McNamara hugs Boeheim, is swarmed by some teammates and eventually slumps on the bench and buries his face on the shoulder of Syracuse assistant coach Mike Hopkins as a national TV audience looks on. "I'm glad coach took me out when he did because I don't know how much longer I could've held it together," McNamara says.

The congratulatory bouquets continue in the post-game but Boeheim sums up the day best when he says, "Gerry McNamara's going to be remembered for his work here, not for one game or two or 10 or 20 or 30. You look at the four-year career that he's had here and you really don't need to say anything. He did it all."

$$\left(\textbf{16} \right)$$

March 7; New York City

Tonight is the evening where the Big East opens its prize vault. The conference not only introduces its player, coach, defender and rookie of the year but also holds a big banquet in the ballroom of the Grand Hyatt Hotel for the 12 teams participating in the conference tournament.

Over the years, players have squired home leather jackets, sweat suits and boom boxes. This year, everyone enjoys some steak and a door prize. The players and coaches at Providence, St. John's, DePaul and South Florida get their trinkets in the mail.

Before the celebration kicks off, Mike Tranghese holds a half-hour news briefing in an adjacent conference room. As usual, he is engaging and forthcoming and with Connecticut and Villanova sitting 1-2 in the polls and as many as 10 teams still clinging to NCAA tourney hopes, he has plenty to smile about. Even a heavy touch of the flu that will end up sending him home for most of the week's events can't dampen his spirits.

"It's been an unbelievable year, starting with the very first game when Marquette beat Connecticut and Stevie Novak went for 41 points." he said. "From there things just got better."

Reporters from around the East pepper the commissioner with queries about the conference's pluses and minuses, everything from the qualifications of teams for the NCAA's to the unbalanced schedule that helped keep some teams home this week.

"Gary Walters (of the NCAA's tournament committee) has the Big East and he knows the Big East, inside and out," Tranghese said. "He dissected our schedules before we even started playing. We just went through it again on the phone this week. Syracuse has played a schedule that's as difficult as anyone. They've played Connecticut twice, Villanova twice. I think they can get rewarded for that."

He wouldn't back off the merits of the unbalanced schedule, either. While the league is committed to all teams playing each other at least once, that won't happen until 2007-08.

"At the top, I know some of the coaches don't want to hear me but I will argue that all the unbalanced schedule does is provide more opportunities to get important wins," he said. "There's no way you can get into the tournament without quality wins. Those games they complain about, those are the ones you need to win. My concern is at the bottom or the middle. Do they get enough chances? If you're only playing Connecticut and Villanova and West Virginia once and you don't beat them, then you're under a lot of pressure to win these other games. The selection committee wants to see who you've beaten and who you've beaten on the road."

Several questions include references to the Ratings Percentage Index, a measuring stick of a team's achievement and schedule strength.

"Personally, I'd like to blow the RPI up. I wanted to blow it up when I was on the committee. The RPI cannot tell you what you need to know. They can talk to me until they're blue in the face. You look at games, see who've people played. There are too many flaws in the RPI," he says.

It's clear that the Big East has six teams already in the NCAA's. UConn and Villanova are favorites for number one seeds. Pittsburgh, West Virginia, Marquette and Georgetown are safe as well. But with jumpy nerves at Syracuse, Seton Hall and Cincinnati, Tranghese needs to campaign just like the leaders of other leagues.

"I can tell you our coaches are nervous about it. They always will be," he says. "I could have 16 teams who were 26-0 and they'd still be nervous. That's coaches. But I am absolutely convinced that no one will get left out because of the size of our conference. I just think that's a fallacy."

That 8-10 teams are in contention for a coveted NCAA bid is the Big East's greatest strength. A league with 16 teams naturally must have more good teams (and bad ones) than smaller ones. In a great year like this one, the Big East is a near-lock to break the record of seven bids awarded to one conference.

"Long-term the strength of this conference is its depth," he said. "Just look at what we have here this week. I know one thing, Pitt is not happy about playing Louisville. Georgetown isn't thrilled about playing Notre Dame. Those are tough games. Cincinnati and Syracuse, they're fighting for their lives. I don't know if we've ever seen games like this in the first round. These are wars. And I don't think this is a one-time thing. I think we'll see this every year where there are a lot of teams on the board in position to get into the tournament and they'll be playing each other."

The Big East names Randy Foye its Player of the Year, Jay Wright the Coach of the Year, Dominic James the top rookie, Hilton Armstrong the Defensive Player of the Year and Aaron Gray Most Improved. Wright, looking dapper as always in a double-breasted, pinstriped suit, is thrilled to win the award for the first time.

"This is a humbling experience looking at the other coaches in our league," he said. "I voted for Louis Orr. He did a great job. I don't think we all realize what this league is all about yet. This weekend will help. Notre Dame is the last team to get in the conference tournament and we were lucky, very lucky, to beat them. Our point guard (Kyle Lowry) tipped in a shot at the buzzer or we would've lost. And they're our 12th team."

The Big East's coaches love James and Tom Crean knows he's lucky to have him. Crean is one of the country's top young coaches, someone everyone in the conference respects. He came of age as an assistant at Pittsburgh and working for Tom Izzo with Michigan State's national championship team in 2000. His excitement to coach again at the Big East Tournament fills his body.

"Madison Square Garden is such a great feeling," he says. "You're sitting in the locker room before the game and hearing the crowd, it's like they're right on top of you. There are walls and concrete separating you but you can still feel it. Anybody that tries to downplay the feeling of playing in this tournament, in this arena, really isn't telling the truth. It's a big time thing."

Off in a corner standing away from the award winners is George Blaney. At 66, he's the oldest assistant coach – and some say the best – in the league. He's certainly the most experienced. Blaney enjoyed a great head coaching career at Holy Cross, leading the Crusaders to seven 20-win seasons and frequently knocking heads with Dave Gavitt's best Providence teams in the 1970's. He jumped to Seton Hall in 1994 but ran into problems following a great run by P.J. Carlesimo and left coaching with 459 wins over 30 years.

Jim Calhoun, an old friend from New England's basketball circles, asked Blaney to join him in Storrs in 2000 and he happily accepted the offer. Now he is Calhoun's right hand, the coach who's always in the office helping run one of the elite programs in the country. This year, Blaney's job hasn't been easy. The Huskies' off-the-court issues are heavy and on the floor he knows as much as anyone that anything less than a national title won't go over easily.

"From a team standpoint, it's been as easy a season as we've had because of the type of kids they are," Blaney said. "They're a fun group to be around, they enjoy each other, they're pretty loose. More than some of the other groups we've had. I think it's being 27-2. When you have only two losses, it's harder to get upset at anybody."

Blaney has helped tutor veterans Armstrong, Denham Brown and Rashad Anderson and really enjoyed sculpting the talents of Rudy Gay and Marcus Williams.

"Our 2004 team had Ben (Gordon) and Emeka (Okafor) and Taliek (Brown) was the heart of the team. This team has more answers, if not those kind of dominant answers," Blaney says. "It could be Hilton one night, Josh another night, Rudy the next night, Denham, Marcus, or any group of those guys together."

Blaney is asked how an All-American like Gay, the unquestioned top NBA prospect in the conference, can leave award night empty-handed.

"It's not like Rudy has caused us to lose a lot of games," Blaney says with a smile. "I think it's his place in the pecking order, really. I think the great expectations have been hard on him but I don't see that it's a whole lot different than it was for Ben (Gordon) in his sophomore year. It takes a great player a long time to realize how great he can really be. It took Caron until late in his sophomore year. It took Ben until his junior year. Rudy is late in his sophomore year and he doesn't know it yet. But the numbers are still there because of his talent."

Blaney may not say it but he's also a bit miffed that UConn's 14-2 conference record can be so easily dismissed. "Do people really realize how good a coach Jim is," he asks. "I think that's also a reflection of where Jim has taken the program. The expectations are so enormous and in a state like Connecticut where they have the coverage that we do, it makes it almost impossible to live up to those expectations."

Blaney is asked how he thinks his team is playing, if it's ready for the post-season run that the entire East has feared for months. "I think we're a good group, we could use another penetrator but we're playing well right now," he says. "I don't see us losing a number one seed if we lose here but our goal is to win this tournament. No one is looking at the NCAA's. We're looking at this pretty hard. Championships mean a great deal to Jim and he really likes winning here in New York against all our friends."

March 8; New York City

It's tournament day in New York. At last.

This is what the players and coaches have worked so hard for, the start of the post-season where the stars become legends and dreams go to die. For most of the 12 teams in New York, this week's games are only about improving seeding in the following week's NCAA Tournament. For others, it's the last gasp at an NCAA bid.

For everyone, however, it's a chance to play in one of the special settings in the sport. New York and college basketball have been great dance partners for years, dating as far back as the 1930s. The city first embraced the game when the City College of New York and New York University traded places as the top dog. Legions of fans were weaned on the game at the 'old' Madison Square Garden, a dark, historic building at 50th Street and 8th Avenue that overflowed with memories of great players and greater teams.

Many of those heroes came to life in the National Invitation Tournament, the post-season tourney of choice from the 1930s until well into the 1960s when UCLA's dominance helped elevate the stature of the NCAA Tournament. New York basketball revolved around Red Holtzman's Knicks in the 1970s, a special era dominated by two championship teams and the flash and dash of stars Walt Frazier, Earl 'The Pearl' Monroe and Willis Reed.

Those Knicks helped christen the 'New Garden' that operates today. The building sits 15 blocks downtown from the original and lies atop the city's Pennsylvania rail station. The area is a 24-hour hub of activity with trains snaking in and out of town to Long Island, New Jersey and all across the East as fans pour into the Garden several times a week to see the Knicks, the Rangers, the Westchester Dog Show, the rodeo, the circus and every other event imaginable.

But when the Garden hosts basketball, a special magic fills the air and the Big East Tournament has become a Garden staple. The league shifted its first three tournaments from the Providence Civic Center to the Carrier Dome to the Hartford Civic Center before Gavitt struck what became one of the conference's most important deals with Madison Square Garden.

For the next 23 years, Big East week at the Garden grew into a must ticket for basketball people from Boston to Washington, D.C. For years, Gavitt sat with Boston Celtic legend Red Auerbach in the same loge section 15 rows off the floor. Jerry West, Jerry Colangelo, Billy Cunningham and other NBA scouts often sat nearby, not to mention celebs like Donald Trump and Spike Lee.

"The Garden has been good to us and we've been good for the Garden," is the way Gavitt puts it.

"I still get goose bumps when I walk into the Garden. It's just different," said Tranghese. "There are a lot of other great tournaments in the country but I think we have the best venue in America. It's been a great home for us."

"I almost feel bad for these conferences that move their tournament around," said Syracuse's Jim Boeheim. "We have it perfect, playing in New York. The kids really appreciate that, too.

The scene in and around the Garden for Big East week is unique. It's only 10 a.m. and Seventh Avenue is awash in orange (Syracuse) sweatshirts, red (Cincinnati) windbreakers and blue and gold (Notre Dame) jackets and hats. Sounds of one pep band after another waft through the plaza that lead to the building's gates. Two of New York's leading sports radio stations, including ESPN's ubiquitous Stephen A. Smith, have set up shop outside the front door.

The 19,594 tickets for each session were all sold to the 16 Big East schools. For the first time, not a single ticket was available to the general public. Scalpers love the fact that the Big East is hot. One 30-something man, who shot back a 'you've got to be kidding me,' look when asked if he wanted to give his first name to a reporter, said, "tickets for college basketball are bad all year. We can't give St. John's tickets away. This is big. Thursday afternoon with Connecticut will be real big. Friday night's semifinals are huge. I just need more tickets."

The conference tournament is a major money maker for the Big East's 16 schools and is the central piece of the TV deal with ESPN, which telecasts the entire event. The network has two full crews on hand to work the day-night doubleheaders but that's only part of the media blitz in town. A back area of the Garden is cordoned off by large blue curtains and filled by newspaper, TV and radio staffers from all over the country.

"I got here at 10:15 and there were four members of The Horde already here. And they don't play until tomorrow," said Jim O'Connell, the Hall of Fame writer from the Associated Press.

The two teams with the most at stake all weekend meet in the first game of the day. Cincinnati won 19 games and finished 8-8 in its first trip through the Big East. A two-point loss to Villanova at home likely cost the Bearcats a clear-cut spot in the NCAA's but a 78-75 win over West Virginia in the season finale clearly improved Andy Kennedy's chances.

The Bearcats face Syracuse, whose NCAA chances are on life support. The Orangemen (19-11, 7-9) have lost three in a row (Georgetown, DePaul, Villanova) and none by less than 10 points. Boeheim has talked about the strength of the league but even he can't politic his team into the big tournament without a win (or two) here this week.

Cincy jumps out to a quick lead but a Gerry McNamara 3-pointer and a tip-in by Mookie Watkins tie things up and set up a seesaw first half. Watkins and Terrence Roberts are playing well, always a good barometer for the Orange. Two Watkins layups give SU a 30-21 lead but Cincy gets back in the game before the end of the half and cuts the lead to 39-34 at the break.

Syracuse breaks fast in the second half and builds a 50-36 lead after five minutes. But Cincinnati starts to slowly whittle the lead down behind seniors James White and Eric Hicks and a pesky defense. A 57-44 Orange lead is cut to just 62-60 with just under eight minutes left after a Devan Downey floater in the lane. Downey strips Eric Devendorf at midcourt with 3:39 left for a layup that gives Cincy the lead, 67-66, and sets up a finish for the ages.

First, White nails a 3-pointer to put the Bearcats up, 70-68, with 2:25 left. Syracuse misses at the other end but White misses another trey and Watkins dunks to tie it up with 1:14 left. White takes an ill-advised three and misses and Roberts takes a nice pass from McNamara on a pick-and-roll and is fouled going to the hoop. He makes one of two foul shots to put Syracuse back up, 71-70, with 30 seconds left. Cincy goes right back to White and this time he delivers by knocking down a 13-footer with 10 seconds left for a 72-71 lead.

Panicked by the moment, Syracuse's Demetris Nichols looks for McNamara on the inbounds but instead throws to Devendorf and Downey steps in front and makes a steal. He's instantly fouled and hits the first of two free throws for a 73-71 lead. But the freshman misses the second shot and gives Syracuse a chance.

Cincy wastes a foul with six seconds left but McNamara takes the inbounds pass, rushes up the court, goes behind his back to get past Jihad Muhammad just inside half-court and lofts a one-handed runner as Hicks rushes at him. The ball hits nothing but net and pandemonium erupts at the Garden. A check of the TV monitor shows McNamara's foot is clearly outside the 3-point line so the Orange lead, 74-73, with 0.5 seconds on the clock.

Muhammad catches the inbounds near midcourt and heaves a shot that nearly goes, hitting the front of the rim and bouncing away. "That was the longest point-three seconds ever," McNamara said. "I was right there with (Muhammad) and when he shot it I watched and said to myself, 'it's in.'"

As two exhausted teams walked off the court, McNamara made sure to look back to the baseline and into a sea of orange. He quickly caught his parents eyes and waved, just as he always does before he walks off the floor.

Right after the game, the media filed into a large, open wing under the Garden stands for a news conference. The coaches are always the stars of these rituals but some are better than others. Boeheim is one of the very best. So are seasoned players like McNamara and when the two walk to the podium, they are armed and ready.

Boeheim has repeatedly said that his star has made more winning shots than any player he's ever coached but this one took things to another level.

"I think with the situation we're in, under the circumstances, this is probably the most important shot that I've hit," McNamara said. "In the situation we're in, we're fighting and trying to battle for every game. We needed this one. There was no doubt about it."

He went on to describe a truly pulsating shot, one that drew the breath out of the sold out Garden.

"I wanted to take what I got," he said. "You know, if I'm going to take a runner, I'm not gonna step on the (3-point) line. I made sure I was behind the line. Plus there wasn't much time so I wouldn't have gotten a layup."

Then things got hot. Before the game, Boeheim was tipped off on a note in that day's Syracuse Post-Standard where reporters Mike Waters and Kim Baxter had polled several assistant coaches in the league and asked their opinions on various subjects. In between categories like 'Best Dunker' and 'Worst Referee' was 'Most Overrated Player.' The response to that one read, 'Sorry Syracuse fans, but Gerry McNamara gets the nod here. He got more than twice as many votes as Rudy Gay and Taquan Dean, the next nearest competitors.'

This slight followed a Feb. 8 column in the Syracuse student newspaper, the Daily Orange, which also criticized McNamara. During a question about the play of center Darryl Watkins, Boeheim interrupted and opened fire.

"I have to laugh a little bit when our own paper, our own student paper, is calling him 'overrated.' They actually listened to a couple of assistant coaches who I guarantee will NEVER be head coaches if they think Gerry McNamara is overrated.

"Without Gerry McNamara we wouldn't have won 10 fucking games this year. Ok? Not 10. The other guys just aren't ready. They needed him. Without him, we wouldn't be here to even have a chance to win this game. And everybody's talking to me and writing about Gerry McNamara being overrated? That's the most bullshit thing I've seen in 30 years. And especially when it comes from people in our own papers. An anonymous assistant coach. Let the assistant coach come up to me and say 'Gerry McNamara is overrated.' He's been double-teamed every game this year and the coaches voted him first team All-Conference. The head coaches. They don't know shit, I guess."

The curse words were vintage Boeheim. In such a formal setting, 99 percent of coaches refrain from using foul language. But he always tells you what he feels, rules be damned. If he feels you're wrong, he's singling you out and slicing and dicing you. Don't like it? Too bad.

Boeheim has exploded at other Big East Tournaments. His best performance came back in the early 80s after a loss to Patrick Ewing's Georgetown team in the championship game. Ewing had taken a roundhouse swipe at his star player, Pearl Washington, but came up air and stayed in the game. Ewing had also decked his burly center, Andre Hawkins, and Boeheim's frustration at both incidents caused him to pound the interview table and spew invective at the game's referees.

McNamara was as upset as his coach when he found out about this latest slight. He had read the 'overrated' column in the Daily Orange back in February and called the writer out on it. But he hadn't seen the coach's poll just yet. "A poll of assistant coaches? Wow. That's amazing," McNamara said. "I wish I was a head coach. Coach Boeheim said everything I would say. We lose a couple of games and we're getting blasted from all sides."

Back in his locker room, Boeheim was still a bit steamed. "Why I was so mad up there was people saying 'well, he's not shooting good this year.' That's bullshit," he said. "When I take him out, teams press and steal the ball. Over and over. These other guys aren't ready for that. We have a freshman guard and a sophomore guard. They're just not ready. Gerry has to be on the court. When he's not, no one can get anyone else the ball. We can't play without him.

"Now is he the best player in the league? No. But he's the most important player in the league. When Allan Ray is hurt, Villanova wins. When somebody at Connecticut doesn't play well, they win. Two guys don't play well and they still win. If Gerry doesn't play well for us, we can't even be in the game. That's how important he is. He's won one hundred-and-something games for us and he's the main guy with the ball in his hands. All he did was win the national championship, win the Big East Tournament and his NCAA record is 8-2. How many guys have won 80 percent of their games in the NCAA Tournament? Not too many."

With the fantastic finish, Syracuse has improved its record to 20-11. In the history of the Big East, 100 of 102 teams that have won 20 or more games have moved on to the NCAA's. In between games, TV's around the Garden are tuned to ESPN and the network replays McNamara's shot over and over. Analysts, including the influential Dick Vitale, quickly begin debating the Orange's NCAA chances. As the last few reporters leave his locker room, Boeheim is asked if he thinks his team is in the big tournament.

"I don't usually say it, but our league is so much better than these other leagues. It's not even close," he said. "Just look at the teams. That doesn't mean we're going to win the NCAA but we have so many good teams. I can't say it yet but I think we're in trouble and not just because we play Connecticut next. Our RPI after tomorrow will be the same as Cincinnati's. We beat them two out of three times but it shouldn't be us or them. They should be in. And so should we."

The other three games on day one are a big letdown after McNamara's heroics. Notre Dame's tough-luck season ends with a 67-63 loss to Georgetown. It is Mike Brey's 11th loss against a Big East team on the season and each has come by six points or less. The Irish may love New York but the Fighting Irish are now 3-11 all-time in the Big East Tournament.

The first game of the night session features the Battle of New Jersey with one coach on the hot seat (Louis Orr) and another on ice (Gary Waters). The game is horrific, a rock fight dominated by Seton Hall's awful shooting. Rutgers leads 50-38 with five minutes left and the Hall never mounts much of a charge and loses rather meekly, 61-48. The quick analysis has the Pirates (18-11) in deep trouble and on the NCAA bubble come Sunday afternoon.

"I feel confident in what we've done," said Pirate coach Louis Orr. "I'm going there with the anticipation of hearing our name called on Sunday. I'm a guy that does a lot of praying anyway, so I will continue to pray. I know God is a good God. He's got good things in store for this team. I'm going to keep the faith."

The final game sees Pittsburgh face Louisville, a horrible match up for the Cardinals. Rick Pitino's team isn't suited for the push-and-shove, grinding game that the Panthers put their foes through. When The 'Ville fails to score in the opening eight minutes and falls behind 16-0, the team's fans are more red-faced than their Cardinal dress shirts. A Taquan Dean 3-pointer makes it

22-5 but the nightmare only gets worse as Pitt races to a 33-5 lead and ends the half up, 39-16.

After a halftime tirade by Pitino, the Cards come out of the locker room with much more energy. They storm back thanks to a press and some 3-point shooting, outscoring Pitt 22-5 to make the score 48-38 with five minutes left. Louisville keeps charging and a Dean 3-pointer with 24 seconds left cuts the lead to 57-54. Pitt's Carl Krauser and Antonio Graves make free throws down the stretch to end the charge and extinguish any Louisville hopes for some New York magic.

Pitino comes into the interview area and a reporter asks him to talk about his team's comeback. "It's your question," he says. "You want me to play reporter, you come up here."

He then talks about a truly awful first half. "We just got destroyed on the backboard, and then panicked a little bit and took bad shots and got weighed down because of it. But the rebounding was so dominant on one side. We were just taken to the woodshed on the glass."

He then sums up the season when he describes the first 10 minutes and says, "it's one of those nights where in the first five or six minutes everything goes wrong and if you're a veteran team, you can play through it. If you're a good defensive team as far as size, you can get through it. We're not an overly physical basketball team. We just couldn't get through that stretch."

With that, Pitino walks off the podium with his eyes fixed on a stat sheet and the floor in front of him. A reporter takes a step toward him and begins to ask a question but the security guard Pitino always travels with halts the man. "Not now. He's all done."

(17)

Thursday, March 9

New York City awakens to find Gerry McNamara on the back pages of the city's tabloids. 'McNAMARA-CLE' screams a headline in the New York Post. While Syracuse fans wake up with celebratory hangovers and chants of 'Gerry-Gerry' ringing in their ears, Jim Boeheim and his coaching staff spent Wednesday night worrying about the large roadblock sitting between them and the NCAA Tournament: No. 1 ranked Connecticut.

The Orangemen were handled easily in their two matchups with UConn, cutting a 25-point deficit to eight in garbage time at home and getting whacked by 23 in Hartford. More than any other coach, Boeheim has sung the Huskies' praises all year.

"Connecticut is a great team. I've said it from the beginning of the year," he said. "Jim (Calhoun) keeps telling me not to say it. They're a great team. There's no way to hide it, you know. We were not in either game when we played them."

Over the years, Syracuse has knocked virtually every Big East team around a bit in March but not Connecticut. The Orange did beat UConn on the way to the 2005 Big East title but since Calhoun came to Storrs, Syracuse is 2-5 versus the Huskies in the Big East Tournament.

UConn-Syracuse kicks off the quarterfinal round. And the Orangemen start fast, still on fire from the day before. Three layups get Syracuse rolling and when Marcus Williams fouls McNamara while he's hoisting a 3-pointer, SU's leader drains three free throws for a 10-0 lead. Before the game is three minutes old, Calhoun has pulled Hilton Armstrong, Marcus Williams and Denham Brown in disgust. That type of shuffling continues throughout the half as Calhoun searches for something to wake his team up. After a UConn flurry, Syracuse answers with Terrence Roberts scoring every which way on the Huskies' vaunted frontline. UConn counterpunches to cut the lead to two with two minutes left but the Orangemen end the half with two Roberts' dunks and an Eric Devendorf 3-pointer to lead at the break, 39-28.

"Syracuse, just as we thought, that shot yesterday carried their momentum right into this game," Calhoun said. "They took it right to us. We were the team that looked slow."

The one thing UConn did right in the half was frustrate McNamara once again. He's 0-of-4 from the floor but is passing superbly with 10 assists. UConn loses him early in the second half and McNamara's first 3-pointer of the game pushes Syracuse's lead to 14 points, 49-35. UConn settles down and finally starts to play its game but McNamara's second trey of the day keeps the underdogs up, 65-56, with 6:35 left.

But that's when the real UConn makes its run. Williams answers with a 3-pointer of his own and a Rashad Anderson steal leads to a big Rudy Gay dunk. A rebound foul at the other end on Darryl Watkins gives Armstrong two free throws and the lead is down to two. Another rebound foul, this time on Roberts, sends Armstrong to the line again and he makes two more free throws to tie the score, 65-65, with 5:09 left and sets up a frantic finish.

The game is still tied at 69-69 with two minutes left when Devendorf deflects a Williams' shot and takes a long feed for an easy layup. Gay misses a 3-pointer with 40 seconds left but McNamara rolls his ankle chasing a loose rebound and UConn gets another chance. This time, Mr. Big Shot delivers. Anderson, a senior who falls out of bed ready to shoot, bombs away and swishes a corner 3-pointer that gives UConn the lead, 72-71. Syracuse looks for McNamara at the other end but he can't get the ball and reserve guard Josh Wright squeezes into the lane and misses an open 10-footer. Brown rebounds and is fouled. With 11 seconds on the clock, Brown makes two free throws to push the lead to 74-71. Calhoun calls time-out.

"We talked a great deal about who to play McNamara," Calhoun said later. "We thought about one of the younger guys, maybe Craig Austrie, Marcus Johnson, Rob Garrison. But we stuck with Rashad because he's done a good job on him. I said to him 'the only job you have is to deny the ball to McNamara.' Denham had Devendorf and we told him to let him catch it."

In the Syracuse huddle, Boeheim was also preparing for someone else to shoot. "I told him to drive and throw it to one of three guys. He looked at me and said 'Can I shoot it?' I said, 'They're not gonna let you shoot it. But if they do, shoot it.'"

With everyone in the packed Garden (except those wearing Husky blue and white) pulling for the Orange, Syracuse ran a quick cut in the backcourt and inbounded the ball to Devendorf. The move somehow caused Anderson to lose McNamara and with Calhoun stomping his foot and screaming 'Rashad!' the SU star caught the ball as he neared midcourt. Josh Boone, UConn's 6-10 center started to come at the ball but wouldn't leave Watkins alone under the hoop. McNamara seized the opening, pulled up from about 24 feet and swished the tying 3-pointer with 5.5 seconds left.

Marcus Williams quickly pushed the ball up the floor, snuck into the lane and lofted a lefty runner that rolled off the rim and sent the game into overtime.

"The thing was I stopped (and shot) pretty far out. I think that's why it mixed them up a little bit," McNamara said. "I took the shot early just in case I did miss it. I stopped behind the NBA line. I did it quick because I wanted to get the shot off clean.

Williams agreed that McNamara's quick shot approach stunned the Huskies a bit. "We were saying that we'd foul him if it's under 10 seconds but he pulled up really fast beyond the NBA line. He made a tough shot."

Syracuse went back up in the overtime and this time Connecticut couldn't escape. Two McNamara free throws gave SU a 83-78 lead with 48 seconds left. A contested 3-pointer by Brown from the right corner cut the lead to 83-81 but Watkins (a 50 percent foul shooter) made two free throws. Brown drained yet another tough 3-pointer with 18 seconds left to cut the lead to 85-84. This time UConn fouled McNamara. He made the first free throw but shockingly missed the second, giving UConn a chance to tie with 17 seconds left.

Williams again took the last shot and missed, but UConn tied the ball up and had the possession arrow with 5.6 seconds left. Williams took the inbounds pass and missed an open 10-footer and when both Boone and Gay couldn't get follow-up tips to fall, Syracuse's run was alive and kicking.

With cheers ringing in his ears, Boeheim walks over to ESPN's crew and asks Sean McDonough and Bill Raftery "are we in now?' Boeheim's month-long trip on the bubble is finally over.

"I've been there before and it's not pleasant," he said. "I thought we could've gotten in after (the Cincinnati win) but it would've been 50-50. I think we should've moved ahead of Cincinnati but I don't know if (the committee) would've seen it that way. We didn't really talk about it. The kids might talk about it but I just get them focused to play. We played really good today. That was something. Gerry has not penetrated like that. They all usually stop and watch him. Today the big guys moved and they were getting layups."

UConn scored 84 points but shot just 30 percent from the field and generated a lot of its offense through 23 offensive rebounds. "Against a zone, you have to get a feel for the game and today they had guys in and then they're out. In and out," Boeheim said.

Calhoun is gracious after the loss and tells the media that his players will head back to the Drake Hotel, pack and bus back to Storrs.

"I'm proud of the way the kids came back," he said. "I'm incredibly, incredibly disappointed in the loss and incredibly disappointed in myself. I would have changed a couple things in the last two, three minutes and into overtime. But we'll go home at 27-3 and give some people a chance to write."

Even after what was clearly a stinging loss, Calhoun somehow had his feud with The Horde on his mind. It seems that after the Huskies clinched the regular season championship with a win over Louisville, Hartford Courant columnist Jeff Jacobs wasn't at the game and wrote a story on the future of the Greater Hartford Open. The coach couldn't understand why and says he heard Jacobs would only write about the team again once it lost.

"By the way, there is some good news," he said near the top of his post-game remarks. "A couple of guys in our state can now write about us. We won a championship on Saturday and they wrote about horse racing or the GHO. The only thing I feel good about is some of those columnists who haven't wrote about us the last couple days – and they've been writing about everything else – they said they were only going to write about us when we lost. And, by the way, that's a true statement. It's not bullshit. They said 'we'll write about him when he loses.' So now you got a chance to write."

Toward the end of UConn's press conference, Calhoun realized it was time to look ahead and said, "this team is to be reckoned with in the NCAA Tournament. This team has a chance to get itself to Indianapolis and, just like anybody else, has a chance to go home."

Even after he left the podium, Calhoun couldn't stop talking. As the words fell off his lips in rapid fire, you could sense his temper rising and falling, his frustration clearly leaving him empty.

"The bottom line is it has a raw feel to it," he said. "Some games you say 'well, we didn't show up and play very well.' This one has a raw feeling because when your team responds the way we did respond and makes all those clutch plays and has a lead with 11 seconds to go. You're right there.

"It's one of the most hurtful losses we've ever had here at Madison Square Garden. We should've won and closed this one out," Calhoun told a smaller group of reporters. "I'll go back to the Drake, tell Pat (his wife) to pack, drive home and cry. We don't want to go home and rest. We wanted to win."

The second game of the afternoon doubleheader isn't as thrilling as Syracuse-UConn but it certainly wasn't bad. Georgetown and Marquette struggle through a sluggish first half (22-22 tie) but crank it up in the last 20 minutes and race to the finish. Steve Novak fires from all over, pours in six 3-pointers but fouls out down the stretch. Star freshman Dominic James makes just 2-of-15 shots and trailing 62-59 with the ball for the final shot, James over-dribbles and passes up the tying shot. Instead he gives the ball to Jerel McNeal with precious few seconds left and his shot misses badly.

As the horn sounds, Marquette coach Tom Crean darts right to midcourt to comfort McNeal. The two embrace and Crean comes back to the sideline to shake hands with the Hoyas' John Thompson III.

"He's my guy, he's our guy," Crean said. "I mean we wouldn't be in New York without guys like Steve (Novak), Dominic and Jerel, this whole group. He took a shot and he'll take it again and he'll make it. It's just his freshman year."

Thompson has a unique sense of Big East history and he puts everything into perspective when he says, "it's Georgetown-Syracuse in the Garden. That says it all if anybody knows anything about the history of this league."

Thompson is asked what the two wins in New York have done to improve his team's NCAA seeding but he cuts off the question. "That's too big-picture for me. I don't think big picture. We'll figure that out once this tournament is over. Then we'll start thinking about the NCAA, hopefully the NCAA. Right now it's not time to sit back and say 'ooh, look at what these two wins did.' Hopefully we're sitting here Saturday night saying 'look at what these four wins did.' That's what we want to do."

The start of the Big East Tournament reflects the craziness of the regular season. Just 28 points decide the opening six games as memorable finishes captivate the country and lead ESPN's Championship Week highlights. That streak ends on Thursday night when No. 2 Villanova begins its postseason by blowing out Rutgers in the second half for a 87-55 win. Allan Ray pours in 26 points and leads all four 'Nova starters in double figures.

The second game has plenty of sizzle with a renewal of the Backyard Brawl and two sure-fire NCAA teams in Pittsburgh and West Virginia. The Panthers (15th) and Mountaineers (19th) are both ranked, a rarity for a conference quarterfinal game. The Mountaineers come out firing and nail six 3-pointers in the first half to claim a 31-24 lead at halftime. But the second half is a different story. Aaron Gray (19 points, 15 rebounds) and Sam Young (14 points, 11 rebounds) rip apart the Mountaineer defense and lead a 68-57 win. WVU is the third of the four teams that earned first round byes to lose.

West Virginia's patterned offense created good shots like it always does but tonight the ball doesn't go in. Afterward, John Beilein is asked if running into an athletic team like Pitt in the NCAA's concerns him.

"I mean, I've been concerned all year that we weren't as athletic as we were last year. D'or Fischer and Tyrone Sally were very quick, very good defensive players," Beilein said. "Any time we lose, I'm concerned. But we played a very difficult schedule. We came in here and we're probably the only three seed in the country that played a team that was a six seed that was higher ranked than us. It wasn't like we came in here and lost to Cupcake U. This was a heck of a team we just lost to that I think had a tremendous season. There's a reason why they're nationally ranked and ahead of us in both RPI and the rankings."

Friday, March 10

The Big East Tournament may be nirvana for any blue-blooded fan of basketball in the East but for the assistant coaches of the teams that advance, it's a major grind. But Mike Hopkins isn't complaining.

Hopkins crunches much of the tape for the Syracuse staff and while he's thrilled with the stunning wins over Cincinnati and Connecticut, he's also tired. But it's a good tired. "Hey, we needed them both and we got them both. You can't ask for more but everyone's dead tired," he says.

Hopkins has seen more Gerry McNamara moments than anyone in Syracuse. He recruited the kid from Scranton where he hit big shots all over the state of Pennsylvania. He's watched him light up Syracuse teammates in practice for four years and carved out a sacred spot among the school's all-time greats in big arenas nationwide.

"But nothing like this," Hopkins said in the lobby of Syracuse's hotel, the East Side Marriott. "We were watching the Connecticut game and it's almost funny. Rob Murphy (another SU assistant) was sitting there and he's never experienced anything like this before with Gerry and he's laughing. I saw him in high school hit four last-second shots in the same game. The same game. I saw the BYU game where he went for 43 in the NCAA's. So it's not that surprising to me."

Like any gym rat, McNamara's drug lies in the competition. He'll often bet teammates in a trick shot ritual that is downright scary, if not prophetic considering the events of the last two days.

"After practice, Gerry shoots halfcourt shots," Hopkins said. "He's like that kid in the gym who instead of working on his game, he'll try circus shots. Behind the backboard, hook shots. We have 'Syracuse' painted out near mid-court and he'll go down the alphabet and let it fly from the S, then the Y and so forth. And he makes them."

Hopkins is standing in the lobby, nursing a bottle of water, waiting for tonight's semifinal doubleheader. After two big wins, the Orangemen are playing with house money. The Garden has become McNamara's stage and it's Georgetown's chance to knock him off. What the public doesn't know is he's played with major pain, the type that no man enjoys. A lingering groin injury has morphed into some type of ugly infection that is hard to even look at.

"The kid can't walk, do you understand? He's all swollen up there. Bill Raftery likes to say 'onions!' Hey, this is Idaho potatoes. He's taking three-hour ice baths. He basically said he couldn't move to his left. It's nasty.

"That's not an excuse but we just don't know how far he can go playing for the third straight day," Hopkins said. "What is amazing to me is that he's done it at this level, this magnitude a game. That is the most impressive thing. Gerry has always loved the moment. Like the national championship game (against Kansas). And he's always taken advantage of the moment. That's the key. He wants it. He was pissed off yesterday (against UConn) when he didn't get the first opportunity to tie it. He was like 'Hop, I need the ball!' That's what the great ones have."

Outside of the Final Four, there are few college basketball nights as special as the semifinal doubleheader at the Big East Tournament. The Garden is buzzing as Orange-clad Syracuse fans storm the building and begin a war of words with their long-time rivals from Georgetown. Unlike the previous two days, the rest of the building is close to full since fans from Pittsburgh and Villanova don't want to miss a play of the opener.

From the opening tip, the McNamara magic is gone and the 'Cuse is in big trouble. The hero's leg has clearly sapped him of his energy and Georgetown's guards lead a quick 12-4 start. The Hoyas keep rolling and shoot nearly 60 percent on the way to a commanding 36-21 halftime lead.

McNamara struggles through 12 ugly minutes where he manages more turnovers (2) than field goals (1).

"We were in bad position at halftime, probably as bad as you can be against a team that controls the tempo like Georgetown does," said Boeheim. "We just said 'let's cut it to ten in the first six minutes.' We did a little better than we thought."

McNamara was struggling in the locker room at the half and Boeheim said a trainer told him his star was playing at 50 percent. "But I looked at him and said, 'yeah but he'll be there.' He's gonna be there. He got tired quick but then he got going. He's a gamer. That's all. He's going to play. I don't worry about him."

McNamara opened the second half scoring with his first 3-pointer of the game, then made a steal and fed Eric Devendorf for a layup. A Watkins slam dunk gave the Orange the first seven points of the half and Georgetown's lead had already shrunk to a manageable eight points. Then McNamara really caught fire. When he drained three treys in a dizzying two-minute span near the 11-minute mark, the Garden became Gerry's House once again and the Orange were down by just 45-41.

With chants of 'Ger-ry, Ger-ry, Ger-ry' filling the building, the Orange kept charging and when McNamara passed to his roommate and pal Matt Gorman and he drained a 3-pointer, the game was tied, 49-49, with 7:18 left. Georgetown answered and never let SU grab the lead with 7-foot-2 Roy Hibbert and forward Jeff Green making the big plays. Two free throws by Green and another by Hibbert gave the Hoyas a 57-53 lead with 2:15 left. Syracuse's Nichols missed an open 3-pointer at the other end but the Hoyas couldn't take advantage by missing two chances of their own.

With 53 seconds left, a time out on the floor gave Syracuse a chance to breath. The Orange inbounded the ball to McNamara who took a few casual dribbles across midcourt, went to his right and fired an NBA-range 3-pointer over the skyscraping Hibbert that hit nothing but net. The Garden clock read 48 seconds and the Hoyas were in full panic mode. Content to melt the clock with a 57-56 lead, Georgetown patiently moved the ball around and Syracuse sat back and waited. As the shot clock reached 10, the Hoyas were clearly flummoxed and with two seconds left, Ashanti Cook threw a pass that Nichols stole. He quickly found McNamara who looked ahead to Devendorf streaking toward the basket for an open layup and Syracuse's first lead of the game, 58-57.

Georgetown still had 9.3 seconds to play with and the Hoyas resisted the chance to call a time-out and raced up the court. This time McNamara cut off a Cook drive to the rim and forced a travel with just 1.5 seconds left, completing one of the most stirring comebacks in Big East history. Georgetown managed only one point in the final 4:51, helping Syracuse overcome the largest half-time deficit in tournament history.

As the final buzzer sounded, the Syracuse alumni club fell out of the stands and into the arms of McNamara, Nichols, Watkins and the coaching staff. Pearl Washington, Derrick Coleman and Lawrence Moten led the charge, past and present stars from the Boeheim Era meeting at center court while thousands of fans chanted "Ger-ry, Ger-ry, Ger-ry," into the night.

This game wasn't about one great shot like the Cincinnati and Connecticut wins. This one was about a team that looked dead and buried and needed plenty of help to storm to the finish and grab its only lead on the last basket of the game. That the game's hero just happened to be in and out of an ice bath for most of the previous 24 hours only added to the drama.

"The first half, like Coach said, we were just trying to monitor my minutes and take it minute by minute and see how I felt. Second half, there was really no question what was going to happen because I saw the scoreboard at half-time. We went down 15 at the buzzer so how I was feeling or not, it didn't matter. It was time to play," said McNamara. "We didn't want to come down here just to win two games and go home. We wanted to come down here and try to win it, you know. That's why you come here. That's the purpose of coming here. We didn't want to just say, 'Oh, we beat UConn, hopefully we're in the tournament. Now let's go home.' We didn't want it to be like that."

At the post-game press conference, Boeheim was almost giddy. "We keep playing all these teams, we're going to find that assistant coach that said he was overrated pretty soon," said Boeheim. "We're either gonna find him or that guy's already home."

As he limped back to the locker room, McNamara shared some of the same euphoric feeling. "This is a great thing. We know we've done something great, that we'll remember forever. But now we want to win it all. That would be great to win it two years in a row."

Without skipping a beat, McNamara wore a shocking look and said, "hey, how cool was it that Derrick Coleman and The Pearl were out there with us? I mean, Derrick Coleman is the reason we're all here. You had three of the legends of Syracuse celebrating and hugging you. It's funny, I thought my farewell game was last week but the Garden has been just great. I have to stop doing it like this. I'll give myself a heart attack right out on the floor."

The nightcap features two Pennsylvania schools with deep New York roots. Villanova's heart and soul comes from the city and Pittsburgh's roster is filled with important New York prep stars. The Big East schedule makers failed to pair the two teams up this season and that turns out to be fortunate news for Villanova whose quick, active but small lineup isn't a good match against the physical Panthers.

Villanova jumps out to a 9-2 lead but Pitt's defense collars the 'Cats and an 11-2 run gives the Panthers control and leads to a 32-21 halftime lead. The second half began with everyone in the Garden expecting the type of 3-point shooting Villanova push that's come all season. But 32 seconds into the second half, tragedy struck. Chasing a loose ball in front of his bench, 'Nova's Allan Ray is poked in the eye by Carl Krauser and immediately begins rolling on the floor and kicking his legs in obvious pain. Coaches, referees and tournament officials rush to the scene and are clearly alarmed at what they see.

"They said my eye was hanging out," Ray said several months later. "I thought I was going to be blind. I thought it was over for me."

Ray is quickly rushed off the floor with trainer Jeff Pierce covering Ray's eye. Ray's parents, Allan, Sr., and Larnel, rush to the locker room area and accompany their son and team chaplain Father Rob Hagen to St. Vincent's Hospital. Ray sees an ophthalmologist who secures the area but no fresh updates filter back to the Garden. The Wildcats are clearly distracted and play one of their worst games of the season and lose, 68-54. As Jay Wright leaves the floor, he's asking anyone in the Villanova party or Big East officials if he can get an update on Ray. Other than being told the injury "is very serious," Wright knows next to nothing when he meets the press.

"He said he couldn't see anything when he left here," he said. "I heard him yelling so I knew he was in pain."

Wright glumly walks back to his locker room and as soon as he arrives, the Big East's Dan Gavitt and some Villanova athletic staffers grab him. Ray is fine, they report. A devastating injury is avoided.

"An ophthalmologist rushed across town and examined him. Now they said his vision's good and they're going to release him," a smiling, relieved Wright reports. "It actually looked a lot worse than it was. It'll be a day-to-day prognosis now, but it's much, much better than they initially anticipated. There's no scratched cornea and the official injury is soft tissue injury to right eye."

Saturday, March 11

An hour before the Big East championship game, Jim and Marge Dixon are already in their seats a couple rows behind the Pittsburgh bench. Their son, Jaime, is in his second title game in three seasons as the Panthers' coach and they couldn't be any prouder.

"It's just great. You couldn't plan it or think it or even dream it. In a word, it's great," said Jim Dixon.

The Dixons are natives of The Bronx but the movies gave them a life in North Hollywood when Jaime was just a boy. Marge Dixon worked for Warner Brothers for years. Jim Dixon is still building a 40-year career as a character actor and screenwriter. "I was an actor and you had to go to California," Jim Dixon said.

But the City Game remained in Jim Dixon's blood and he made sure to hang a hoop outside the family's home. Jaime and his two sisters, Julie and Maggie, grew up to the sound of the ball bouncing in the driveway.

"We'd tell the babysitter to let Jaime stay up and watch the UCLA games when John Wooden was the coach," Jim Dixon recalled. "He was glued to the set. That's a pretty good role model to have."

A few minutes later, Maggie Dixon arrives and hugs her parents. She's a first-year women's coach at Army who made big news a few days earlier when her team won their league title. The male Cadets stormed the court and helped carry the coach off the floor in celebration.

"I wouldn't miss this for the world," said Maggie Dixon. "I think it's Jaime's turn to win this thing."(A month later, Maggie Dixon died tragically from a arrhythmic episode in her heart. She was 28 years old. The Army embraced her legacy by burying her at West Point, an honor normally reserved for senior military officials.)

Alumni Row is filling up behind the Syracuse bench. John Wallace, Rafael Addison and Wendell Alexis have joined Derrick Coleman and Pearl Washington for the title game. Big East associate commissioner Tom Odjakian has spent the better part of a year helping plan this week's tournament and he's telling a friend about the special feel in the Garden tonight. "It's a big-game atmosphere. It's really impossible not to feel your spine tingle when we shut the lights out and play the national anthem," he says.

When the lights come back up, the Garden is buzzing with electricity. The big crowd edge goes to Syracuse and its New York roots and, sure enough, the Orangmen are ready to deliver. Quick 3-pointers by Devendorf, McNamara and Nichols give Syracuse a big 21-7 lead after eight wild minutes. The lead stays at a comfortable 34-25 by halftime with McNamara cruising along with 10 points and 5 assists and SU's defense blocking six shots and limiting the Panthers to 27 percent shooting.

"We really played great early, as well as we can play really," said Boeheim. "But they were getting inside and we were blocking a lot early. Sooner or later we had to run out of gas and they'd get some of those inside plays."

Sure enough, Pitt starts the second half sharply and trails 45-41 with 12 minutes left. Syracuse rides the play of its two much-maligned big men, Roberts and Watkins, for long stretches of the second half. They both do a great job on Pitt center Aaron Gray but it's clear the sellout crowd and ESPN national audience is going to see another great finish.

Two Krauser free throws, a 3-point play by Gray and a layup from high-flying freshman Sam Young give Pitt a 48-47 lead with 8:34 left. Seventeen seconds later, almost on cue, McNamara fires in a deep 3-point shot to give Syracuse the lead back. Despite yeoman's efforts from Krauser, Young and Antonio Graves, Pitt can't go out in front again.

A Krauser 3-pointer with 2:32 left cuts the lead to 55-54 but Devendorf answers with a tough 17-footer just before the shot clock rings. After a hoop by Gray, Devendorf is fouled and hits two pressure-packed free throws to make it 59-56 with 35 seconds left. Krauser then gets in the lane and appears to be bumped but there is no call and he loses the ball to Nichols, who pushes it to McNamara and on to Watkins for a big jam and a 61-56 lead. A stupid foul by Devendorf gives Graves two free throws but little-used Josh Wright knocks home four free throws in the final 17 seconds to secure the win and Syracuse's fifth Big East tourney crown.

As the final buzzer rings out, the Garden floor is again flooded with Orange. Nancy Zimpher, the school's new chancellor, is wearing an orange No. 3 jersey in honor of McNamara. Pearl Washington is carrying a small camera and snapping pictures, including one of McNamara as he receives the Dave Gavitt Trophy as the tourney's Most Outstanding Player.

"I can't compare because I never won this thing," said The Pearl. "You have to have luck but these guys are dangerous because they bust their ass. They never quit."

Syracuse, which won four games in four days by a total of eight points, stays on the floor while Pittsburgh heads back to its locker room. Boeheim is surrounded by well-wishers and shakes his head at the scene.

"It's one thing to come down here and win one or two games but to win four in a row, with that kind of pressure, these guys deserve all the credit.

They have huge, huge hearts," he says. "But Gerry McNamara, this is his tournament. No one has ever done what he's done in this tournament. And I've seen them all. No one."

By the time the Pitt players shed their uniforms, any hurt from the night's defeat was already easing. The Panthers are 24-7 and heading to the NCAA Tournament in a few days. There are bigger games to play.

"I think we should have nine teams in the NCAA tournament. I think we should set a record," Dixon tells the press. "I think our conference, we talked about how great this conference was going into this season. Just like our guys tonight stepped up, our conference stepped up. We deserve nine bids. I think, if given the chance, we're going to get nine teams playing great in the NCAA tournament."

When Syracuse arrives in the interview room, a smiling Boeheim is thrilled. After losing their last three games heading into the postseason by an average of more than 20 points, Syracuse's fate was on life-support. Then McNamara became Chip Hilton, living out some boyhood fantasy on one of the biggest stages in the sport. That he received more than a little help from Nichols and Roberts, Devendorf and Watkins only made the week sweeter.

"When we came down here, we were on the outside looking in," said McNamara. "Now there are a lot of teams looking at us."

Boeheim says that outside of the 2003 national-title finish, "this week was probably the best stretch I've been involved in. This team showed more heart and guts than any team I've ever coached."

It may have taken his team until March to come together and play with the elusive combination of fire and execution he's craved but Boeheim knows there are no guarantees in this sport. A Big East Tournament win guarantees nothing, especially next week in the NCAA's. He's more than happy to take some time and enjoy his team's second straight New York moment for awhile first.

"This is still a great feeling. This is still a great league. To win it is a great feeling," he said. "The unfortunate thing is that in college basketball, for a program like ours, the only thing that matters is what starts next week. Shouldn't be that way, but that's life. That's the way it is. You have to accept it. I accepted it a long time ago. We just got to get ready for next week. This will help us."

$$\left(18\right)$$

Selection Sunday; March 12

After all the hours spent practicing and playing games from Alaska to Tampa, the NCAA selects the lucky 65 teams to play for the national championship.

The tourney means different things to different programs. For teams seeded in the 12-16 range, it's the rare chance for basketball's Davids to take the national stage and get a shot at Goliath. For the remainder of the field, the NCAA's hold very different meaning. This is the chance to elevate your program and build a legacy that can last forever. Win enough games and players become heroes, coaches become legends.

The lucky team that cuts down the nets at the end of the national championship game is rarely the focus of Selection Sunday. Over the last 20 years, CBS has masterfully leveraged its billion dollar investment in the tournament by hosting a nationally televised kickoff party that earns higher ratings than many of the actual games. Players, coaches and fans are glued to their seats to see who gets into the event and where they'll be sent to play.

It's must-see TV for anyone involved in the sport and truly great theater. It's also the day when dreams do indeed die. Good teams that could easily win a game or two in the tournament are always left out. No one wants to be the team without a seat when the music stops.

The selection committee meets in a hotel in Indianapolis, not far from the NCAA's offices. The Big East staff has been busy all weekend answering any questions the committee could come across. The most important regards the health of Villanova guard Allan Ray, who is home in Philadelphia nursing his injured eye. He isn't practicing but both Mike Tranghese and Dan Gavitt assure committee member Gary Walters that Ray is expected to return to full health and play in the tournament. At the worst, he could miss an opening round game.

What the league can't help with is how the committee rates Seton Hall and Cincinnati, the two Big East teams currently on thin ice. The Pirates (18-11) have lost four of their last six games and own an RPI of 58, shaky credentials. The Bearcats (18-12) appear to own a stronger case with a 40 RPI, the fifth stiffest schedule in the country and a 14-year appearance streak in the event.

From the moment Gerry McNamara's 3-pointer ended his team's hopes in New York, Cincinnati's interim coach Andy Kennedy has been a worried man. Deep down, he says he's confident. But on Selection Sunday, you never know.

"I hate to use the cliche 'collective body of work,' but the one thing that I think separates us from the 'bubble' is strength of schedule," Kennedy said at the Big East Tournament. "The one thing the committee has consistently said is if you control the part of your schedule you can, which is obviously the non-league part, and you play people on the road and you're able to survive that, as we were, I think that's what's going to put us in a good position. We're going to have a top five strength of schedule in the country. I thought getting to 8-8 in the most powerful league in the country put us in a good position, too."

Seven Big East schools know they're in the tournament. An eighth would break the record for the most bids awarded to a single conference. At the top of the CBS show, the announcers report that Connecticut, Villanova, Duke and Memphis are the four number one seeds. The only other time the Big East had ever produced two top seeds was in 1985, the same year the conference made history by qualifying three teams in the Final Four in Lexington, Ky.

Then CBS rolls out each of the four regions. Pittsburgh (5-seed), Syracuse (also a 5), West Virginia (6), Georgetown (7) and Marquette (7) happily accept their walking papers. When Seton Hall learns that it's matched up against Wichita State, pandemonium breaks out in South Orange, N.J. The players pile on top of each other while coach Louis Orr runs down the hallway with his arms upraised.

"It almost reminded me of a preacher running through the aisles of a church. I guess I got full of the Holy Spirit and just moved," the coach told the

Record of Bergen County. "It wasn't planned. It just happened. I've still got about 10 or 20 good yards in me. After that, I'm done."

The scene was not repeated in the Queen City of Cincinnati. Despite a resume filled with positive numbers, the committee clearly looked at the Bearcats' efforts after the season-ending knee injury to Armien Kirkland in early January and wasn't impressed. A 15-point loss at Seton Hall on Feb. 28 clearly didn't help, either. The Cincy players were so heartbroken that Kennedy didn't let them speak to reporters after hearing the news.

"Obviously the committee's criteria for making the tournament does not hold true," a clearly peeved Kennedy told the Cincy press. "I need an explanation for why we don't make it. I need something better because this just isn't working for me. My players are devastated, emotionally devastated and I have not tried to say anything to them because I too am still in shock. They deserve better than this."

Kennedy proceeds to tick off his team's accomplishments and compare them against a few of the final at-large teams – such as Air Force, Utah State and Texas A&M – that did get the nod.

"I know every year there are two or three teams that do not make the tournament that feel as if they were justified in making it, and this year we are one of those teams," Kennedy said. "But I would dare to say that never in the history of determining the teams that get included into the NCAA tournament, is a team that has a strength of schedule a six, a non-league strength of schedule of 23 and an 8-8 record in the most powerful league ever formed, be in the position or deal with what we are dealing with today."

The snub leaves Kennedy with one overwhelming feeling. After Tranghese and other Big East power brokers insisted that the size of the league wouldn't hurt anyone's NCAA chances, reality hit the conference square in the face.

"To me the only explanation is that despite the rhetoric that we have heard about there not being a cap on how many teams could go from one conference, I really feel like they were not going to put nine teams in from the Big East," he said. "I need the truth to be told and the truth to be told is that we can't give one (conference) nine bids, so for every head coach in the Big East, today was a frightening day."

Tranghese was as stunned as anyone else. While praising the record selection of eight teams, the commissioner said he could not understand the snub of Cincinnati.

"I just don't know what their thinking was," he said. "You never know what goes on inside that room."

Getting a definitive answer from the selection committee is impossible. There are so many criteria in play that once the group narrows down the final few, it simply pins decisions on a couple of the numbers and discards others. How else to explain Cincinnati trumping Air Force in virtually every category that matters yet still coming up empty?

Asked about Cincinnati later, committee chairman Craig Littlepage praised the Big East for its record eight bids but also criticized its bulky size.

"I think, number one, it means that they were a very big conference," said Littlepage. "I think it also means, more importantly, they have a very good conference. I think that what we saw in terms of the Big East this year created some very, very unusual challenges for us as we looked at this era of the imbalanced conference scheduling, that is conference teams with identical records that have had varying degrees of difficulty to get to that point in the season where they would be ranked and placed in their conference tournaments."

With eight teams in the tournament, the Big East's fortunes were scattered throughout the country. Syracuse received the glamour locale, traveling to Jacksonville to face Texas A&M. Marquette fared pretty well, too, taking its sun tan lotion out to San Diego for a game against Alabama. Pittsburgh and West Virginia are both sent to Auburn Hills to face Kent State and Southern Illinois, respectively. Georgetown will travel to Dayton and face Northern Iowa.

The most important site was clearly Philadelphia, where the two No. 1 seeds and all their fans happily descended. Connecticut is matched up with Albany, with possibly Kentucky waiting in round two. Villanova plays Monmouth but faces a tough second round game against either Arizona or Wisconsin.

March 16

Today is the opening round of the NCAA Tournament, a day that college basketball fans can't get enough of. It's also a day where it's impossible not to think about money.

Out in Las Vegas, you can't find a seat in a sport's book. With 16 games today and 16 more tomorrow spread out from noon to midnight, it's a fan's (and gambler's) paradise. With few exceptions, the NBA arenas and domed stadiums hosting the games are packed with fans. The stakes can't be higher and the pressure on the collegiate players looks and smells an awful lot like the pros.

The financial windfall a conference can receive from excellent play in the NCAA Tournament is impressive, but not on a par with the bounty football's bowl games deliver. The NCAA budgets a large portion of its multi-billion dollar CBS TV contract, along with the proceeds from the huge gates at the games, to the teams that make the tournament. It assigns units to each contest whereby if you play in one game, your conference is awarded one unit. If you win a game, your units increase with each succeeding round. In 2006, each unit is worth approximately $164,000.

By landing a record eight teams in the tourney, the Big East is assured of $1.3 million even if it falls flat on its face. That's good money but a mere pittance compared to what the football powers pocket. In fact, a relatively meaningless game like the Holiday Bowl pays its two teams over $2 million each. In 2006, the Big East pooled its bowl money and then distributed it on a tiered basis, with the participant in a BCS game earning $2.4 million, the team in the bowl with the second-highest payout getting $1.6 million, the third $1.3 million and the fourth and fifth $1.1 million.

In basketball, the conference is hoping for as many teams as possible to play as deep as they can into the tournament. With UConn and Villanova looming as Final Four favorites, the possibility of the Big East pocketing as many as 20 'units' is very real.

After the first day of the tournament, it looks like the Big East doesn't deserve any of the NCAA's money.

Syracuse, Marquette and Seton Hall all go down in flames. The Orangemen don't get a break on two fronts. First, Jim Boeheim would've loved to play on Friday and rest Gerry McNamara and his injured groin as long as possible. Instead, Syracuse traveled on Tuesday and played Thursday against an opponent who clearly merited better than a 12 seed. Texas A&M was fast, quick and aggressive and basically shut the Orange attack down in a 66-58 loss.

McNamara was a shell of himself, failing to score a single field goal and managing only two points, which tied his career low. It was the first time in his career he never made a shot. Neither McNamara nor Boeheim acknowledged the groin injury after the game. "We don't make excuses," the coach said.

McNamara seemed to aggravate the groin injury just five minutes into the game when he left a scrum for a loose ball in pain. After he played the first 8:06 of the second half, the senior guard returned to the floor only one more time. He sat the final five minutes of the game next to his coach.

"I'm not going to make excuses. He's not going to make excuses," Boeheim said. "If you watch the game, you know why he wasn't in the game. Gerry could not make plays tonight. If anything, I played him too much."

What Syracuse didn't want to say was that McNamara didn't practice all week and simply couldn't move. The groin injury only intensified and, truth be told, the four days of heroics in New York proved to be too much for him to handle. While McNamara's legacy as one of the greatest SU players was safe, the story of this year's team was probably crystallized in Boeheim's foul-mouthed explosion at the Big East Tournament.

Without Gerry McNamara, the Orangemen would not have won 10 games. While a bit of an overstatement, Boeheim was largely right. He patched a thin team together around the leadership of one player and without him playing at top efficiency, Syracuse was barely a top 12 team in the Big East.

"I said all year that we needed our big guys to play better and when they did, we were pretty good," Boeheim said a few weeks after the season-ending loss. "That held true most of the year. We could've used another guard and just the consistency of our junior class was a problem most of the year."

Seton Hall went down in flames, falling behind by 20 points in the first half and losing to Wichita State, 86-66. The Shockers came in ready to claw the Big East beast, especially after CBS analyst Billy Packer openly spoke out against the Missouri Valley Conference earning four bids into the tournament, the same as the Atlantic Coast, Big 12 and Pac-10 conferences.

The ugly loss was the final entry in a season-long referendum on the fate of Pirates' coach Louis Orr. While getting his team to the NCAA's for the second time in three seasons should've been cause for celebration, Orr clearly lacked the deep-rooted support needed to keep his job. As the NCAA Tournament rolled on for the next few weeks, his destiny was clearly an unanswered question.

Marquette played infinitely better in its 90-85 shootout loss to Alabama. The day started in bizarre fashion when a security sweep of Cox Arena in San Diego caused a 70-minute delay. The MU players returned to their hotel rooms while the arena was checked by bomb-sniffing dogs. Nothing suspicious was found.

The delay bothered the Golden Eagles who fell behind by 14 points by halftime. To their credit, the team roared back in the second half and nearly grabbed an exciting win. Down three with eight seconds left, Marquette had the ball and found the dangerous Steve Novak open in the corner.

But Marquette's greatest 3-point shooter ever missed and Alabama escaped with a win.

"It felt good. I was wide open. It was probably the first wide-open shot I had all night. Some go down, some don't," Novak told the Milwaukee Journal-Sentinel.

Novak's career ended with the miss and he finished with 17 points. The future of the program, Dominic James and fellow frosh Wesley Matthews and Jerel McNeal each played well. James finishes with a team-high 20 points and as the players leave the floor, coach Tom Crean collared his freshmen trio and made sure that they remembered the painful feeling of an NCAA loss. After all, everyone in Milwaukee expects the James Gang to return to this stage again.

March 17; Philadelphia

The ugliness of the tourney's opening day shined a brighter spotlight on today's games.

If the Seton Hall-Wichita State game was seen as a sort of referenda on the worthiness of the Missouri Valley in some parts of the country, this afternoon's matchups were circled in the East. Georgetown-Northern Iowa and West Virginia-Southern Illinois were true grudge matches, the type of games that were perceived to go either way, but in reality were ones the Big East needed to get. The other key game featured Pittsburgh against Kent State, yet another chance for a mid-major team to knock a Big East bruiser down a few pegs.

Quick starts and some dominating offensive basketball helped West Virginia and Pitt to relatively easy victories. A poised Mountaineer team ripped into the Salukis and won going away, 64-46. Pitt's physical style and 67 percent shooting wore out Kent with Aaron Gray leading the way with 17 points and 13 rebounds in a 79-64 win.

Georgetown's battle with Northern Iowa didn't go as smoothly. The Panthers jumped out to a quick lead and still led, 30-26, at the half. A few defensive adjustments altered the game dramatically, however. Led by Roy Hibbert (17 points, 9 boards), the Hoyas grabbed the lead and then held UNI scoreless for over 12 minutes. That smothering Hoya defense continued the rest of the way and delivered a 54-49 win, giving the Big East a convincing 3-0 sweep over the upstarts from The Valley.

Serving almost as an after-thought to that nip-and-tuck game in Dayton were the first round games in Philadelphia. Up first was Villanova, playing on its second home court at the Wachovia Center. But this wasn't like the Connecticut or Louisville games earlier in the year. This time the 'Cats didn't even sleep in their own beds a half hour away on the Main Line. The NCAA assigns (and pays for) each team a hotel and you have no choice but to use it.

As a No. 1 seed, Villanova and Connecticut enjoyed the choice digs. The Cats stayed at the downtown Westin Hotel, the Huskies at the Ritz Carlton. Albany, a 16-seed, bedded at the Courtyard Hotel downtown.

Villanova faced Monmouth, the winner of the NCAA's play-in game over Hampton. Monmouth is a fairly typical 16-seed, a team that started 1-7 against stiff competition but eventually righted itself in time for Northeast Conference play. But as their 19-14 record indicates, the Hawks must try something different to push Villanova off its game and their deliberate style is the best weapon.

'Nova comes out to a hero's welcome, serenaded by the big hometown crowd that drowns out the small Monmouth fan base. The game starts slowly. Very slowly, in fact. The Wildcats make just one of their first seven shots but a 3-pointer by Ray seven minutes in makes the score 8-1 as Monmouth can't get out of its own way (0-for-12 start). But Villanova isn't much better and with six minutes left in the half, the score is an amazing 12-6 as Ray, Randy Foye and Mike Nardi are relying too much on NBA-range 3-pointers.

Villanova leads 27-16 at the half as neither team shoots better than 32 percent. Lute Olson, the legendary Arizona coach, has to like what he sees as he sits behind the Monmouth bench. His team ripped Wisconsin, 94-75, in the day's opener and is gearing up for 'Nova next. Slowing down Villanova's guards is a huge challenge but if Monmouth can do it, can't Arizona?

Monmouth keeps hanging around in the second half and actually cuts the lead to 47-40 with 6:22 left on a corner 3-pointer from Dejan Delic, a shooter from Belgrade. When that shot falls in, the quiet crowd suddenly awakens with a roar. "I looked up and wondered 'where did all these people come from?" said Jay Wright. "This was supposed to be a home game.

Even though the 'neutral' crowd at the Wachovia Center certainly sat in Villanova's corner, everyone else clearly was cheering for an upset. That's what the first four days of the NCAA's have become, the Little Guy's Big Chance. If a big upset is possible, CBS trains its cameras on the game and the nation watches with gleeful anticipation. When Delic had another open three with the chance to cut the Wildcats' lead to four, the big crowd held its collective breath as the shot pierced the air. When it hit the back rim and bounded away, Delic said he heard the fans groan instead of roar and felt the air disappear from his confident chest.

This was the only moment of truth Villanova faced. Foye answered with a runner in the lane and Kyle Lowry made a steal and went on to make four straight free throws to bump the lead back to double figures and secure a 58-45 win. Afterwards, Wright took to the podium and shocked the throngs of reporters when he said, "I thought we played a pretty good game."

Later he spoke about Monmouth's patient style and the fact that his team needed to return to action after staying on the sidelines for a week.

"They're a tough team to play in the first round," he said. "I just wanted to see us defend and rebound and we held them to 34 percent (shooting). That's good, in my mind. I thought we played well until I started talking to the press. All I know is if we defend and rebound like that, we give ourselves a chance even when we don't make shots."

The good news for the Wildcats is Ray made shots. Despite being the prime point of medical conversation around college basketball for a week, the senior from New York hit five of 'Nova's seven threes and looked comfortable all day.

"I wouldn't say it but I was concerned," said Wright. "But now I'm convinced. He's golden, he's good."

By this point, Ray is sick of questions about his eye but he's mature enough to understand the inquisitors aren't backing away. During the tournament, the NCAA instructs teams to open their locker rooms for a half hour after each game. Villanova, and many other teams around the country, chooses to close its dressing room to reporters during the regular season. With its games in Philadelphia, the Wildcats are besieged by the press and wave upon wave keep walking through the door and asking Ray, Foye and Nardi the same, repetitive questions.

Ray brushes off the focus on his eye, saying "it was no factor today. Everything is fine. Once the doctor cleared me, I was full speed ahead."

Ray's teammates are gratefully relieved. They had seen him in practice the previous few days and knew he looked good but until they saw his sweet stroke return in a game, they weren't taking anything for granted.

A few hours after Villanova leaves the floor, UConn arrives. The day before, Albany coach Will Brown spelled out the task facing his Great Danes when he said, "their kids are signing NBA contracts. Ours are sending out resumés. If they play their 'A' game, they probably can beat the Knicks."

The words are a smoke screen, of course. Jim Calhoun is sharply dressed in a black suit with a green tie signifying his Irish heritage on St. Patrick's Day. But it's the Albany kids who can't wait to play. Quick, penetrating guard Jamar

Wilson leads the upstarts to an 11-5 lead right out of the gate. UConn's big men bobble the ball so much that they can't take advantage of a huge size edge and 11 first-half turnovers keep the Husky attack in check. After every Albany score, an enraged Calhoun turns and stares at a scorned player sitting on his bench or screams at George Blaney, looking for answers.

UConn shoots 65 percent for the half but the turnovers and inability of any guard to slow down Wilson makes the score 31-30, UConn, at halftime.

The second half features more of the same and as Albany continues to frustrate the Huskies, the chance of a shocking upset captivates the country. No 16 seed has ever beaten a number one, although several have come close and the Great Danes clearly have the Huskies on the ropes.

With Wilson tooling Marcus Williams, Albany opens the second half with a 13-2 run that staggers Connecticut. With 11:34 left, Wilson hits a running 10-footer and Albany's lead peaks at 50-38. With the crowd at the Wachovia Center roaring for the underdogs, UConn somehow finds its game. Williams, of course, is the catalyst. He feeds Josh Boone for a dunk and then follows a Rudy Gay steal with a deep 3-pointer. Williams strips the ball from Jason Siggers and swoops in for a layup and the lead is down to only 50-45.

UConn keeps rolling with a scary offensive onslaught. Williams breaks a 52-52 tie with another 3-pointer and after he finds Hilton Armstrong for a jumper, the crafty point guard nails his fifth 3-pointer of the game, good for his career-high. The Husky explosion closes the game on a 34-9 run and secures a deceiving 72-59 victory.

"We were letting guys get to the rim on defense, especially myself," Williams said. "We had to buckle down and get stops. Experiences like this will help us. We know now we have to go out and take the first hit."

Teammate Denham Brown summed up his team's confidence when he said, "we weren't that concerned. We're a championship team at heart. These are the games that will make us great."

Their coach wasn't as pleased. He called the offensive sluggishness, "our poorest offensive effort in maybe 20 years at UConn. It looked like we were going one-on-five and had never been coached before.

"They tell me the entire country was drawn in to see history," Calhoun said. "But history wasn't made, thank God. CBS brought all of its viewers here to see a team in peril. Did I think my kids felt the pressure of being a one (seed)? No question. A 16-seed is going to beat a one. The gap is closing. We all know that."

The UConn win wrapped up a busy, and productive, day for the Big East. Five teams survived first round upsets and moved on. With a berth in the Sweet 16 one win away, a very important round two awaited.

March 19; Philadelphia

Eight of the Sweet 16 teams were decided on Saturday with the only big surprise coming in Wichita State's win over Tennessee. But that doesn't even qualify as an upset as compared to what George Mason is doing in today's opening game.

The Patriots shocked Tom Izzo's Michigan State team in round one but now faced one of the game's blue bloods in third-seeded North Carolina. But sure enough Jim Larranaga's team shocked the world again. This time a few plays late did the trick in a 65-60 win that sent the Virginia commuter school onto the next round in Washington, D.C.

A little more of that upset magic was floating in the air in Auburn Hills. Bradley and its impressive center Patrick O'Bryant (28 points) proved to be the perfect match for Pittsburgh. The Panthers fell into early foul trouble and could never quite catch the Braves in a tight game that wasn't decided until the final minute, 72-66. The loss continued a frustrating string of NCAA defeats for a Pitt program that's won more games than any other Big East team over the last five seasons but has just three Sweet 16 finishes to show for it.

That set up a critical two-hour window where three Big East teams faced chances to advance. West Virginia had the easiest task and took advantage by rolling out to a 41-19 lead and walloping Northwestern State, 67-54. The Mountaineers will move on to Atlanta and play Texas in the Georgia Dome.

Georgetown was next and the Hoyas came in as slight underdogs to second-seeded Ohio State which enjoyed a home-court advantage playing in Dayton. The Hoyas took that edge away early with a 17-4 start led by some dominating post play by Hibbert. An 11-2 run to end the half left the Hoyas with a comfortable 38-25 lead at the break. Ohio State and its star, Big Ten Player of the Year Terence Dials, made several pushes in the second half, most notably one that cut the lead to 54-48 with five minutes left but Hibbert (20 points, 14 rebounds) and Jeff Green (19 & 8) closed the door and Georgetown left with a convincing 70-52 win.

In just his second season as the coach, John Thompson III had returned the Hoyas to their first Sweet 16 since 2001 and 10th since 1980. As the coach left the floor, he received a big bear hug from his father who was on-site calling the game on radio. Only four Hoyas reached the scoring column, with Ashanti Cook (17 points) and Darrel Owens (14) joining Hibbert and Green. But when it was over, the rest of college basketball knew Georgetown was back.

"It's something I've always wanted to do as a Hoya – to get a win that really, truly meant something," Owens told the Washington Post. "To go to the Sweet 16 – I've been walking into the gym the last four years, looking at that Sweet 16 banner, always wondering what it'd feel like to get there."

With two teams moving on, now it was time for the Big East's leaders to join in. In order to do so, Connecticut and Villanova needed to stare down two of the biggest names in the game in Kentucky and Arizona. The day before, Calhoun went out of his way to praise Kentucky's tradition. He also spoke about how difficult it is to keep winning like the Wildcats have, from Adolph Rupp to Rick Pitino and now under Tubby Smith.

"We're not new to this but Kentucky has kept it going forever," he said. "I think we're working to get up there with the royalty of college basketball like at Durham, like at Chapel Hill, like in Lexington, Indiana and like in Storrs, Connecticut. It's nice to have the ability to get players and have them waiting for you to call them. So to be compared to those kinds of programs after a 20-year run at UConn, I think we've made great strides heading that way."

If anyone appreciates that the path to such greatness runs through the NCAA's, it's Calhoun. That's why he recites his team's records so often and remembers the great shots that have won and lost the biggest games.

"We've said simply that we wanted to become one of basketball's better programs, and the way you're going to have to do that is continue to get to the tournament, continue to march. Probably throw another championship or two up there," he said. "Along the way if you don't get the championship, if you don't have a great, great tournament in that particular year, come right back the next year and throw up another 20-something season and go from there."

Unlike the Albany game, UConn answers the bell against Kentucky and enjoys a superlative start. A 14-2 run gives the Huskies a 22-10 lead midway through the first half and they keep it in place thanks largely to Rashad Anderson's four 3-pointers and 14 first half points for a 43-31 halftime lead.

UConn still holds a comfortable 66-57 lead with 8:40 left but wrapping up a Sweet 16 bid doesn't come easy. Three-pointers by Bobby Perry, Sheray Thomas and Rajon Rondo slice the deficit to a mere two points (74-72) with 3:16 to play. UConn's Williams answers with a driving layup while being fouled. He misses the free throw but Armstrong scoops up the rebound and scores, putting UConn back in control, 78-72.

Boone is fouled but he air balls the first free throw and misses the second badly. But Armstrong is on the glass yet again and Craig Austrie hits his biggest hoop of the season to extend the lead to 81-74. Kentucky keeps fighting behind Rondo and Patrick Sparks, who nails a big 3-pointer that helps the Cats claw to within 81-79 with 52 seconds left. But Williams, yet again, saves the day by making four clutch free throws and Gay adds two more with three seconds left to preserve a 87-83 win.

Williams finishes with 20 points and 8 assists while Gay plays very well with 19 points. UConn's big men are another matter entirely. Boone doesn't score and grabs one rebound in 24 minutes. Calhoun plays Ed Nelson for 12 unproductive minutes, taking time away from Armstrong who manages 10 points and 5 boards in only 21 minutes.

"I haven't been on a team that's gotten past this round so these were the two toughest games of my life," said Gay. "Today was all business."

Calhoun is clearly relieved. Getting past the first two rounds was all but expected by everyone back in Husky Nation but for whatever reason, the team isn't playing well right now. Kentucky shoots 56 percent in the second half and nearly out-rebounded (35-34) a much bigger Connecticut team.

"I'm so proud of my kids the way they took every shot that Kentucky gave us," Calhoun said. "In this tournament sometimes you're thrust into a game that evolves entirely different than your game plan. I thought we would eventually take control of the game but Kentucky kept fighting back. That is not in the game plan. That's a credit to Kentucky, not just to UConn."

UConn takes its expected spot opposite Washington in the round of 16 next Friday in Washington, D.C. But what's truly stunning about the Huskies road is the game opposite them matching the tourney's two biggest underdogs, George Mason and Wichita State. No one is looking past Washington but as one UConn insider says, "George Mason-Wichita is a lot better than looking at North Carolina or Tennessee."

With Connecticut safely moving on, the spotlight shifts to Villanova and its home court advantage was in full bloom as only a smattering of the 20,050 fans sported Arizona's red and white colors. The home fans were treated to a bravo first half performance by star guard Foye who poured in 20 points to lead 'Nova's Cats to a 42-35 lead at the break.

But even with the lead, Jay Wright was troubled by Arizona's aggressive inside play. Worried that his small team couldn't work the backboards like it needed to, Wright scrapped his 'traditional' four-guard lineup in favor of a two-guard set where freshmen Dante Cunningham and Shane Clark were asked to help Will Sheridan inside and Cunningham came up big, grabbing a team-high nine rebounds. That didn't offset Arizona's 20 offensive boards or 42-24 scoring advantage in the paint but it was enough to help deliver a 82-78 win.

"Shane and Dante came in and helped us out on the glass. That was important," Ray said. "It doesn't really matter if they score or anything like that. They did a tremendous job of helping us out on the glass. Arizona was killing us on the boards, and coach put those two guys in to help us rebound."

Foye was held to four points in the second half but Ray fires in 20 of his 25 over the final 20 minutes. Foye and Ray are so close personally that they clearly play with no jealousy. That's made them the best 1-2 guard combo in the country.

"I didn't say it was his turn or my turn. We just read the defense," Foye said. "He knew every time I got the ball, everybody was loading to my side. So we swung the ball over and he had a one-on-one on the other side. We just kept adjusting."

The Villanova win gave the Big East four members of the Sweet 16, a sweet quarter of the teams still dreaming of a national championship. Not bad.

$$\bigodot_{19}$$

March 23; Atlanta

If any team isn't going to be intimidated by an opponent, it's West Virginia. The poised, veteran Mountaineers have made a living for two years making opponents adjust to them and not the other way around.

That's certainly the case heading into a matchup with Texas at the Georgia Dome. The second-seeded Longhorns think they can win the national title, and with good reason. Rick Barnes has a group that's almost as experienced as WVU's, but with more talent. Sophomore center LaMarcus Aldridge is a likely lottery pick who's expected to leave school after this year. P.J. Tucker was the Big 12's top player and talented guards Daniel Gibson, Kenton Paulino and A.J. Abrams bring some explosive scoring to the table.

The Longhorns threw all of that firepower at West Virginia early on and threatened to run away with an easy win. Texas led 39-27 at the half and it seemed like the 'Horns grabbed every rebound. That trend continued all night as Texas won the board battle 45-16 and West Virginia managed a mere three offensive rebounds all game.

But size and strength didn't measure the heart of the Mountaineers. After getting a half time pep talk from John Beilein, the seniors came out firing and a 8-0 spurt to open the second half sent Texas back on the ropes. With Pittsnogle (19 points, 5 threes), Mike Gansey (18, 3 threes) and Patrick Beilein

(14, 4 threes) firing from all corners, the Mountaineers kept charging and went ahead, 61-58, on a tough 3-pointer by Gansey.

Texas regrouped and rode the broad shoulders of Aldridge (26 points, 13 rebounds) and Tucker (15 points, 14 boards) to the finish line. Aldridge hit a free throw and Abrams tacked on two more with 27 seconds left to give Texas a 70-65 lead. Gansey then shook free from the top of the key for a 3-pointer to make it a two-point game with 14.7 seconds left. Aldridge was fouled and had a chance to ice the game but he made just one of two free throws to make it 71-68.

WVU calmly came up the floor, spread the Longhorns out and looked for an open bomber. The ball settled in Pittsnogle's eager hands and he fired in a trey with 5.1 seconds left. Texas raced up the floor and Abrams found an open Paulino on the left wing. The senior nailed it at the buzzer, giving Texas a stunning win.

After losing to Louisville in overtime for the right to go to the Final Four a year earlier, the Mountaineers are left to swallow another painful defeat. The class of Pittsnogle, Gansey, Beilein, Joe Herber and J.D. Collins led WVU to back-to-back Sweet 16 appearances for the first time since the Jerry West days of 1959 and '60, a legacy that should be remembered for decades.

"I think it's sunk in that for the seniors that was our last game at West Virginia and I think that's what we're more sad about than losing the game," said Pittsnogle. "It's a great game. They made a great shot, they deserved to win, they're a better team. But I think it's more or less that we're not ever going to play again as a team because we have so much fun together. We love each other and it's – that's probably the main thing."

March 24; Washington, D.C. & Minneapolis

One of Tranghese's toughest duties during the NCAA Tournament is determining which games he'd like to see in person while not missing any on television. It's a difficult balancing act, especially when you have eight teams to follow like this year.

Tranghese is a NCAA veteran, serving as a Sports Information Director for a Final Four team at Providence in 1973, a top conference official cheering on Big East teams at numerous Final Fours and as the head of the men's basketball committee a few years ago. He's seen innumerable games decided in lots of crazy ways, by a great shot, an awful miss, a defensive stand or an errant pass. The action that unfolds in the final seconds is what makes the NCAA's great.

"The thing about the NCAA Tournament is at one point you just have to make a play. One play," he says. "It happens to every team. Look at North Carolina last year. They won it all but against Villanova they were in deep trouble and had to step up and make a play and they did it. If one play goes the other way, they're not there.

"I look back at all of our national championships and that was the case. When Connecticut won the last time (2004), everyone remembers they beat Georgia Tech big in the final. But they had to get past the Duke game in the semifinals. In '99, they had to get by Gonzaga out West. Jimmy Boeheim and Syracuse, they were down 14 points to Oklahoma State in the second round in 2003. Georgetown in '84, people forget, but they won their first round game against Southern Methodist, 37-36. And Villanova, everybody knows how many scares they had (in 1985). I think if you have toughness and you can defend, that can get you through it."

With three teams playing within a four-hour span, the stakes can't get much higher for Tranghese and everyone else in the Big East. The first game in the Metrodome matches top-seeded Villanova with an old nemesis that's fallen out of favor with the rest of the Big East. Boston College enjoyed its first taste of Atlantic Coast Conference basketball immensely in 2006. The Eagles feared some type of adjustment penalty switching to a new league but, if anything, the ACC proved to be much tamer than the Big East for Al Skinner's team.

That had more to do with the relative softness of the new league and the powerful bodies of Craig Smith, Jared Dudley and the rest of an Eagle team that proved it could win a lot of games in whatever league it called home. BC (28-7) has its eye squarely on the school's first Final Four berth.

"A lot of times you get deep in the tournament playing somebody you haven't seen," said 'Nova coach Wright. "I don't know if that is any type of advantage because they know us also, but it kind of feels like a conference game. You know each other. You know what you have to do. You just have to go play the game. That's the way we look at it. They are tough. They are really tough."

That toughness shines through from the opening tip as BC's defense checks Villanova's guard-dominated attack and limits the Wildcats to 4-of-20 shooting out of the gate. BC builds a 16-point early lead but falters with some shaky passing and carries a 28-24 edge into halftime. In order to counteract BC's inside power, Wright again limits Nardi's playing time in favor of more size with Cunningham, Clark and Jason Fraser but with Ray struggling (3-of-15 FG) like he hadn't all season, Villanova's offense limps along squarely on the shoulders of Foye.

Not surprisingly, the All-American delivers. With BC also struggling to score thanks to a pesky defense that causes 21 turnovers, Foye carries 'Nova to the finish. He hits two tough jumpers in the lane and his two free throws with 2:18 left give Villanova its first lead of the game, 49-48. Another tough pull-up jumper in the lane pushes the lead to three points with 45 seconds left. BC's Dudley answers with a 3-pointer from the wing that ties the game at 51 with 29 seconds left. 'Nova sees a chance to win in the final seconds but Lowry's open jumper is swatted away by the Condor-like Sean Williams to force overtime.

The extra session features more Foye and more critical plays. With BC defenders draped on him, Foye keeps rolling with a 3-pointer and a tough driving lay-up for a 58-55 lead. Dudley and Smith come right back with lay-ups for a 59-58 BC lead with 12 seconds to go. Foye drives to the hoop but the ball is knocked away. 'Nova retains the ball under its own basket with just 3.5 seconds on the clock. Wright calls a play, the same play that beat Cincinnati in the final seconds a few weeks ago and one the Wildcats practice a few times a week.

Lowry is the inbounder and wants to find either Foye or Ray coming off a pick for a quick jumper. BC won't let Foye free but the Eagles shade him and Ray a bit too much and Sheridan pops open on a roll to the hoop. Lowry hits Sheridan who puts a wide-open lay-up up on the glass. Williams swoops over and knocks the ball away but the block is clearly goaltending and Villanova escapes, 60-59.

"It's just a play we sometimes run. It worked," said Sheridan. "I mean, what can I say? It was a good read by our guard, Kyle. It was one of the biggest shots in my career and I didn't get to make it."

Villanova had won so many shootouts all season, flashing its high-scoring backcourt whenever possible. But tonight it emerged as a ragged victor in a street fight against an old neighbor.

"Coach Wright stresses this to us, when shots are falling and, you know, you are playing good offensively, it is easy to win," said Ray. "But the real good teams and the real great teams find a way to win when you are not making shots and your shot is not falling. So, as a team, that's something that we really take pride in. In the locker room that's one of the things we were talking about. We shot the ball poorly, but we still were able to come up with a win. You know, like Coach said, that's what great teams do."

Georgetown and Florida are up next in Minneapolis. The Gators are a young and talented team that's seen as being a year away from contending for a national championship. That youth shines through most of the game but so does the impressive talent on Billy Donovan's squad. The Gators are led by Joakim Noah, a long 6-10 center who grew up wanting to go to Georgetown. Then-Hoya coach Craig Esherick never really called on him though, and as his national profile soared Noah eventually settled on the sun of Gainesville. Georgetown countered with big men Hibbert and Green and the Hoyas wisely slow the Gator attack and make the game play at their pace.

A 30-28 halftime score remained tight the rest of the way. The game was tied at 49-49 with three minutes left when a string of strange events began unfolding. Down 52-51, the Hoyas received a gift when Cook's foul line jumper banked into the hoop. With the game knotted at 53-all, it was Florida's turn for a gift. Noah missed a lay-up in traffic but Al Horford won a scramble for the loose rebound and directed it to Corey Brewer. As Brandon Bowman nearly tied the ball up for a jump, Brewer flipped an off-balance shot up toward the glass that somehow fell through as he landed on the floor.

"Al tipped the ball off the offensive rebound and it came right to me," said Brewer. "I was driving and I really didn't see the guy behind me. I spun and the guy grabbed my arm. I threw it up and it went in."

At the other end, Georgetown quickly found Darrel Owens open at the top of the key after Brewer fell coming around a pick. Owens looked at a 3-pointer from point blank range but the shot bounced way. Florida rebounded, made two free throws and the game was over, 57-53.

"I couldn't have bought a better shot for a million dollars. I guess it just wasn't meant to be," Owens said.

The last-minute action the NCAA's are known for has cost the Big East two teams. West Virginia gets beat on a last-second prayer. Georgetown's final plea goes unanswered. Players and coaches from both sides know how close the game-turning plays can be.

"The only time I was nervous was on the last play when I tripped and fell and, in my mind, I seen (Owens) hit the three," said Brewer. "That's the only time I was nervous in the stretch. My heart was in my mouth."

Asked if a loss like that stays with a coach, Thompson said, "Does it stay with you? Oh, yes. Look, we come down and we miss a lay-up. At the other end, we don't get a rebound and they get a 3-point play. We come to our end and we get the shot we wanted for the person we wanted to get it. It didn't go in. So that's how close this all is. It is a game of inches."

At Washington's Verizon Center, the stunning ride of the George Mason Patriots continues with a 63-55 win over Wichita State. 'Go Mason' placards and T-shirts fill the arena and give the Colonial Conference team a strong home-court advantage.

The final game of the night is set to start and Jim Calhoun isn't happy. The Battle of the Huskies doesn't begin until a little after 10 o'clock, emphasizing that CBS can do whatever it wants after paying a few billion dollars for the rights to show these big games.

From the start, it was clear that UConn's Huskies were in for a major battle. Everyone knew that Washington's Brandon Roy was a star but the aggressive play of Jamaal Williams, who scored a game-high 27 points in 29 minutes, was stunning. With the game tied at 26-all, Calhoun is assessed a technical foul by official Patrick Adams for no clear-cut reason. The coach was in the midst of his usual bait-and-switch routine with officials but wasn't overly bombastic and is openly shocked and upset with the T. The call starts Washington on a 14-4 run that leads to a 40-30 lead and a 45-40 half-time lead.

Gay was all but invisible in the half, missing all four of his shots and grabbing one rebound. That changes out of the gate in the second half as he scores five quick points but at the 13:48 mark, Gay and Roy go chest-to-chest after a hard foul by Roy. Both players are slapped with quick technicals, a devastating turn of events for Washington because the fouls are Roy's third and fourth of the game. Only a few seconds later, another Washington fouls puts UConn in the bonus and Marcus Williams begins a lengthy UConn parade to the foul line.

The game stays tight and goes back and forth the rest of the way with neither team playing good defense and UConn draining loads of free throws (34-of-47). But Calhoun's team can't grab the lead and when Roy hits a lay-up in traffic and Jamaal Williams cans a 3-pointer over Boone, Washington leads 78-72 with 1:55 left.

A Boone free throw and Rashad Anderson 3-pointer cut the deficit to 78-76 with 34 seconds left but UConn has to foul and Justin Dentmon makes two free throws for a 80-76 lead with 21 ticks left. UConn catches a big break when Mike Jensen reaches in and fouls Marcus Williams on a drive to the hoop and a lay-up. The bonus free throw cuts the lead to one with 11 seconds left. Roy is quickly fouled and he makes two shots to give Washington a 82-79 lead with 7.9 seconds left.

As soon as the second shot falls in, UConn inbounds the ball to Williams who races up the floor and runs the 'Hand Off' play where he gives the ball to Anderson coming off a high screen. "I told Marcus make or miss, do it like we always do and I'll knock it down," said Anderson.

Sure enough, with 1.8 seconds on the clock, Anderson received the ball and fired a 23-footer over Ryan Appleby that swished through the hoop and miraculously forced overtime. "I just knew if Marcus got me the ball, I'd knock it down. You give me that shot 30 times, I'm making it 30 times," Anderson said.

Williams and Anderson scored for Connecticut to open the overtime. and the Huskies appeared safe with a 94-89 lead with 24 seconds left. But this wild game had one more twist to it. Appleby swished a deep 3-pointer with 16 seconds left and then stepped in front of the inbound pass from Gay. With the ball and a chance to win, Washington got the ball to Joel Smith but he tried an inadvertent crosscourt pass that Marcus Williams stabbed out of the air with 11 seconds left. He made two free throws to make it 96-92 and finally end the wackiness at 12:55 a.m.

"I said in New York after we lost to Syracuse that we have a champion's heart and we do have a champion's heart," Calhoun said. "Someone asked me when we'll see the Connecticut we hear so much about. Well we're 30-3 and they find a way to win. We have guys who refuse to lose. We were five down with 1:17 left and they think they can win."

As reporters fill his locker room, a drained Calhoun sat slumped in a small room away from the fray. Blaney, Tom Moore and Patrick Sellers were in the room and looked spent as well. Calhoun is moaning about getting his team home by 2 a.m. and back to the arena less than 12 hours later for more media obligations. He's looking at a stat sheet filled with big numbers and is clearly shocked that his once-dominating defensive club was torched for 92 points. "We can't win like this. This isn't what we do. We're not guarding anyone. This whole tournament people are scoring on us too easily. It's no way to live."

March 26; Washington, D.C. & Minneapolis

Two spots in the Final Four are already filled. UCLA overpowers Memphis and surprising LSU beats Texas to move onto Indianapolis. Now it's time to see if a Big East team can join the party.

Villanova and Florida will play a rematch of an NCAA game a year ago where the Wildcats posted a second round upset. Joakim Noah played very little for that Gator team but that's certainly not the case now. Wright knows all about Noah, a New York City kid whose father is tennis star Yannick Noah.

"When he picked Florida, it was bittersweet because we were recruiting him and we were one of the finalists," Wright said. "He grew up in New York City playing for a guy named Tyrone Green, who is a good friend of mine, and we thought we were going to get him. I was crushed when he picked Florida, but I was happy because I thought at least he's not in the Big East so I won't have to play against him. That didn't work out too well this year."

It's a recruiting loss that ultimately hurts the Wildcats in the program's biggest game in 20 years. Most of the season, Villanova rarely ran up against the dominant big man who could wear out the team's fragile frontline. Until today, that is. Noah (21 points, 15 rebounds, 5 blocks) and Al Horford (12 points, 15 rebounds) combine to crush the Wildcats off the glass all day long and the big men shut down Sheridan, Cunningham and every other Villanova forward.

That puts loads of pressure on the guards and this time they can't deliver. Ray grew frustrated quickly when he picked up a silly technical foul for bouncing the ball off of Walter Hodges' head. Ray earned his third foul later in the first half and watched helplessly as his team fell behind by as many as 12 points and trailed 35-30 at half time.

The final 20 minutes were uglier. Florida kept sweeping the glass (53-40 edge, 19 offensive boards) and none of Villanova's shooters found the range. Foye finished with 25 points and helped cut the lead to three with 11 minutes left but Ray (5-of-19) and Nardi (2-for-11) were ice cold and as a team Villanova shot just 25 percent from the floor. That helped the Gators break away late for a 75-62 win.

With 28 seconds left, both Foye and Ray came out of the game to a big ovation and plenty of tears on the Villanova bench. "I just told Coach Wright 'Thanks for the ride, thanks for pushing me these four years for me being the man that I am today.' He just told me just keep my head up and keep working hard, and he would always be there for me," said Foye.

Foye and Ray both spoke about the shocking feeling of their college careers ending one game short of the Final Four goal. The college season ends bitterly in the NCAA's but especially for seniors whose great expectations aren't fulfilled.

"I know we have to answer questions, but I want to make sure that our guys and our team feel great about this great season they have had and how I think they got everything out of what they had, and that's all we can ask of them," said Wright. "We asked these guys to give us everything they have. This team did. And care about each other, love each other and they did. So we are going to suck up this hurt a little bit tonight, but I am going to make sure these guys feel real good about themselves. I am going to start working on that right after this."

•

When Rashad Anderson woke up the morning after his heroic shot to force overtime against Washington he was both tired and ecstatic. Still filled with excitement when he went to bed around 3 a.m., Anderson couldn't sleep. He ordered a movie ("Aeon Flux, a Super Hero flick") and didn't fall asleep until about 5:30.

When an alarm woke him a few hours later, Anderson said roommate Marcus Williams caught his eye and said 'Man, we won last night.' I turned to him and smiled and said 'yeah. We sure did.'"

That gleeful feeling carried the Huskies through Saturday's light workout in preparation for the regional final game against George Mason. After all, if a team needs to see its life flash before its eyes, Connecticut certainly saw the light against Washington. And if anyone would've told Calhoun, Anderson or anyone else in Storrs a few weeks back that George Mason would present the last hurdle before the Final Four, everyone would jump at those odds.

The differences in the two programs could not be any starker. According to Department of Education statistics, UConn reported $1.9 million in operating expenses for men's basketball in 2004-05. George Mason spent $237,000. The Huskies raked in $7.8 million in revenue to the Patriots' $1.1 million. NBA scouts followed UConn's players around all season long. The same scouts wouldn't know where to find George Mason. UConn has won two national championships and loads of NCAA tourney games under Calhoun. Before the last two weeks, Mason had zero NCAA wins.

Jim Larranaga, the Patriots' coach, actually owns deep Northeast roots. He was a high school star in New York and played for legendary coach Jack Curran at Archbishop Molloy before going on to score more than 1,200 points at Providence where his coach was Dave Gavitt. Larranaga's first head coaching job came at Calhoun's alma mater, American International in Springfield.

"I called Jim at Northeastern and asked him to play and he said, 'ok, let's play at Northeastern.' I made a play at his ego and said he should also come and play at his alma mater and he agreed," Larranaga said. "We lost at Northeastern and when they came to AIC, we won by one point. I like that story a lot."

Larranaga knows that at this point in the tournament, he's playing with house money. The 11th seeded Patriots are a loose group that knows how to have fun. The players were pleasantly surprised when they even got into the tournament and they've poked fun at each other over the various Cinderella references they've heard ever since. After practice last week, Mason's players and coaches played a little Whiffle ball to lighten up the mood. Before going out to face Connecticut, Larranaga told his team, "I want to be playing baseball again on Tuesday in the Patriot Center. That's what we've done the last two Tuesdays to finish out practice. I think they got the message."

The game begins and it's very clear from the opening tap who the favorite is in the Verizon Center. As Calhoun and his players are introduced, boos rain down from every corner of the building. Everyone loves an underdog and college basketball hasn't seen an underdog like George Mason since Pennsylvania of the Ivy League crashed the Final Four party in 1979.

The game begins and the Patriots are clearly stunned by UConn's size advantage as Armstrong and Gay combine for 12 quick points and the Huskies go up early, 16-8. But threes by Sammy Hernandez and Lamar Butler jump-start the Patriots, get the crowd rolling and before you know it the game is tied, 21-21. Mason takes a 29-28 lead with 3:09 left before UConn races to the half-time horn with four 3-point shots in a 15-5 run for a 43-34 lead.

Connecticut shot an impressive 57 percent in the half but two other stats aren't very comforting. For one, the Huskies made 5-of-9 shots from 3-point range, a lofty percentage that likely would not last. Also, Mason out-rebound-ed UConn, 16-15.

Those trends played out in the second half. While UConn made just 1-of-8 threes the rest of the way, George Mason's Jai Lewis and Will Thomas kept taking the ball right at Boone, Armstrong and the Husky frontcourt and ended up winning the rebound battle, 37-34. Mason tied the game at the 12:33 mark and the two teams staged a thrilling fight to the finish where no more than four points separated the action.

A Lewis hook over Armstrong gave Mason a 64-63 lead with 5:53 left and a deep, pull-up 3-pointer by Tony Skinn pushed the lead to 67-63 and was the Patriots' sixth trey in seven attempts in the half. The Patriots still led by four (71-67) with 1:09 left when Thomas willed his way inside for a tip-in of a Lewis miss.

With the season on the line, UConn's Williams raced end-to-end and scored on a tough lay-up while getting fouled by Butler. He made the free throw to make it 71-70 but Lewis draws a foul on Armstrong and hits one of two free throws. Williams gets caught off-balance and loses the ball, and UConn quickly fouls Butler. He makes two free throws with 17 seconds left, pushing the lead to 74-70. Williams again answers, this time with a runner in the lane with eight seconds left.

UConn calls time-out and instantly fouls Skinn as soon as the ball is put in play. The senior guard is an 81 percent foul shooter and can ice the game but he misses the front end of a 1-and-1. Gay rebounds the ball, gets it to Williams and he races up the middle of the floor and finds Denham Brown cutting to the hoop. The Canadian elevates to the basket, reverses the ball under the rim to avoid a block attempt by the beefy Lewis and spins the ball up on the glass. The ball hesitates for a moment on the rim, almost freezing the moment in time, before falling in at the buzzer and tying the game, 74-74.

"I thought we had dodged a bullet because I thought we had let up," Calhoun said. "When we got into overtime, I said we were in pretty good shape now. We had new life and we needed an adrenaline shot and we got it."

But instead of new life, the Huskies simply had prolonged their demise. The 6-foot-7 Thomas hooked in a shot over Boone to get Mason off and running and hit another tough shot in the lane to give his team a 82-78 lead with two minutes left. After two Brown free throws, Folarin Campbell made a difficult, fall-away corner jumper over Gay to stay ahead, 84-80. The Patriots still led 86-81 with 25 seconds left and UConn looked dead but Williams nailed a 3-pointer with 10 seconds left to cut the deficit to two points. Anderson fouled Lewis with seven seconds left and when the Patriots' big man missed both free throws, the college basketball world braced for another frantic finish.

This time Brown rebounded Lewis' shot with six seconds left, dribbled up the left sideline and kept rambling until he reached the 3-point line with a second left. He rose and took a contested three for the win but the shot missed and George Mason was headed to the Final Four with a 86-84 win.

"I didn't see anyone else at all," Brown said of the final play. "I came across midcourt with three seconds left so I knew I couldn't go to the rim. It was a real good look."

Reporters were coming at Brown in waves, asking about the thrilling shot he made to force overtime and the one that missed at the end. At one point he grew frustrated at the questions and blurted out, "This isn't good enough, 30-4. Not with the caliber of team we have. This season is incomplete. If you're not winning a championship with our record, we came up short."

Calhoun was more than graceful after the game, congratulating Larranaga and his players for an unbelievable achievement. He also spent time praising his own team and appreciated the strong personal characteristics of his players.

"We're 30-4 and disappointed, for sure, but we had a great year," he says. "I think if we keep winning 30 games a year we can break through and play in a few more Final Fours. I'm confident of that. I know that doesn't help the hearts of my kids now though and that's what hurts the most."

$$\text{\large(}\textbf{20}\text{\large)}$$

May 17; Storrs, Conn.

It is six weeks after a loss that still elicits headshakes in all corners of the state of Connecticut. Jim Calhoun has had time to think through a frantic end of a season that will be talked about for years to come and, sure enough, the coach of the Huskies is ready to share some strong opinions.

Calhoun is sitting at a large conference table that fills more than half of his office. Pictures of UConn's great teams and players, as well as mementos from the coach's Hall of Fame career, fill every corner. The coach has just returned from a golfing vacation in South Carolina with his two sons, George Blaney and a few other close friends. It was a time to relax, put a little perspective on a 30-4 season and start looking ahead to 2006-07.

Calhoun is asked what his dominant feeling is as he looks back on the '06 season: satisfaction, turmoil, or regret.

"Some reporters have written that, unequivocally, the season has to be a failure. Well, if that is all we're going to do in college basketball, then it's sad that a Final Eight year can be a failure," he says. "What would you call Duke then? A disaster? Of course not. It wasn't a disaster by any stretch of the imagination. You can't get to the Final Four every year. You just can't."

Two dominant themes developed as Calhoun rolled the replays of the Big East Tournament loss to Syracuse and the Huskies' four NCAA games in his mind. One was the brilliance of Marcus Williams, the fact that he was clearly indispensable and the only playmaker on the roster.

"The key to college basketball is guard play. I've become more and more convinced of that," he said. "If you took our top seven guys, we certainly were talented enough to win it all. But I would have traded two of my wings, or even maybe two of my big guys, for a good guard. An experienced guard who could come in and get us 8-10 points a game, play defense and get us 4-5 assists a game.

"I'll always say that if we had A.J. Price, if he was cleared, he was our best player. We needed another guard. We couldn't make enough plays. I never disputed we didn't have the best talent in the country. It just wasn't spread out evenly enough," he says.

While guard play was indeed shaky at times, the Huskies' season ended because of shortfalls on the defensive end of the floor. After allowing 67 points a game in the regular season, UConn surrendered 83 or more in four of its five postseason games. For some reason, the team with better big men than the Celtics stopped dominating the boards and scaring shooters with all the chips on the table.

Calhoun quickly begins rattling off statistics that illustrate his point that the team's passion, especially on defense, somehow waned. In the regular season, UConn out-rebounded foes by nine a game. In five postseason games, the number was down to five. "Blocked shots, nine a game, four in the postseason. Field-goal percentage defense, 37 percent, second in the country. Postseason, 45 percent," he says.

Finding reasons for the defensive slide has been a tormenting process for the coach. Calhoun values defense as much as anyone in the country and if he ever had a team capable of shutting down the best opponents under the brightest lights, this one seemed to have all the ingredients. Instead, the opposite came to fruition.

"In 35 years of coaching, the one thing you can kind of figure is we'll guard the hell out of you and rebound the ball," he says, "but at the end of the year we were a terrific offensive team but couldn't guard a chair. I can't imagine George Mason's two big guys - when Pittsburgh's big guys couldn't shoot over us – shooting right over us. They're 6-foor-5, 6-foot-6 making shots over two 6-foot-10 kids who led the country in blocked shots. We had 19 blocked shots against Notre Dame and we can't block shots or rebound against George Mason."

One plausible dynamic Calhoun thinks contributed to his team's ragged March effort was a fear of the future for virtually half the team. After rolling to a 27-2 record, the Huskies checked into the Drake Hotel for an expected long week at the Big East Tournament. Calhoun contracted an undercover Connecticut State Trooper to tag along and keep peace for the week.

"The last thing you have to understand is, especially in 2006, we had Denham, Hilton, Rashad and even Ed. Rudy, Josh and Marcus. That's seven players. Seven," he says. "We go to New York, and this is so vivid in my mind. I started to see, for the first time, that the NBA was out there. And I had never seen that very much at all during the season. We brought an undercover state trooper (to New York) and his job was to walk the corridors in the hotel and see who doesn't belong. We've done that just about every year but especially with the number of kids we had this year that could possibly play in the pros. When you take that into consideration, it's hard on these kids.

"So the trooper comes to me after the first night and he says 'coach, your kids go out to get a pizza and they're all over them.' So he asked me to come down to the lobby at the Drake and watch. Our guys would get off the elevator, walk through the lobby and they'd be on them. Runners for agents, adults, kids looking for autographs. Then they'd step outside and there would be three more of them.

"For the first time, and I mean this honestly, Rudy Gay is 19 going on 15. He's just a nice, nice kid. This was a lot on his shoulders, living like that. And what can you do? As we got down the stretch, an awareness grew in these kids that the pros were there. All of a sudden, the bad stuff became a bitch. Really. We had seven kids who were either leaving the womb or had to make tough decisions about (the draft) and for the first time they started thinking about their own future."

One player who clearly limped home over the final few weeks of the season was Josh Boone. The junior center is just days away from declaring for the NBA Draft, following in the footsteps of Gay and Williams. Boone's chances of landing in the first round are rated as shaky, unlike his teammates, but he and Calhoun clearly had issues all season.

"It became apparent to some of these guys that 'I'm actually leaving. Oh shit,'" Calhoun says. "In Josh's case, 'should I leave or not?' Josh played awful in the tournament. The body language on Josh in the George Mason game was the worst I've ever seen. And I love Josh Boone. He was going to leave all season but over this year, he went backwards a bit. His own teammate (Hilton Armstrong) had a better year. That wore on him."

A popular theory for UConn's demise floating in the nation's media is that the players weren't properly motivated for the tournament. That they were somehow distracted or lacking a focus to get the job done. Calhoun admits that the NBA monster was a distraction, but bristles at the thought that he hadn't pushed his team as hard as he could.

"I always said this team had a champion's heart," he said. "We couldn't stop any guards in the NCAA's. Albany, that kid (Jamar Wilson) killed us. Kentucky, we couldn't stop (Patrick) Sparks or (Rajon) Rondo. Then we play Washington and we couldn't stop anyone there either but we hung in there and won that one. You don't do what we did if you're not inspired. In the Albany game, we don't come back if we're not inspired. You cash it in a little bit. We should've lost the Kentucky game. Washington had us beat. Beat. And we come back in overtime to win. So no one can convince me we weren't motivated. But in the last five games we lost focus mentally on what we were."

A few days before his golf trip, Calhoun received a phone call from Rashad Anderson. He had wrapped up a strong performance at the Portsmouth (Va.) Invitational Camp for prospective NBA draftees. On an opposing team was Tony Skinn, the George Mason guard who torched the Huskies.

"Rashad goes down to Portsmouth and plays against Tony Skinn. Rashad had 30 points and Skinn gets two. Rashad says 'coach, he can't play. I can't believe it's the same guy' Well he had 23 against us," Calhoun said.

He uses the anecdote to illustrate the greatness of the NCAA Tournament where anything can happen.

"I agree with what Billy Donovan said. He said if you played the tournament over, you'd have four different teams in the Final Four," said Calhoun. "I know one thing. George Mason wouldn't beat Michigan State and Connecticut again. But it happened. The tournament is always wide open. Did the best team win this year? I don't think so. Billy had a good team and they're going to be a great team. But I think there were better teams. Were we the best? We were in the mix but in this sport that doesn't always equate to the championship, which is great, I think."

Calhoun is asked if he has any regrets after finishing 30-4. It's an almost silly question but also somehow apropos considering the expectations his players carried on their shoulders all season. One regret is the long faces he's seen when Marcus Williams and Rudy Gay walked into his office and told him they were heading to the NBA without winning a national title.

"They've all talked about what they've missed out on," he said. "It became so in vogue that they were going to win the national championship, hands down, that it's a disappointment. It shouldn't be and that's what I've tried to tell them, but I can see that it is."

As Calhoun keeps talking, you can almost see his mind racing, searching for answers to a question that will stick in his heart forever.

"Again, we had enough talent to win the national championship even despite the fact that we didn't have another guard but the distractions at the end of the season, which we avoided into a 30-4 season, hurt us," he said. "Given everything, the conclusion will always be disappointing but I don't know what I could've done. It was the most helpless feeling in the world. We almost did it in spite of ourselves, playing entirely different than we played all year. We still won three games in the NCAA's playing awful, which isn't bad."

Not bad. In most college basketball towns, an Elite Eight finish is a lot more than not bad. But in Connecticut in 2006, not bad isn't what anyone's heart was set on. Greatness was the one and only desired destination and the realization that the Huskies fell short of their destiny left everyone with an empty feeling.